PROBLEMS OF LIBRARY ACQUISITIONS

PROBLEMS OF LIBRARY ACQUISITIONS

By

Tariq Ashraf

ANMOL PUBLICATIONS PVT. LTD.
NEW DELHI - 110 002 (INDIA)

ANMOL PUBLICATIONS PVT. LTD.
4374/4B, Ansari Road, Daryaganj
New Delhi - 110 002
Ph.: 23261597, 23278000
Visit us at: www.anmolpublications.com

Problems of Library Acquisitions

First Published, 2004

ISBN 81-261-1857-1

PRINTED IN INDIA

Published by J.L. Kumar for Anmol Publications Pvt. Ltd., New Delhi - 110 002 and Printed at Mehra Offset Press, Delhi.

Contents

Preface

One of the important aspects of acquisition work is the pivotal role that it plays in relating the practice of librarianship to publishers and sellers of library material. Publishing industry, in fact sets the limits within which librarians have to operate, as most of the documents which libraries acquire are in published form. Collection development remains an immensely important yardstick in determining the nature and, to a considerable extent, the level of service which a library is able to provide. The availability of good books largely depends on their continuous production by good publishers and their timely marketing. Libraries, on their part, constitute the biggest clientele of book traders and consume largest chunk of books produced by them.

The present study is an attempt to understand the process of acquisition in special libraries in India and looks into the procedures, problems and the linkages with the book trade. The purpose of this study is to find answers for various deceptively easy problems that an acquisition librarian has to face. The questions concern publishing and the decisions that affect the cost and life of the documents, their acquisition and procurement of periodical publications, the world of vendors and how one decides if a vendor is performing well for the library. The study, it is hoped, will help the librarians in improving the system of acquisition of documents in their libraries and also to have a better understanding of the book trade.

Before launching the work of collecting data, extensive literature survey was undertaken to understand the problems and research trends in the area. Library and Information Science Abstracts (LISA) was used for identifying the related articles on various aspects of the research topic. The topic was segmented into various sections and literature was scanned on each section of the study. The literature survey helped to understand the problems related to acquisition in a proper perspective and broaden the framework. It also helped in gaining clarity and in developing different questionnaires.

The study is based on survey approach of research. Besides questionnaires, data has been collected on the basis of personal interviews. Four different questionnaires have been used for eliciting responses from librarians, publishers, distributors and vendors on various issues related to acquisition of documents and role of book trade. The questionnaires were tested before finally administering them to the respective population groups. Questionnaires were distributed personally and were also sent both by post and email as attachments. The sample size for the survey relating to four groups of questionnaires was chosen on the basis of their estimated strength and the practical constraints of space, time and economy in administering the questionnaires.

The data has been analysed using SPSS software and results have been tabulated in four sections based on respective questionnaires.

The entire study is divided into 10 chapters. A brief outline of each chapter is given below:

Chapter 1—Introduction: This chapter introduces the research topic, its background, statement of the problem, scope of the study and its limitations. It spells out the objectives of the research and the hypotheses upon which the study is based. It also gives the operational definitions of various terms used in the study.

Chapter 2—Review of Related Literature: This chapter is about the literature which has been scanned and surveyed to study the various trends in this area of study. It deals with various aspects like collection development policy, publishing and collection development, ordering and acquisition process, pricing and discounts, distribution and electronic publishing, etc.

Chapter 3—Research Design: This chapter relates to the method of study, construction of the questionnaires, selection of variables, development of scale, organisation and administration of the questionnaires. The chapter further mentions the process of data collection and its analysis.

Chapter 4—Collection Development: This chapter discusses various components of collection development process, factors affecting collection development, collection development policy with reference to special libraries.

Chapter 5—Acquisition of Printed Documents: This chapter describes the acquisition procedures of printed materials, selection aids and links with publishing industry. Books being important component of library collection, it also describes problems faced by libraries in acquisition of books.

Chapter 6—Acquisition of Periodical Publications: Since periodical publications occupy most important position in special libraries, the problems related with them have been separately dealt with. The chapter describes categories of periodical publications, their role in library collection, selection principles, and acquisition sources of these publications. It describes in details the problems related with the acquisition of periodical publications in special libraries in India.

Chapter 7—Acquisition of Non-print Documents: This chapter defines non-print materials, their importance in special libraries. The chapter discusses all such material category-wise like audio-visual material, filmstrips, slides, microforms and electronic formats. The chapter also describes various problems related with the acquisition of such material in special libraries.

Chapter 8—Indian Publishing Industry: This chapter discusses the origin and growth of Indian publishing industry. It profiles the present status of publishing trade and also discusses the various problems which Indian publishing industry is afflicted with.

Chapter 9— Analysis and Interpretation of Data: This chapter analyses the data collected during survey. The analysis is divided in 4 different sections as per four different questionnaires which were designed and distributed.

Chapter 10—Findings, Recommendations and Areas For Further Research: This last chapter is devoted to the important findings of the study which have come out of the research. It gives recommendations to improve the existing situation. Areas for further research have also been suggested.

Acknowledgements

It is my proud privilege and pleasant duty to express my gratitude and sincere thanks for guidance, support, encouragement and assistance, I received from several individuals and institutions during the course research study.

First and foremost I am indebted to my supervisor, Dr. (Mrs.) S.P. Singh for shouldering the responsibility of guiding me through the course of this research work nearly for four years. Despite her demanding administrative and academic responsibilities as Head of the Department, she freely gave her time by rescheduling her work to accommodate me and provided a motivating, critical academic atmosphere during the discussions and deliberations we had. It was a great pleasure for me to conduct the research work under her supervision.

I am deeply indebted to Prof. Krishan Kumar for providing critical input at various stages and important junctures of the research. His words of encouragement, comments, criticism and suggestions helped me to a great extent in conducting the study purposefully.

My thanks are due to Chairperson of Institute For Integrated Learning in Management (IILM), Mrs. Malvika Rai and Director of the institute, for their constant support and encouragement to complete the doctoral research.

I am also thankful to my colleagues at IILM, Prof. Deepa Majumdar, Dr. Naseem Abidi and Mr. Sachidanand Mishra for helping me in analysing the data. I am also thankful to Yusuf Siddiqui, Gauri Shankar and Kamal Din for their help.

My friends deserve my special thanks, Dr. Dev Raj Singh, Library & Information Officer, National Institute of Public Finance and Policy, New Delhi, for allowing me to use his doctoral experience and Sanjeev Kumar, Deputy Director, National Institute of Fashion Technology, New Delhi, for using his laptop which helped me immensely to complete the research work.

I am also thankful to Prof. P.B. Mangla, Prof. J.L. Sardana, Prof. Shahabuddin Ansari, Dr. (Mrs.) Neela Jagannathan, Prof. K.C. Sahoo, Prof. Sabir Hussain, Dr. Shailendar Kumar, Prof. C.P. Vashisht, Sh. O.P. Sachdeva, and my friends Dr. Devraj Singh, Sanjeev Kumar, Satendar Singh Dhaka and Akhtar Parvez for their help, advice and assistance in completion of my research work in their respective capacities.

I am also thankful to all the librarians, publishers, distributors and vendors for responding to the various questionnaires sent to them for collecting data for the study and also providing very valuable information through personal interaction.

I would be failing in my duty if I do not express my thanks to Sh. O.P. Sachdeva, Librarian, Department of Library and Information Science, University of Delhi and his other colleagues for helping me in locating various important references required during the course of this study.

Lastly I wish to put on records my success thank to Sh. Ahuja and M/s Anmol Publications Pvt. Ltd. for publishing this research study.

—Tariq Ashraf

Abbreviations

AACR	Anglo American Cataloguing Rules
Adv in Libr	Advances in Librarianship
Acq Libr	Acquisition Librarian
ALA	American Library Association
Am Libs	American Libraries
Am Soc Inf J	American Society for Information Journal
Annals of Libr Sc Doc	Annals of Library Science Documentation
Bull Inf Tech	Bulletin of Information Technology
CNA	Central News Agency
Cathol Libr world	Catholic Library World
CDI	Comprehensive Dissertation Index
CD-ROM	Compact Disk Read Only Memory
CMIE	Centre for Monitoring Indian Economy
Coll Res Libr	College and Research Libraries
Collect Manage	Collection Management
Collect Build	Collection Building
CSIR	Council for Scientific and Industrial Research
DELNET	Developing Libraries Network

Deptt	Department
Desidoc Bull Inf Tech	Desidoc Bulletin of Information Technology
DAI	Dissertation Abstracts International
Ed	Editor
E-Journals	Electronic Journals
Electron Publishing	Electronic Publishing
ELBS	English Language Book Society
GOC	Good Offices Committee
Govt	Government
Hr Lib Sc	Herald of Library Science
HTML	Hyper Text Markup Language.
IASLIC	Indian Association of Special Libraries and Information Centres
IASLIC Bull	IASLIC Bulletin
ICSSR	Indian Council for Social Science Research
IILM	Institute for Integrated Learning in Management
ILA Bull	Indian Library Association Bulletin
Inf Manag	Information Management
Inf Proc Mang	Information Processing and Management
Inf Technol Libr	Information Technology and Libraries
Inf Today	Information Today
INPADOC	International Patent Documentation Centre
INSDOC	Indian National Scientific Documentation Centre
ISBN	International Standard Book Number

ISRO	Indian Space Research Organisation
IT	Information Technology
J Acquis Libr	Journal of Acquisition Librarian
J Elec Pub	Journal of Electronic Publishing
J Inf Sc	Journal of Information Science
J Libr Adm	Journal of Library Administration
J Libr	Journal of Librarianship
J Sch Pub	Journal of Scholarly Publishing
Libr Acquis Prac Th	Library Acquisition Practice and Theory
Libr Coll Acq Tech Serv	Library Collection Acquisition and Technical Services
Libr Inf Sc Res	Library and Information Science Research
Libr Media Q	Library Media Quarterly
Libr Resour Tech	Library Resources &Technology
Libr Trends	Library Trends
Libr Technol Rep	Library Technology Reports
Libr Q	Library Quarterly
LISA	Library and Information Science Abstracts
MRDF	Machine-Readable Data File
Music Libr Assoc	Music Library Association
NASSDOC	National Social Science Documentation Centre
NPM	Non-Print Material
NCERT	National Council of Educational Research and Training
OCLC	Online Computer Library Centre
P	Page
PC	Personal Computer

PDF	Portable Document Format
Ph.D	Doctor of Philosophy
PIN	Patent Information Network
Public Access Computer Sys Rev	Public Access Computer System Review
Pub Weekly	Publishers Weekly
R&D	Research and Development
Sc Tech Libr	Science and Technology Libraries
Ser Libr	Serial Librarian
Spl Libr	Special Libraries
SPSS	Statistical Package for Social Sciences
STC	State Trading Corporation
UGC	University Grants Commission
UK	United Kingdom
UNIDO	United Nations Industrial Development Organisation
URL	Unified Resource Locator
VHS	Video Home System
WI	Weighted Index
Wilson Libr Bull	Wilson Library Bulletin
WPI	World Patent Index

1
Introduction

Background

The mission of a special library is to serve as a gateway to information and to promote intellectual discovery of its users. The basic requisite in the accomplishment of this mission lies in acquisition of a variety of materials in all subject areas covered in its objectives so as to fulfil the information needs of its specialised clientele. Accordingly, the collection development programme in a special library aims to develop the collection that supports its research and developmental activities and fulfils the basic objectives of the parent organisation.

Collection development is not ordinarily perceived as a very demanding activity but it certainly brings great personal satisfaction to the librarian if the material needed by a particular user can be provided to him immediately . Such fulfilment is only possible if the organizational needs are properly assessed and anticipated before the acquisition of the documents in the library. For this purpose, it is essential for the libraries to be well aware of the goals of the parent organisation, information needs of the users and on-going research and development activities of the organisation.

However, the process of identifying what the library ought to acquire, determining how and from whom it can be obtained, and actually getting it, is time consuming and often a complex process. Without an effective acquisition management and collection development programme, the expectations of library patrons can never be met. Thus, "the collection development is an effective audit aspect of a library, closely linked with its use".[1]

Statement of the Problem

The task of collection development, however, has never been easy in India particularly in special libraries as these libraries need to develop specialized need-based collections for their clientele who are always keen to keep themselves up-to-date with the latest developments taking place in their area of specialization. Such information is generally available in non–traditional documents including conference proceedings, patents, standards, etc. All these types of documents are very special in nature having their own problems of acquisition as many of these are not usually available through normal trade channels. Thus, for acquisition of such materials, a viable mechanism has to be developed, appropriate vendors have to be identified, acquisition librarians have to monitor their functioning constantly which requires good knowledge of publishing and book selling also. "The acquisition librarian, in addition, has to have a lively appreciation of the economics of purchasing plan and weigh its efficiency and convenience against the obvious costs".[2]

It is commonly felt that despite the availability of reasonable funds, libraries often lag behind in building up a need-based quality collection of documents. In this backdrop, it becomes a moot issue to probe whether the fault lies with the collection development policy of the library, the publishers, the booksellers or the vendors or there are other reasons. To what extent does the, publishing industry influences the collection development process and what are the problems of publishing industry itself which have a bearing on timely supply of books, periodicals and non-print material, etc? In this context, we need to identify not only the problems which special libraries in India face in collection building in relation to the publishing trade but also understand the functioning and dynamics of publishing industry vis-a-vis special libraries, so as to find the suitable solution

Need for the Study

Collection development remains an immensely important yardstick in determining the nature and, to a considerable extent, the level of service which a library is able to provide. The availability of good books largely depends on continuous production of a variety of books by good publishers and their timely marketing. Thus, both book trade and libraries not only compliment each other but are also mutually dependent upon each other for their survival. Hence, any study relating to the collection development programme will not be complete without looking into the publishing trade, its problems and its linkages with libraries. Though several studies have taken place related to acquisition of documents but there has not been so far any research which has investigated linkages between publishing trade and acquisition of documents in special libraries. Thus, the study intends to fill up this gap

Objectives

The objectives of the study are:

(i) to study acquisition of print materials (books, periodical publications, etc.) as well as other non-print materials in special libraries in India.

(ii) to understand the problems relatesd to collection development of selected special libraries in India in relation to publishing industry;

(iii) to trace the growth and development of publishing industry in India and its role in collection development in special libraries;

(iv) to understand the dynamics of book industry, its operations, problems;

(v) to identify the developmental changes that are taking place in the publishing industry in India in relation to technology, manpower and their impact on libraries;

(vi) and also to suggest a omprehensive plan for improvement of services provided by book industry related to collection development.

Scope of the Study

Population

The population covered in this study includes:

(i) Librarians/Information Officers/Documentation Officers;

(ii) Publishers;

(iii) Distributors; and

(iv) Vendors.

For the purpose of this study, printed materials, like books, periodicals, patents, standards, reports etc. and non-print materials, like audio-visual aids, electronic documents constitute the terms 'documents'. As the study is empirical in nature and acquisition of these documents is inseparably linked with the publishing industry, all the important constituents involved in the acquisition of these documents have been included in the survey. Four separate questionnaires were developed for and distributed among librarians, publishers, distributors and vendors for this purpose.

Given the constraints of time, space and economy, the study is confined to the selected libraries in India listed as special libraries by *Association of Indian Special Libraries and Information Centres* (IASLIC).[3] Similarly care has been taken to include important publishers, distributors and vendors dealing in special material. The names have been selected from the *Directory of Indian Publishers and Distributors*.[4] The study analyses the present position of

Indian publishing industry in terms of its publishing policies, system of pricing of publications, publishing of Indian reprints of foreign books, system of discounts and distribution. Distributors of Indian as well as foreign books have been included in the study as they play a very important role in the development of specialised collection in special libraries. In addition, the study also includes aspects like import policy of library documents, ordering and procurement process, and the problem of remainder titles, etc. A good number of publishing houses have obtained rights for publishing Indian versions of foreign books from their respective publishers. This has several implications for libraries in their acquisition programme, the study also looks into their problems.

Hypotheses

This research work has attempted to study the acquisition of documents in special libraries in India and its linkages with publishing industry. In this connection the following hypotheses are aimed to be tested:

(i) The acquisition of documents in majority of special libraries is being guided by a written and comprehensive collection development policy

(ii) Librarians are influenced by many variables while purchasing library material ranging from favourable reviews, to inclusion on a vendor's approval plan, to publishers advertising, to faculty request. They also order materials through many different channels; direct from publishers; through a varied number of booksellers, both wholesalers and retailers and from subscription agents.

(iii) Electronic formats and online databases, slowly but surely are becoming an important part of collection of special libraries.

(iv) Special libraries are maintaining their traditional services and collections even as they use technology in new ways to deliver services and provide access to information on networks or through document delivery services.

(v) Acquisition of documents in special library is dependent upon a strong book trade . Indian book trade has not been successful in fulfilling the requirements of special libraries for a need-based and up-to-date collection of library materials.

(vi.) Publishing trade in India is a loosely organised enterprise lacking sufficient capital and trained manpower to run its operations

Limitations of the Study

Due to large geographical dimensions, it has not been possible to conduct the study on a truly national scale. Sheer logistical constraints do not permit to include all the special libraries in the survey. Similarly it has not been possible to include all the publishing houses. Therefore, only selected libraries, publishing houses, distributors and vendors have been included in the study. Another limitation of the study is that it is confined to English language publishing. The same is the case with the distributors and vendors. The study has looked only into the contemporary problem without going into the detailed history except a brief backgrounder.

Operational Definitions

Some of the key terms and concepts which form part of the study have been defined as follows:

Acquisition

"The process of obtaining books and other items for a library, documentation centre or archive".[5] The term has been used here as a process to get the documents in library on being selected and approval granted by concerned authorities for their purchase. A strict definition of acquisitions will include the ordering, claiming and receiving of materials.

Bookseller

"A retail dealer having a varied selection of books covering a wide range of subjects".[6] In this study terms bookseller, vendor and jobber have been used interchangeably.

Book Trade

Refers to the complex of arrangements for publishing, distribution and sale of books to the general public and libraries, etc. It includes retail bookstores, bookseller's organisations and publishers and their organisations.

Collection Development

"The process of planning a stock acquisition programme not simply to cater for immediate needs, but to build a coherent and reliable collection over a number of years, to meet the objectives of the service".[7] The term collection development describes a cluster of functions such as evaluation, selection, approval, acquisition, and payments which together shape the holdings of materials in a library.

Distributor/Wholesaler

A book dealer who buys books directly from publishers and sells to library supliers like booksellers, vendors and jobbers .

Document

"A record which conveys information; originally an inscribed or written record, but now considered to include any form of information, graphic, acoustic, alphanumeric etc. such as maps, manuscripts, tapes, videotapes, computer software".[8] For this study documents are meant to be all published materials such as books, journals, reports, standards, patents and non-print material such as audio-visual material, magnetic disks and CD-ROMs.

Librarian

"One who has care of a library and its contents; the work includes selection of stock, its arrangement and exploitation in the widest sense, and the provision of a range of services in the best interest of all group of users".[9] The term librarian here includes both information officers and documentation officers also.

Linkages

The term linkages here refers to "a series of systems of links to unite or connect".[10]

Print Material

The term here refers to printed publications like books, periodical publications, reports, patents, dissertations, trade literature, standards, maps and government documents.

Non-print Material

Non-print material can be defined as "library materials that require some form of media enhancement to be used".[11] A common characteristic of these media is their reliance upon equipment for access. These include audio recordings, audio and video tapes, slides, filmstrips and electronic formats like floppies and CD-ROMs, etc.

Periodical Publications

According to Ranganathan[12] periodical Publication is a documents with the following attributes:

1. Periodicity.-A volume or small or small group of volumes of it, is published or intended to be published or completed normally once in a year or at other regular intervals though irregularity in interval is not ruled out;
2. Distinguishing Number.- Each successive volume or periodical group of volumes, is usually distinguished by the year of publication and/or by

a number belonging to a system of single or complex ordinal number usually called a Volume Number; and

3. Continuity.-The intention had been to continue the publication for ever and with the same title in all the volumes though not actually carried out."

Publisher

"The person, firm or corporate body responsible for placing a book on the market, as distinguished from the printer. Relates also to publication of music, maps and photographs".[13]

Special Libraries

The term special library is used here to denote the libraries "having collection of books and other printed, graphic or record material dealing with a limited field of knowledge, and provided by a learned society, research organisation, industrial or commercial undertaking, government department or educational institutions".[14]

As a generic term it has been used to include different kinds of libraries, such as libraries attached to industrial and commercial organisations, libraries of learned societies, government agencies and departments, etc. Special libraries serve a limited and well-defined group of clientele, usually limited to its parent organisation. These libraries contain in-depth working collections, to provide support for information services, the emphasis being on current and up-to-date information in its primary area of interest.

Vendor

A person who takes books from several wholesalers and supplies to different libraries on commission basis both on approval and against confirmed orders. The term vendor and booksellers are here used interchangeably. Vendor usually work without maintaining any office.

Organisation of the Study

The entire study is divided into 10 chapters. A brief outline of each chapter is given below:

The first chapter 'Introduction' introduces the research topic, gives statement of the problem, scope of the study and its limitations. It also gives the operational definitions of various terms used in the study.

The second chapter 'Review of Related Literature' is about the literature which has been scanned and surveyed to study various aspects like collection development policy, publishing and collection development, ordering and acquisition process, pricing and discounts, distribution and electronic publishing, etc. pertaining to acquisition of documents in special libraries and publishing trade.

The third chapter 'Research Design' deals with the method of study adopted to investigate the problem under study, selection of variables, development of scale, designing and administration of the questionnaires. The chapter further mentions the process of data collection and its analysis.

The fourth chapter 'Collection Development' discusses various components of collection development with special reference to special libraries.

The fifth chapter 'Acquisition of Printed Documents' describes the acquisition of printed documents, selection aids, acquisition methods and links with publishing industry. It also describes problems faced by libraries in acquisition of these documents.

The sixth chapter 'Acquisition of Periodical Publications' describes categories of periodical publications, their role in library collection, selection principles, and acquisition sources of serial publications. It also describes in details the problems faced by libraries in India in their acquisition.

The seventh chapter 'Acquisition of Non-print Documents' defines non-print materials, their types and importance in special libraries. It discusses various problems related to the acquisition of such materials in special libraries in India.

The eighth chapter 'Indian Publishing Industry' discusses about the emergence and growth of Indian publishing industry. It profiles the present status of publishing trade and also discusses the various problems which Indian publishing industry is afflicted with.

The ninth chapter 'Analysis and Interpretation of Data' analyses the data which has been collected. The analysis is divided into 4 different sections as per four different questionnaires which were designed and distributed among librarians/information officers/documentation officers, publishers, distributors and vendors.

The tenth chapter 'Findings, Recommendations and Areas of Further Research' is devoted to the important findings of the study which have been grouped under separate headings. It also gives recommendations for librarians and book trade as a whole. Areas for further research have been given at the end of this chapter.

Chapter 10 is followed by appendices and bibliography.

Conclusion

Book trade and libraries, both directly and indirectly have a bearing on each other's existence. Development of need-based, balanced and up-do-date collection is a continuous process in a special library. This demand is being fulfilled by the publishers with an active support of vendors. Therefore, the trinity of librarian, publisher and vendor plays a very important role in this process. "Although some of the problems in publishing world are peripheral to the daily operations of an acquisition department, however, the knowledge of this related industry helps the librarian to recognize the acquisition cycle, to talk intelligently with vendors, and to understand and allow for the continued shifting within the publishing world".[15] The acquisition librarian recognizes the need for maintaining an appropriate relationship with the vendors and their representatives. The ability to balance the needs of the library and pressures of the vendors or its representative is a skill that comes with experience. As libraries have to rely on vendors to acquire their material, they must know the strengths and weaknesses of the vendors they appoint, as well as of their competitors. The library world is not immune to upheavals among their business partners; a knowledge of what else is out there is as an alternative if catastrophe strikes one's long-time vendor. The publishing and vending worlds have their own jargons and initialism, just as the library world does, the understanding of which and use of signals, a commonality of purpose and degree of professionalism. But "what should be a simple producer/distributor/consumer relationship becomes complicated and emotion charged because of the complex and often chaotic nature of the publishing industry and mythology surrounding the books and libraries".[16] The librarians, as consumer of information, publishers as producer and vendors as link between these two are part of a separate but intersecting systems. Though, libraries, publishing and vending are very different systems, but they are dependent on each other. Only by learning about the weaknesses and strengths of the respective systems and dealing with them constructively, can help them form a truly symbiotic relationship.

References

1. Sharon (W Propas). Publishers' trade discounts and public libraries . *Libr Acquis Prac Th* . 8; 1984; 95-97.
2. Pemberton (J Michael). A handbook of acquisition personnel. 1984. Scarecrow Press, N.J. p 10.
3. Indian Association of Special Libraries & Information Centres. List of members. 2000. Calcutta.
4. Directory of Indian publishers and distributors 2000. 2001. Indian Bibliographic Centre, Varanasi.

5. Prytherch (Ray), *Ed.* Harrod's librarians glossary. Ed 9. 2000.Gower Publishing Company Limited, England. p 7.

6. *Ibid.* p 71.

7. *Ibid.* p163.

8. *Ibid.* p 235.

9. Hodge (Stanley P). Future development by book publishers. jobbers and networks; their impact on library collection development. *Libr Acquis Prac Th_.* 5; 1981; 15-16.

10. Webester's deluxe unabridged dictionary. Ed. 2. 1979.Dorset and Baber, USA. p 1052.

11. Pemberton (J Michael). A handbook of acquisition personnel. 1984. Scare Crow Press, N.J. p 8.

12. Ranganathan (S R).Prolegomena to library classification. Ed 3. 1967.Asian Publishing House, Bombay. p 212.

13. Boss (Richard W) and Judy (McQueen). The uses of automation and related technologies by domestic book and serials jobbers. Library Technology Report No 35; 1999; 125-251. Available at: *http: / / staffweb.library.vanderbilt.edu / libtech / reports / 1999 May-Mr.html*

14. Prutherch (Ray), *Ed. Op cit.* p 687.

15. Alessi (Dana). Vendor selection. vendor collection. or vendor defection. *J Libr Adm.* 16, 3; 117-30.

16. Schmidt (Karen A), *Ed.* Understanding the business of library acquisitions. 1990. Books on Demand, Ann Arbor. p 336. Available at: *http: / / www.books-on-demand.com / index-int.html.*

2
Review of Related Literature

Introduction

Books have been regarded a primary means of communicating the knowledge. They are crucial to providing information, entertainment, analysis and education to millions worldwide. Publishing is a central activity to countries' educational systems, to the creation and distribution of knowledge, and to the nurturing of an independent and intellectual culture. Without books and other published material, a civil society can not exist, educational system suffers, and knowledge can not be communicated. Despite the advent of new technologies for knowledge distribution, such as Internet and other computer based innovations, traditional books and newspapers very often remain the primary source of information.

In building up the resources of the libraries in a proper manner, the book trade as a whole plays a vital role and there is always a need for closer collaboration between libraries and book trade. A good library is known by its collection and a good collection is impossible without the existence of strong publishing trade.

In the first fifty years of the development of the library profession, acquisitions, as we commonly refer to it today did not exist. From the beginning of this century, well into the late 1930s, students of librarianship studied "order work", which embraced some, but not all of the work, we now commonly associate with acquisitions. Training at that time paralleled the general organization of larger libraries, which had the order department as well as periodical department and receipt division. The word acquisition itself did not come into common usage until around 1940s, a few years after Columbia University published its syllabus on the principles of library organisation and administration.

A review of literature related to the research topic reveals the existence of a wide variety of research work but in most of the cases, the focus of research is either on collection development or on publishing trade exclusively. Excepting a few cases, there is absence of literature focussing on inter-relation between book trade and library acquisition programmes. Nevertheless, the scanning of literature has enabled to gain an insight into existing research trends in the field and widen theoretical perspective of the researcher. The scope of the present review of the literature is confined to the related aspects of the research topic such as collection development policy, acquisition and ordering process, problems related to publishing trade in general and Indian publishing trade in particular.

Acquisition

Over the years, the books encompassing the work of acquisition have been produced sporadically and reflected the growth of this area of expertise. The first was a text by F.F. Hopper[1], under the auspices of the ALA Committee on Library Training, which published the *ALA Manual of Library Economy*. Revised in 1930 by Carl Cannon,[2] this work, as well as a text by Francis K.W. Drury,[3] was for more than forty years the essential publications in acquisitions. In the early 1970s, two more books appeared, one was a series of essays by Daniel Melcher,[4] whose experience over the years at the R.R. Bowker Company convinced him of the need for librarians to have a better understanding of publishing. The other was by Stephen Ford,[5] who published *The Acquisition of Library Materials*, a text that has remained since then as the handbook of acquisitions. In addition to these books, two journals are devoted entirely to the topic : *Library Acquisitions: Practice and Theory* and *The Acquisitions Librarian*, which appeared in 1977 and 1989 respectively,

Collection Development Policy

Acquisition section of a library is virtually akin to nerve centre of a human body. Bereft of a sound and up-to-date acquisition policy, libraries will only have a lopsided growth of its collection. There are some studies which have explored and analysed the various elements of collection development policy. According to Carpenter[6], collection development is perhaps the type of library work most often assigned low priority as a harried librarian struggles to manage time effectively. He lays emphasis on a written collection development policy at least for three reasons: (i) writing a collection development policy requires the articulation of a plan for acquiring materials. A policy must answer two basic questions: what is the library acquiring and why; (ii) a written policy provides for rational planning and allocation of the acquisition budget; (iii) a written policy is a communication tool, permitting a library to address several audiences such as faculty and students, administrators who control resources and library's consortia partners.

According to Aldredge[7] a collection development policy consists of four elements viz.: historical record of what has been done in the past; a description of parameters of the existing collection; a blueprint for the future of the collection and a contract with users in the way collection is to be developed. Librarians can use it to create a rationale for funding, to inform the faculty about the strengths and weaknesses of the collection, and to establish a hierarchy of needs.

Ferguson[8] defines a collection development policy statement as a communication tool for management, librarians, users and other libraries; detailed outline of collecting levels; a description of collection development responsibilities; and a budgeting tool that helps librarians decide where to place resources. According to Mastejulia[9] the basic function and purpose of acquisitions can be stated simply to purchase for and receive into the library materials that have been requested and /or are required.

Sharon[10] identified the characteristics of collection management as economically efficient control of library resources, and the identification of coherent patterns in the collection and in user needs. Whaley[11] argues that librarians have the responsibility to have proper materials in proper formats in the proper languages for an undefined and often indefinable patrons.

Osburn[12] predicts that technology will play an increasingly important part in shaping the environment in which collection development must function.

Bavakutty[13] states that in Kerala all the College libraries invite quotations for purchasing books, as per the instructions of Directorate of Collegiate Education. The main disadvantage of this system of book ordering are that booksellers who quote the highest discount were supplying those books on which they get a liberal discount. This has resulted in non-availability of to a certain extent of books essential for the academic programme of the college.

According to Esperanza[14] the college library should try to make available to its readers the latest edition in print. The aim should be to acquire the most important intellectual resources to the academic community of readers. College libraries must aim to show the richness of our Indian heritage while respecting the Western and Eastern thought.

Anand[15] in his work emphasises the need for a written collection development policy statement to enable the book selectors to work with greater consistency towards defined goals. A written collection development policy helps assure continuity in collections development because library staff members as well as the members of the library committee, who select book, often keep on changing. In this situation a written collection development policy serves as a reference tool for new library staff members and the members of library committee.

Similarly Tejomurty[16] states that each library should have a developing acquisition policy, which should be constantly revised. Close co-operation will be necessary between library and academic staff in formulating, developing and implementing acquisition policies. It is essential that a high proportion of funds should be available in the library as soon as possible after its publication·

According to Mehta[17] in the matter of building national collections, in the field of science and technology, the goal would be that the scientific and technical research libraries of national, state, branch and local taken together should ensure that at least one copy of everything worthwhile published in the field of science and technology in the world is accessible within the country for use, no matter where it is kept.

Mishra[18] in his paper notes that the development of a good collection is essential for satisfying user's need in any library, but accepts that most libraries do not have a clear cut policy statement for the development of their library collection. In the absence of policy statement, the collection grows in a haphazard manner affecting the utility of the documents acquired. He emphasises the need for a policy statement for collection development and elaborate levels and components of a policy statement for thus purpose.

According to Wasan[19] books are not selected and procured according to the genuine needs of the users and librarians in some cases are found reluctant to know the needs of their clientale.

Jones[20] states that basic functions of collection development in the digital library remain the same as for the traditional science technology and Math library. Applying these functions to electronic resources at this time requires increased collaboration and a broadening of the skills and experience of collection development personnel. A primary objective of collection development is to give structure to a collection of resources by organizing them in a meaningful manner. New approaches are being used to define what the collection development.

According to Raina[21] increasing financial constraints have left the libraries, attached to the 4 national level management institutions of India (IIM), with no option but to acquire learning resources on cooperative basis. He proposes some broad policy indicators for fine tuning the existing acquisition policies of IIM libraries.

Maheswarappa and Karsidappa[22] have emphasised the need for collection development as a systematic approach to the building of the library's collection in the context of economic recession and involves the application of comm inity analysis and use studies, collection development policy, selection, acquisitions, and collection management aspects such as weeding, storage, preservation and collection evaluation, and notes the problems associated with each of these processes in special libraries in India.

According to Navaneethan[23], the exchange of reprints comprises an existing, effective network among authors. The proper collection and organization of reprints helps authors to obtain needed information instantly and the enables the librarian to save money by discontinuing costly periodicals from which few articles actually needed. He highlights the role of reprints and suggests a low cost method of acquiring reprints using the current awareness service.

Garg and Gupta[24] have found that special libraries customarily maintain a regular and systematic information service covering the immediate and future interests of the organisations of which they are part. This necessitates the development and management of an adequate collection of books, periodicals, reports, patents, standards, government publications, maps, audio-visual records. In house publications, market surveys, data files, are also brought together in these collections.

Ordering and Acquisition Process

Ordering and acquisition of documents brings libraries into direct contact with publishers and book suppliers. Various researchers have looked into the problems pertaining to the actual book acquisition process.

According to Alessi[25] libraries began to apply the techniques of computerization in 1960s to their ordering process, the generation of purchase orders, claims and cancellations, fund accounting and the like. Automation will provide easier access and delivery of materials. It will also allow the libraries to have more control over purchases leading ultimately to cooperative collection development through link-ups or through common vendor or any other system of acquisition. But it has also created a fear among book vendors that electronic transmission of orders from library to publisher directly may have adverse effect on their own position.

Eaglin[26] states that libraries should buy all their books from wholesalers because this is more efficient and less costly. Only a few publishers are willing to offer equal discount for equal volume. The rest hang on to a century old practice that has alienated libraries for nearly as long and for no good or even valid reason. Most will agree that the cost of the sale to the retailer is greater than it is to the library: why then arbitrarily decide that it is up to the library to pay for the greater cost? She suggests that publishers should either pass it on to the bookseller or amortize it equally by charging a little more to all.

Lockman[27] observes that vendor must actively maintain an up-to-date liaison with publishers, abiding by their terms of sales, communicating with the customer service departments to guarantee earlier possible delivery of out of stock titles, abiding by publishers returns policy, paying publishers invoice.

Bauman[28] has found in his study that ordering directly from publishers usually results in an increase in the workload for the acquisition departments. Vendors provide valuable services. While there is no doubt that vendors are in business to make money, competition works to keep their discount schedule high.

According to Secor "all too often vendors treat their library clients and prospective clients in much the same fashion as some politician treat their voters to a business naivete that pre-supposes that a vendor is indeed a non profit entity. These same non-business oriented librarians tend to view the vendor as a big bookstore in the sky-browsing collections to whimsically order from and return to".[29]

Somers[30] argues that firm orders are important to a successful acquisition program and the factors that are critical when selecting a vendor are speed and accuracy of delivery, a willingness to handle a wide range of publications, a proven track record with other libraries, and service .

Lockman[31] states that in addition to determining which of the vendor services are available, the acquisitions librarians must develop a basic understanding of definitions publishers use in classifying their books. Quite often a title will be available from a publisher in several editions each offering a different discount to the vendor and therefore, a different discount to library. Understanding the different classification of books, as well as knowing the difference between trade publishers, technical publishers, university presses, reprint houses of text book publishers would prove very useful. Each type of publisher approaches the book buyer with such a different marketing strategy that delivery rates, out of stock reports and cancellations will lack consistency when viewed in toto. Each publisher type will invest his capital to achieve his own desired results from selling what is stock today with little regard to out of stock titles, to actively accumulating back orders to justify a reprinting.

Hossain[32] has emphasised the need for librarians getting information about new publications. Every new publication should be duly advertised so that it can be acquired easily.

Regarding fulfilling the library orders, Kaula[33] states that it has been experienced that even though the order for the purchase of books are placed with certain booksellers who agree to supply the books within the prescribed time, the experience of librarians in this respect is quite different. Generally 25 to 30% of the books ordered from abroad are supplied and the library is at a loss.

Acquisition of Government Documents

Gandhi[34] emphasises that the skill of shopping around assessing the cost effectiveness of supplier's goods and services is important for the librarian to develop. The acquisition of foreign publications and government documents require specialised knowledge. In special libraries the acquisition of technical reports, conference proceedings and other fugitive material, not obtainable through normal trade channels is a great problem.

Mohinder Singh[35] in his study of publications of state governments states that there is wide spread dissatisfaction among the users of libraries due to poor stocks of government publications, particularly the publications of state government. At the state level there is no independent central publishing and distribution agency. The attachment of publications units to the printing and stationary departments at a very low level of hierarchy and the decentralised publishing policy presently prevailing in the state have made the identification and acquisition of relevant publications most difficult.The ineligible importance given to promotion and distribution of such publications and lack of proper bibliographic control has further complicated the situation. Even if the relevant publications have been identified from secondary sources, it may be difficult to know about the right source from where publications can be promptly acquired.

Pricing and Discounts

Escalating prices of books and dubious discount policies have always bothered the libraries. A lot of literature is available in this area.

Reidelbach[36] in his study reveals that discounts for most plans typically range from 10% to 13%. Each vendor handles discounts in a slightly different way. Some have flat charges applied across the board to all materials; others have sliding scales depending upon the size and nature of the plan. The primary characteristic is that discounts are negotiable in most cases, depending upon the process included in the plan and its subject and non-subject qualifiers. Most vendors report that all books shipped via approval receive the same type of discounts.

The most confounding issue, Lockman [37] in his study reveals that vendors face from publishers is that of net pricing. With the elimination of any official list price, one is a quandary when determining a fair price. This problem is compounded by the ever growing number of publishers adopting this practice.

Bauman[38] argues that publishers establish their price based on projected sales revenue. If they were to sell at a higher discount directly to libraries, they would simply make up the lost revenue by either raising their prices or cutting down on the number of unprofitable books which are published

According to Mastejulia[39] the final price of a book ultimately determines how many books will be bought by a library. The publisher determines the cost to acquire a manuscript and to print and distribute the book and adds the profit to this cost for arriving at the price of the publication. The price may not appear in any announcement or advertisement and may only be given when an inquiry is made to the publisher. Some may indicate the net price; others, a built-in cost factor. In some cases, once they get their profit from the sale of a book, they do not care what price is charged as long as their sales and profit requirements are met. Publishers often apply one discount policy to wholesalers and another to libraries. Discount may reflect the quantity ordered as well as the type and category of material e.g. single title, agency, continuations, text, trade etc. The suggested list price may appear in journals, resource publications, catalogue reviews and announcements. Accuracy of the suggested list price is determined by the type and age of the announcement, reputation of publisher to adhere to prepublication pricing and the age of the publication.

Schrift[40] argues that a major reason for steady rise of average list price of scholarly books is the smaller print run. There are certain fixed costs usually amortized over the entire length of the print run. When this print run is reduced by 20% to 30%, the list price must be increased to cover the cost.

Layman[41] in his write-up poses an intriguing new approach to publishing costs. Layman summarizes the current situation as one in which scholarly publishing is subsidized by subscription rates. He describes a shift since 1940s from non-commercial to commercial scholarly publishing in which only 15 per cent of scholarly publishing is now non-commercial.The essence of Layman's approach is to change to a distributed economic model which would centralize fixed costs and revenue (authorship, editorial efforts, and composition), but would distribute variable cost and revenues (printing and distribution). He would like the publisher to return to publishing and decentralize the manufacturing aspects.

Continuing the debate further, Secor[42] says that librarians who continue to fan flames of discount gamesmanship by pushing for more and more discount will find that they pay in depressed services. Librarians who continue to incite vendor hype will accelerate the imminent fallout that is going to hit publishing trade in the late 1980s.

Bhatt[43] in his study discusses various factors involved in book selection in India particularly the continuos increase in the prices of the books and the devaluation of thc rupee. He has suggested need for incresed resources sharing for meeting this challenge.

Alvi[44] has described the crisis which has developed in Indian libraries due to the explosion of knowledge in combination with the poor economic environment and rising prices of documents. He suggest solutions which include resource sharing, mechanisation, and commercialisation of services.

Goil[45] in his study takes note of the abnormal escalation in the prices of reading material and rising staff costs are hindering the development of library services. Urges publishers to reduce prices and review the rationale behind their structuring of book prices. He further suggests that libraries should go for microforms of documents to save space and money.

Ismail[46] stresses the need and importance of selection of documents in the face of rise in prices. Discusses the impact of frequent rise in prices of books and the problems faced by librarians due to variations in discount, non-printing of prices and other variations in editions. Refers to the unfair practices of publishers and lack of authentic bibliographical sources to check the original prices.

Problem of Remainder Titles

Narendar Kumar and Saini[47] have studied the problem of remainders in library acquisition and have found out that booksellers in India buy remainders very cheaply often at a half or less of catalogue price and offer these titles at full catalogue price. They further state that sometimes a library needs to order old publications and when he looks sources for bibliographic details, he finds that title is listed in out-of print bibliography. As a result the order is not placed. However, the title, is in fact, available in the market in the remaindered form. The authors suggest that publishers and booksellers association of India and Good Offices Committee should make efforts with overseas publishers for to bring out a bibliography of overseas remainders periodically. The Federation of Publishers' and Booksellers' Association in India has proposed that old editions of titles in print should not be permitted under Open General License and that suppliers from overseas should certify on their invoices that the books are the current editions in print. Commenting on the issue of remainder titles, Patil[48] in his paper argues that wholesalers and booksellers purchase these books at a low price-almost throw away price, sell these books at regular price on par with other books without giving the benefit to the libraries.

Journals

Fiste[49] observes that it will be increasingly expansive to launch journals and more risk will be involved. In popular areas the market will become quickly saturated. In addition, the potential market for journals is diminishing. Twenty years ago new journals could attract 1000 or more institutional subscribers. In the 1970s the figure was between 500 and 1000. In the 1980s, the number drops to several hundred subscribers.

Clack[50] commented that launching a journal involves a long term investment of six to seven years before profits are realized. Profits are realized from a mix of published material; print, on-line, CD-ROM, etc. He does not feel that publicizing a firms' total profits will solve any problem. Libraries should be considering value, quality, and usage in addition to price. Producing first rate materials is worth the risk involved in launching and canceling journals.

According to Markwith[51], "the achievements of a bookseller's profitability is more than sale pitches. It is more than management style and panache. It is more than accountants' fine-point pens and bottomlines. But it is dependent on the customers support of service and capabilities".

Singh[52] in her study of role of subscription agents in serial collection has concluded that agent's service to libraries is absolutely dependent upon its ability to plan for future and to take help of new technologies. Singh has suggested that subscription agents, like their western counterparts should try to maintain a data bank so as to place quick orders without any delay. Instead of renewal list, they should send final perfect invoice so that interruption in service does not arise and should take all efforts to procure the gaps for its clients.

Regarding the acquisition of periodicals, Dey[53] in his paper argues that procurement of library materials through Indian agents directly offers several advantages and disadvantages. He states that these problems can be overcome by introducing procurement through State Trading Corporation. It could be the most appropriate agency to undertake this work, provided it works effectively with a separate division.

Sylvia[54] states that special libraries face serious budgetary problems in the development of library collections for scholarly research due to rising cost of journal subscription prices and the increased number of journals. Bibliographical citation analysis of research papers is one method of evaluating the use of journal collection.

According to McCarthy[55] shrinking funds combined with journal prices are forcing many libraries in the US to conduct wholesale cancellations of journals. The average science journal price is 360 dollars.

Vaidya[56] states that the problem of acquisition of journals and serials get magnified many times because of far flung markets, primitive accounting system, foreign exchange problems, unorganised book trade, bogus agencies, erratic postal services, etc.

According to Puri[57], “It is universal practice that the responsibility for the issue that go amiss in transit can not be that of the subscription agency”

Reddy and Suseela[58] in their study of prices of journals highlight the impact of indiscriminate pricing policies of publishers, foreign exchange, mailing charges and inflation on periodical prices in India by calculating the average price of a periodical in dollars, sterling and rupees. Suggests ways of tackling these problems by increased resource sharing and networking.

Reddy[59] has studies trends in prices for the core periodicals according to the subject, country of origin, type of publisher and frequency, by applying statistical indicators such as: Mean growth rates; compound growth rates; standard deviation; and coefficient of variation over the period 1981 to 1991. Trends in foreign exchange and problems related to Indian inflation are discussed. He concludes that periodical prices have increased by 21 to 31 per cent, foreign exchange by 10 to 15 per cent and Indian inflation by almost 8 per cent. Further, the prices showed significant dispersion and were less consistent.

Anand[60] in his paper highlights the importance of current periodicals in Indian institutions of higher education and research. Discusses the problems of subscription to current periodicals such as inflation, additional cost of special numbers of periodicals, uncertainty of arrears bills, communication gap between publishers and agents, postage and handling charges, additional charges for late orders, fluctuation in international money market etc. Stresses the psychological factor in substituting periodicals which have been subscribed to for decades. Agrees with the observation of the Parry Committee regarding the decision to subscribe to a periodical. Also discusses proliferation and fission of periodicals, with examples. Gives viable suggestions in order to minimise the problems of financing for subscription to current periodicals.

Kapoor[61] enumerates and discusses modes of subscribing to foreign journals for the Indian Libraries and discusses advantages and limitations as experienced by working librarians, and isolates the basic problem of delayed transmittal of subscriptions and losses in transit. Suggests possible ways of reducing the problem: (1) subscribe to foreign journals through agents when possible; (2) subscribe through distributors if appointed; (3) order directly all publications of learned bodies, associations, institutions, corporate bodies, and publishers with multiple publications; and (4) use established foreign vendors for little known private concerns or obscure new publications.

Acquisition: Vendors' Role

Secor[62] says that libraries and vendors form a partnership. In practice, the professional vendor is an extension of the library's acquisition processes and must function on an ethical plane. The library must be concerned with total service; the vendor must be concerned with providing these services while maintaining the fiscal responsibilities inherent in a business setting.

Bonk[63] emphasises that order placement should be dependent upon an ongoing evaluation of sources of supply against the library's objectives in placement of standing order. Evaluation of sources of supply should be dependent upon clear objectives of what is expected from the source of supply and/ or what is not expected because of local capabilities or local priorities. These objectives should be clear to the person making the order decision, the vendor, and the library staff who actually process the materials after initial ordering.

According to Saxena[64], spot selection of books should be done with great caution and vendor should not be allowed to contact individually the faculty members for selection of books, otherwise through aggressive salesmanship technique lot of rubbish or trash literature which does not find easy market at the bookshops is dumped in libraries. In respect of acquisition of periodicals, Saxena observes that in India there is dearth of reliable agents and some of the agents take advance payment from the libraries and do not remit to respective parties either in time or even at all. Experience has shown that it is always economical to order periodicals directly with the publishers or their sole authorised agents.

Sridhar[65] in his case study of ISRO Satellite Centre Library has revealed that 35 per cent of total acquisition of books were against specific suggestions of users and only about 21 per cent of total users have ever suggested books to the library. One of the reasons for such a low participation of users in collection development is book procurement delays. Quick and timely procurement of suggested/ on demand books act as achievement motivator for further suggestions from users. Sridhar further states that as high as 48 per cent demand of users are not met even after 8/20 months of placing orders. Though the ordering policy has a favourable edge to Indian retail vendors, the performance of foreign vendors with an average 50 per cent efficiency is much better than 28 per cent efficiency of Indian vendors. Many Indian book vendors make random supply in an accidental way, depending on match of pending orders with stock based on memory of operating staff. There were instances where books pending for supply for long time came as approval books either from the same vendors or others in the city. Even the feedback about delay or non-availability or cancellation rarely comes from Indian vendors.

Cox[66] in his paper discusses role of subscription agents as interface between publisher and librarians. Development such as document delivery have caused a widening of the gap between large vendors and their smaller competitors, resulting in fewer, larger companies. He asserts that future lies with much reduced serial collections supplemented by a range of information services based on bulletin boards, journal contents, and the delivery of individual articles and other data all from remote suppliers.

According to Marriman,[67] the subscription agent forms a vital link in the information chain of author, publisher, librarian and reader, claims of missing issues, duplicate copies.

Publishing and Collection Development

Publishing is an activity which causes something to be printed and offered for sale and publisher as a person or firm that publishes; especially one that prints and issues to the public newspapers, books and other literary matters. No library can develop its collection without continuous supply of good reading material. There is a very close link between the librarians and the publishers and the book suppliers. Librarians as consumer of information, deal with publishers and vendors. Some of the studies have touched upon this aspect of the research.

Hodge[68] states that they are part of separate but intersecting systems. Publishers, book sellers and libraries depend upon and are affected by the products, requirements or services of one another. The costs, efficiency of services and the products themselves (i.e. books) are influenced by a complex set of factors over which librarians have little or no control. Publishers by changing their organisational structure and adopting more automated procedures are seeking to survive in the competitive marketplace or even strengthen their positions. Many of their internal and distribution procedures will become more responsive and efficient. Book distributors will continue to find the services offered by specialized vendors of turnkey systems competing against their own acquisition and financial reporting system. They will also face stiff competition from library networks as well. With the options provided by competing and diverse services, libraries will be in more favourable position to make their preferences and requirements known and to have a major influence the type of services that will be developed in the future. The result will be that libraries with their differing requirements and wide range of budget may have a greater variety of systems to assist them in realizing their objectives more effectively.

Dole[69] investigating the relationship between publishers, vendors and librarians describe it as symbiotic. Books are carriers and disseminators of ideas. More than any other means of communication, they are the most permanent, reasoned, and essential repository of the thoughts of civilized man. Book trade is in fact, both the guardian and constant creator of our written culture. Librarians have a tendency to sanctify both vending and publishing because these industries are involved in what librarians often view as their sacred mission of acquiring and preserving knowledge. This is why when publishers and vendors act more business-like, librarians often feel as if a sacred trust has been betrayed.

On the contrary Cine and Sinhot[70] in their study argue that most librarians and faculty perceive of the library as eternal. They think of informational value of a work, not of its format or the type of publisher who produced it or the method of distribution by which it must be obtained.

Dole[71], looks into the reason of conflicts that arise between libraries, publishing and vending, and states that each system perceives conflicts within its own frame of reference. They all maintain that they are misunderstood. Librarians and vendors criticise publishers for churning out catalogues and flyers which do not contain the information needed for selection and acquisition. Librarians complain that vendors do not understand the impact of their actions on library operations. If the acquisition librarian of a large library is promised a book shipment on a specific day of the week, he or she arranges the work flow of the department accordingly. If the vendor does not keep that promise and the shipment arrives late or several week's shipment arrive together, the work flow of the acquisition department is disturbed.

According to Grasse[72], "publishers are trying to improve the organisation and method of book distribution. Despite more computers and centralized warehouse, it still takes too long to get books to libraries, booksellers and distributors. The physical flow of books from the manufacturing line to ultimate consumer will certainly be helped by effective automation." A very important aspect of this development will be computerised management of order consolidation for more economic shipping.

Lockman[73] lists the type of publisher's policy, practice that affect supply of books. These are : (i) title changed or never published, (ii) price increase, (iii) multiple ISBNs, (iv) restricting distribution and (v) continued receipt of wrong books.

Boissonnas[74] argues that there are other aspects of title output that influence collection development. Even though there seems to be more money to spend on fewer books, publishers are cutting the number of copies per title being printed. If orders are not placed before or soon after publication, titles may be unavailable when orders are placed. And even though the averages may not be increasing greatly, the actual amount spent depends as much on the type of book purchased as on how many are purchased.

According to Secor[75], the book industry is being punished, like so many other businesses, by the economy and rising interest rates. The library community has been severely shaken and after years of struggling to maintain the quality of their collections, now find budgets inadequate to the challenge. Over the past several years, book sales have been flat with minimal dollar increase in unit sale. There are many single corporations which boast sales far in excess of entire book industry, which is comprised of 15000 to 20000 individual publishers.

Schrift[76] states that publishers release of new titles has become much more conservative in recent years. Many announce titles well in advance of publication and only make the decision to publish when sufficient orders have been received. The most significant change is rather dramatic decrease in units produced of a new title. Fifteen years ago, when the successful title had sold some 75% of its print run, this would have prompted the publisher to reprint additional copies. Today, Shrift continues, when the initial print run is sold out, there is a very good chance it will not be reprinted, and ultimately will be declared out of print.

Continuing the argument Flansburg[77] states that a common understanding of the distribution process is essential to improve dealer- library relations. One of the methods of developing this understanding is through effective communication.

According to Sachdev[78] there is a need for trade on its part to change so as to cater to the needs of specialised libraries more effectively. The need to provide the libraries with easy access to report literature, dissertation or even microform products should be explored by the trade.

Danesi[79] compares and contrasts his different experiences with scholarly, educational and trade publishers. Each publisher has different motives and procedures and authors have to accommodate themselves to these differences in order to be successful.

According to Davidar[80], before the launch of Penguin Books India in 1987, trade publishing in English in India did not have the high profile in bookstores and review pages it has today. Discusses the reasons why Indian writers in English, especially novelists and authors of general non-fiction books, failed to be published in the past by Indian publishers. The publication of Salman Rushdie's *Midnight's Children* in 1981 opened up the world market to Indian writers and the following decade saw an explosion in literary novels. Trade publishing is now coming into its own. There is now a large number of educated, urban middle class Indians to whom English is a first language who need books relevant to their needs. Penguin India began publishing in October 1987 with 6 titles and in 1994 published over 100 original titles and will continue to publish at that rate.

According to Roy[81], India, with its massive and growing English reading population, is a market ripe for expansion. Describes the changing trends in publishing and opportunities for UK publishers in areas such as: manufacturing; distribution; bookshops; book fares; and joint ventures.

Publishing Trade: Current Issues

Publishing trade faces a range of contemporary challenges that have a profound impact on the nature of the industry and indirectly the ways that books are produced and distributed.

According to Altbach and Teferra[82], two basic technological developments are affecting publishing. The first is the reprographic revolution initiated by photocopy technology which has stimulated not only the ubiquitous photocopy machine, bringing challenge to copyright, but has introduced innovation in printing. The second one is of still greater importance than reprography to publishing is the revolution based on computer. Traditional composition technologies have, in much of the world, been replaced by computer based composition and book design. This has also changed business procedures relating to inventory control, billing, and tracing trends in the sale of specific titles. Computer technology has also permitted the effective use of targeted mailing lists, specialized publicity campaigns and the like.

Discussing the economics of publishing, Smith and Datus[83] lament the lack of risk capital, or at least of capital that its owners are willing to invest in the future of their own countries, holds back development in many parts of Asia, Africa, and Latin America. The problem is especially acute in the book publishing trade and under capitalization is perhaps the most serious single obstacle to book publishing development in the developing countries. They further argue that it is lack of business loan at a sensible rate of interest, the publisher is forced to go to bazar money lenders and pay 25 per cent or more. This leads to the escalation of publishing costs.

Graham[84] who has studied trends in European publishing argues that many of the companies in North America and Western European publishing companies have retreated into lagers of affluence because of their deep structural changes. "The information revolution and its accompanying technology have generated publishing enterprise on a scale not dreamt of 30 years ago, and with the book no longer occupying centre stage. These corporations, argues Graham, may not have become multinational, but they have become" multimedia" and have acquired many of the traditional folio publishing houses."

Electronic Publishing

A virtual revolution is taking place in publishing world which has long range implications for the library systems. The electronic revolution is fast threatening the very existence of book in its present physical format. It is being replaced by an electronic form. How real is the challenge and how publishing world is coping with it, is the area of research which some investigators have looked into.

Guedon[85] says that electronic publishing still suffers from a lack of legitimacy so authors, especially young ones that are seeking tenure hesitate committing the fruits of their efforts to a medium that is still viewed in many quarters as if it were little more than a vanity press in a new form. The stock of full texts in electronic form may be steadily growing, but it still amounts to very little in comparison with what is available in print in any university.

According to Clack[86], publishers are developing systems which will allow on-line order processing and full text searching. But still she predicted that there will be dramatic price increase for US periodicals because alternate methods of dissemination of information will be more costly than the present one and publishers will not invest heavily in new technologies until they have a better grasp of their use.

The development of the internet, electronic journals, and questions surrounding the longevity of paper journal have led some to wonder what the role of subscription vendors will be in the future. According to Brooke[87], regardless of the future changes in the variety of information and available media, the subscription or information agency's main role-helping customers efficiently identify, procure and manage a variety of information resources will be the same, although the methods of conducting business will change and additional services will be offered. Even if information becomes more fragmented and the "journal" as we know it ceases to exist, access to articles, through websites, online hosts, or other means, will probably still be available on subscription. Moreover, providing user with coordinated, cost effective access to quality information about serials and articles will continue to a challenge for libraries.

Brown[88] in her report, "Approaches to Internet based collection" lays down the factors affecting the internet, has argued for the need for short-term planning due to rapid changes in resources available and technologies.

Hunter[89] in his work communicates some of the publishing world's problems and concerns in the face of digital technology. This new technology divorces the content from the container and is relegating the journal to the artifact of the paper world. The Internet is a major factor in this divorce, despite which, he believes that the expertise of publishers and librarians will always be necessary. He further argues that pricing is now driven by form, content or use, no longer by just container. Most publishers are floundering and fear is the rule of the day. The loss of sales of reference works to individuals, books for a scholar's home library, or departmental journal can be significant.

Gleason[90] discussing the problems related to piracy and copyright states that ease with which the new technologies allow copies to be made of information published electronically on the web, through electronic bulletin boards, from propriety databases, and so on and then downloaded to a user's personal computer and transmitted by them to other users PCs has been boon to both scholarly and commercial communication and a cause of serious concern to publishers and their owners of intellectual property. Gleason further argues that in the face of piracy problem, while countries of industrialised countries and their publishers have stepped their efforts to combat book piracy in recent years, the economic and social development of some developing countries and the advancement of their publishing industries have induced them to change their attitudes towards the international copyright systems.

Vishwanathan[91], in his write up on electronic publishing in India reveals that electronic publishing is fast picking up in India. At present, the emphasis is more on network publishing than on optical disk publishing. But the complementarity of the two technologies, Vishwanathan argues, is expected to move publishers to both the network and CD-ROM publishing in the coming years. "India with its vast information and knowledge sources, is likely to contribute significantly in terms of vehicles to run on the global information infrastructure that is likely to evolve in the next few decades or so".

Jacso[92] has pointed out growing problem of the proliferation of CD-ROM databases and the pressure this brings to bear on collection development. He has suggested that future collection development decisions will be eased by significant reductions in the price of expansive abstracting and indexing services as cheap full text version of primary periodicals become available.

According to Rao[93], CD-ROM database availability and usage is still in the nascent stage in India. Major factors influencing the popularity of CD-ROMs includes out of reach subscription prices, difficulties with procedures at custom offices for importing databases.

Knibbe[94] describes where the subscription agent fits into the electronic publishing process and how the subscription agent actively contributes to this industry. He concludes that, while electronic publishing offers a great deal of potential in terms of ease of access and content, little (if any) of the actual administrative burden is removed. For that reason, subscription agents will continue to play an active and progressive role in the procurement of electronic periodicals.

Baldwin[95] in his paper focusses on the factors that will make electronic periodicals successful. The research indicates that readers and authors want electronic access to periodicals and they view the key benefits as convenience, time savings, wider circulation, and faster publication times. Ideally they want integrated services within a discipline offering a searchable database, a wide range and a critical mass of full text periodicals and seamless linking among periodicals.

Reviews the initiatives publishers are taking to develop electronic periodicals and integrated services and suggests some of the emerging issues for librarians.

According to Getz[96], higher education faces a significant challenge in discovering what academic information will succeed on the Internet. The cost of launching a new journal electronically seems to be falling. It remains to be seen whether the new electronic journals will attract successful editors and valued manuscripts from authors. In the end, universities should be drawn to electronic information services because of their superiority in instruction, their reach beyond the academy, and their power in the creation of new ideas.

Kovacs[97] considers the complex impact of electronic publishing (e-publishing) on library collections, services and administration. While acknowledging that there are no simple solutions to the problems of managing the collection, archiving and access to electronic publications and including them in library services, notes that there are many good, usable solutions that libraries can learn from each other. Concludes that how the advent and increasing presence of electronic publications will impact the people who will read them may ultimately turn out to be of more importance than what is done with the machines, the storage media or the delivery mechanism. Therefore, emphasis in this special theme issue is more on the human interaction aspects of electronic publishing than on the technology or delivery mechanisms.

According to Scupola[98], the publishing industry, like many other industries, is exploring new markets, new services and new products in response to forces such as advances in information and communication technologies, business strategies such as mass customization, globalization and shorter production cycles. Focuses on the way in which electronic commerce (e-commerce) technologies are changing and could change the publishing processes, and develops a business value complementarity model of electronic publishing. This model gives a theoretical rationale for, and can be used as a methodology to explore, complementarities between different primary activities and supporting technologies when entering the e-commerce arena in order to maximize profitability and improve the competitive position.

According to Chakraborty[99], CD publishing in and about India is increasing rapidly. Some Indian organisations have started storing their data on CD-ROMs and a few libraries and information centres have also started to store and market catalogue and bibliographical data on CD-ROMs. Investigates the variety of such products being published in India and provides information on some 20 Indian producers of CD-ROM databases, drives, software, networking facilities and maintenance services. Includes descriptions of some 33 CD-ROMs covering full text databases, bibliographic databases, dictionaries, business and company information, multimedia, tourism, educational and professional materials.

Amudhavalli[100] has examined the problems of collection development in traditional libraries and how they can be tackled in the IT environment. Also considers the problems faced by library and information centres in procuring electronic publications. She emphasises the need for a clear cut collection development policy in this regard.

Kane[101] in his study takes a look at the advantages offered to libraries by World Wide Web based book retailing companies, noting the lack of the kind of guidance to libraries that is the strong suit of the traditional library vendor. The library vendor sees its role as directing libraries away from some books that it feels are not required, whereas Web-based vendors have no constraints.

Wilhite[102] observes that the acquisition of electronic access to information is characterized by growth and change. Budgets earmarked for electronic access increase year by year. Acquisitions staff endeavour to plan workflow and create records to track trial or free subscriptions as well as paid orders. It is important to retain record flexibility to accommodate changing order specifications and to provide useful management reports.

Kytomaki and Nordinfo[103] have stated in their study that the Finnish collection development policy is regulated through legislation on legal deposit and the National Repository Library and the government's 1972 decision on national resource libraries. Local and regional supply is the responsibility of the university and public libraries, while the national resource libraries supply information in their respective disciplines. Now the Internet and electronic publishing make this policy unworkable. The advantage of electronic publications is their availability and searchability, but they put pressure on funds allocated for new materials and cause additional work. While before some core materials was acquired by all universities, now one joint nationwide license for core databases and publications could surface. Another solution is a government funded national electronic library. The location of the acquired shared electronic materials could be a Pan-Nordic server.

Publishing in Third World

Commenting on Third World publishing scenario Altbach and Teferra[104] argue that most Third World countries do not produce a sufficient amount of "cultural paper" needed for book production and many produce virtually no paper at all. According to them "supplies of cultural paper must be imported in a market dominated by several major industrialized nations as producers and by major western user countries which set prices. The large Western multinational publishers and other major users in the industrialized nation can obtain paper less expensively by purchasing in bulk". According to Zell,[105] who has studied problems of publishing in Third World countries, book publishing is in crisis in most African countries, their economies wrecked by past corrupt regimes, capital flight, devastating years of drought and famine and political unrest. Few indigenous publishers have been able to meet the challenges of the book shortages and the majority of them are still unable to compete with the multi-nationals on real terms.

Zell further states that major problem faced by African readers is poor access to books. Libraries and bookshops are concentrated in urban centres only. "It appears", Zell concludes "that African book industry has entered the final decade of century with many of the same problems that have existed since the early 1970s. Certainly it must be conceded that based on content wide statistical evidence, the prospects for African publishing are not encouraging".

Altbach and Teferra[106] in their study of textbooks in developing countries point out how British, American and Soviet organizations placed a greater number of textbooks either in their original language or in translation in Third World countries at highly discounted prices. The authors point out that "Third World publishers have claimed that the foreign books undercut their own publications and actually hinder the emergence of domestic textbooks".

Graham[107] has studied the impact of multinationals on third world publishing. According to him, the emergence of multinational media corporations has transformed the structure of major book publishing industries of Europe and North America in the second half of the twentieth century. Before World War II book publishing companies were small, nationally based and mostly personally owned. By 1990s more than half of all book publishing in Europe and America was controlled by companies that were largely publicly owned, and international. This transformation is irreversible, at least in the short term, if only for the reason that it makes financial sense.

Chakava[108] has looked into the problems of publishing trade in Kenya. His findings reveal that previously the Kenyan publishing trade was dominated by multinationals but over the last five years, things have somewhat changed. Two of ten largest commercial publishers, Longman Kenya and Heinaman Kenya, have come under the control of the locals. "Their next challenge according to Chakava is to fully "Kenyanize" their list, a portion of which are still written, developed and printed out of country". But the greatest problem being faced by the Kenyan publishers is the lack of capital. A book can take up to two years from the time of commissioning an author to write it to the time of finished copies, and might take longer to sell.

Similarly discussing the problems of publishing trade in Nigeria, Nwanko [109] states that "the problem of combating book shortages in Nigeria is the problem of overcoming the disabilities of under development. A national government's role in book development should be to co-ordinate the nation's economic activities to optimally enhance the growth of book production. The thrust of this guiding role should be to motivate private initiatives, in whose hands the bulk of publishing is in Nigeria and ought to be in any developing country.

Hossain[110] and others in their study of library collection in Bangladesh states that one of the negative factors working against book procurement is the morbid state of the local book trade. As for provisions of badly needed foreign publications of advanced subjects level, the book sellers are found to be woefully unenterprising. Much of the indifference, according to the author stems from restrictive import policy, which does not favour import of books and periodicals from abroad; nor does encourage entrepreneurs to invest much in the book trade. Another problem according to authors is the almost total lack of book trade bibliography in the form of catalogue of publications for current and older books, indexes, abstracting journals and book review literature.

Arboleda[111] looking into distribution problems in third world countries says that distribution is further hampered because publishers in third world countries are often not well versed in the intricacies of consumer demand and, therefore, do not know how many people will buy a book. As a result they tend to produce uneconomically small quantities. He further states that market surveys consistently neglect distribution. Many statistical overviews present a plethora of numbers on manufacturing and production, but there is almost nothing on what happens with the product.

According to Arboleda[112], even though the general picture of distribution in the third world is the same everywhere, the actual situation varies with each country and region. In 1991, Asia with total population of 3.6 billion inhabitants, accounted for 30 per cent of the total world production of 929,000 book titles. The industrialized world accounted for about 80 per cent with only 25 per cent of world's population. As more and more countries in Asia begin to recognize that education is fundamental to development, there is parallel realization of the importance of publishing and, thereby, the need to improve distribution system.

Hasan[113] in his study, lists great number of languages within many countries, the lack of indigenous authorship, copyright problems, the high cost of production as possible obstacles in improving the distribution system. Hasan thinks that it will be "rather difficult to achieve a real breakthrough in book distribution in Asia without national wholesale distribution agencies. He feels that they could "act as a catalyst in movement of the books to every corner of the country".

Moutchia[114] Director of the Regional Centre for Book Promotion in Africa south of the Sahara, characterizes Africa's book industry as young. The vast continent of Africa, with 10 per cent of World's population, produced meagre 2 per cent of the global output of the books in 1981 or 14000 titles in total. Africa remains behind other parts of the world, he feels, because no colonial powers made a deliberate attempt to introduce education or publishing. Distribution, he admits is in dire straits, particularly because transportation system is poor, government actions ineffectual, and interference is excessive.

Augsburger[115] looking into the distribution problems in Latin America argues that problems of distribution in Latin America are ostensibly not as complicated as in the other third world countries mainly because Spanish is spoken in most Latin American countries. According to him, "The movement of books across borders, particularly from larger publishing nations such as Argentina, Chile, or Mexico to nearby countries is simple".

Indian Publishing

The Indian book industry, which took shape towards the early part of this century and gained strength in the sixties is one of the top ten in the world and is largely in private hands. Indian publishers publish books in 14 major languages, including English and the total number of books produced on an average is 20,000 every year. No precise data are available on the number of publishers in the country, let alone their break-up by the types of book published. A survey carried out for the Ministry of Education of the Government of India[116] by the National Council for Applied Economic Research (NCAER), New Delhi, in 1985 had estimated that there were some 3000 active publishers in India of which the large majority are small scale publishers issuing 5-12 titles a year; 300 medium sized, issuing 12-50 titles a year; and 100 large issuing 50 or more titles a year.

Discussing the problems of Indian publishing trade, Tajeshwar Singh,[117] states that "among the most crucial of the these problems is the of lack of distribution channels. Only the metropolis and major cities are well served by bookshops". According to him, there are more than 6,000 colleges and universities in the country but Indian publishers find it difficult to sell even 500 or 600 copies of a scholarly title. That is equivalent to a mere 10 per cent penetration of the core market, without taking into account the additional market constituted by research institutions, individual buyers, and export sales". He further states that "there are publishers in India who do not pay royalties to authors. Booksellers sometimes give higher discounts to libraries just to ensure that they get lion share of business and importers often sell remainders at full price." Graham[118] in his study about Indian publishing emphasises the part played by multinationals in India as local publishers have not been able to contribute in a major way. There are numerous partnerships between

Indian and Western publishers where both sides seem to be content. Indian ventures by American college textbooks houses such as McGraw-Hill, N.Y, John Wiley, London or Prentice-Hall, N.J. based originally on local reprints, are now part of Indian publishing scene. More recent ventures such as that by Penguin or, on a smaller scale by Sage are consciously geared to a rule that a foreign partner can have only a minority share. He credits India for not restricting imports seriously, because the import trade provides a structure onto which local publishing can latch.

A study by Malhotra[119] reveals that it has been assumed unwittingly that Indian publishing, represented by English language publishing is confined to a few metropolitan cities. This segment actually represents only 15 per cent to 20 per cent of the total book publishing. He further states that we have rich literature in every language and all the Indian language publishers have encouraged new writers, and today, India has good authors not only in the field of humanities but in science and technology, computer and any field where ever books are needed.

Gupta[120] in his study argues that by the late fifties the Government of India also entered the publishing field. Central Government ministries started publishing books and reports. Some of this publishing was handled by the Manager of Publications, Ministry of Information and Broadcasting and distributed through private channels. But the basic thrust of the state was in two areas: School books which was handled by the National Council of Educational Research and Training (NCERT) and State Council of Educational Research and Training (SCERT) of different states.

According to Ghai[121], the nationalization of textbooks after independence was a big setback to Indian publishing industry. He opines, "Had school textbooks remained with commercial publishers, this would have yielded considerable revenue to publishers to underwrite creative and other range of books."

Raghavan[122] in his paper on "Publishing in Public Sector" states that "in the field of book publishing, the state has taken over exclusively certain sector of educational publishing".These sectors cover programmed books required by school students in very large numbers throughout the country in the different Indian languages, including English. Cent per cent monopoly in respect of school books is enjoyed by some state governments. Every state government has its own public sector agency such as departmental bureau, autonomous society or corporation to bring out and distribute school text books essentially on no-profit no-loss basis.

Koutchoumov[123] has looked into the current scenario and future of Indian publishing trade. According to him, publishing in 1998 is characterized by an increasing number of titles published at smaller and smaller print runs. The monopoly of books is gradually eroded by the new media, the last of which are the networks of computers. Books are still indispensable for shaping of individuals' future and future of India will have to be proved and shown by those involved in writing, publishing and reading. Koutchoumov emphasises need for shift in publishing priorities and exhorts publishers to publish lighter work which can be accompanied by diskettes or videos. Encyclopaedic work will be totally left to multimedia agencies. Publishers will publish on demand, engage in tailor made publishing with the advantage of sale on subscription, of reduced stocks and no returns.

Looking into ills of Indian publishing Narendra Kumar[124] states that despite the fact that publishing in many ways is an intellectual enterprise, it needs to have sound financial foundation. Kumar laments that Indian publishing in the post independence era has been beleaguered by the problems of an overall shaky economic base. Since a majority of publishing far from enjoying the pride of place has had to suffer from all the drawbacks of an incidental side activity. According to him, "With the general non-availability of bank loans and credit facilities, coupled with a Micawber-like talent for messing up business ventures, many publishers have ended up in the dock".

Distribution

Distribution constitutes the nervous system of publishing trade. No book trade can survive without the existence of a wide and effective book distribution network. Librarians have to spend a good time of their job to acquire books. At time they virtually have to chase the supplier for a particular title. Thus, distribution constitutes an essential part of publishing trade. A literate society is as dependent on its ability to distribute books widely as it is on the authors who writes the books. No publishing trade can adequately serve a nation's needs without the support of a sound and efficient network of competent wholesalers and retailers.

Discussing the problems of distribution, Lee[125] writes that a bookmaker has two basic tasks:(a) to facilitate communication between author and reader, and (b) to make the book a successful commercial product. "Publishers", he points out "often have cultural or personal objectives when they accept a book for publication, but the object of publishing as a business is to sell books".

Mastejulia[126] states that an increasing number of publishers are distributing their books through sources other than their own. Either their entire lists are distributed by other companies or publishers are splitting their lists and giving various parts to other publishers or distributors. The traditional role of publisher as a distributor of its own material is changing. We can no longer assume that the imprint publisher and the distributor will be same. Publishers' moves towards in-house efficiency are making it more difficult and expensive for libraries and vendors to acquire their material. Rising costs, will eventually affect the number of books purchased. The cycle of increasing costs leading to fewer books being purchased causing publishers to provide fewer services will hurt the library and its patrons, the publishers, and the vendor. Unfortunately, the publishers perpetuating this cycle may not be the ones directly and negatively affected.

The difficulties of distribution are also formidable for publishers in industrialized countries. In a speech at the annual meeting of the Book Manufacturers Institute in 1983, Brooks Thomas president of Harper & Row, pointed out that rising cost could be attributed in part to an inefficient distribution system in the United States.

Lottman[127] giving example of Japan states that despite a very-well developed and unique distribution system, readers served by over 4,000 publishers, 60 distributors, and 20,000 or more bookstores throughout the country, are sometimes neglected by the sophisticated automation of the system that is not geared to meet special request outside the distribution system.

Conclusion

It is evident from the above review of the literature that though there exists sizeable literature on the topic but most of the studies on collection development and publishing trade have been conducted in exclusion to each other and there is hardly any study which has examined in depth the mutual relationship between libraries and book trade. It makes it necessary to further explore the areas of mutual linkages so as to assess the problems of acquisition of documents in libraries in relation to book industry.

References

1. Hopper (F F). Order and accession department.1915. American Library Association, Chicago. p 11.
2. Cannon (Carl). Order and accession department: Manual of library economy. 1930. American Library Association, Chicago. p 17.
3. Drury(Francis K W).Order work for libraries. 1930. American Library Association, Chicago. p 45.
4. MElcher (Daniel). Melcher on acquisition. 1971. American Library Association. Chicago. p 23
5. Ford(Stephen). Acquisition of library materials. 1973. American Library Association, Chicago. p 43.

6. Carpenter(Eric J).Collection development policies based on approval plans. *Libr Acquis Prac Th* . 9; 1985; 51-59.

7. Aldregde (Noreen S). Collection development policies as a long range planning tool. *Libr Acquis Prac Th* . 8; 1984; 55.

8. Ferguson (Anthony). Electronic resources collection development policy statement workshop: A pre-conference. *Libr Acquis Prac Th* . 21; 1997; 239-240.

9. Mastejulia (Robert). Publisher policies and their impact on market. *Libr Acquis Prac Th*. 11; 1987; 139-144.

10. Sharon (W Propas). Publishers' trade discounts and public libraries *Libr Acquis Prac Th* . 8; 1984; 95-97.

11. Whaley (John H). Approaches to collection development evaluation: Use and user studies. *Libr Acquis Prac Th* . 8; 1984; 52-53.

12. Osburn. (Charles). New directions in collection development. *Libr Acquis Prac Th*. 8; 1984; 54-55.

13. Bavakutty (M).Development of book collection in college libraries in Kerala . *In* MANGLA(P B), *Ed.* Building library collections and national policy for library and information services. Seminar papers. 1985. ILA, Delhi. p 177-180.

14. EsperanzA (M). Collection development in college libraries. *In* Mangla (P B), *Ed.* Ibid. p 17-19.

15. Anand (J K). Collection development in college libraries: Need for a policy. *In* Building library collections and national policy for library and information services. *In* Mangla (P B), *Ed.* Ibid. p 192-198.

16. Tejmurty (A). Collection development in Madhya Pradesh university libraries. *In* Mangla (P B), *Ed.* Ibid. p 213-222.

17. Mehta (Surendra Nath). Collection development in scientific and technical research libraries in India. *In* Mangla (P B), *Ed. Ibid*. p 295-307.

18. Mishra (S). Role of policy statement in collection development. *In* Chatterjee(A) and others, *Ed.* Collection development in the context of economic recession. Seminar Papers. Indian Association of Special Libraries and Information Centres, Calcutta, 1993. p 29-31.

19. Wasan (R P).Acquisition of literature: Some problems. *IASLIC Bull.* 44, 1; 1999; 1-14.

20. Jones (D).Collection development in digital libraries. *Sc Tech Libr.*17, 3-4; 1999; 27-37.

21. Raina (R).Collection development: A policy indicator for IIM libraries. *In* Chatterjee(A) and others, *Ed.* Op cit. P 33-36.

22. Maheswarappa(B S). and Karisidappa(C R).Problems of collection development among special libraries in India. *In* Chatterjee(A) and others, *Ed.* Op cit. P 77-80.

23. Navaneethan(R). Low-cost collection development method for reprints in special libraries and information centres. *In* Chatterjee(A) and others, *Ed.* Op cit. P 81-93.

24. Garg(K C) and Gupta (S P). Collection development and management in special libraries in India. *Collect Manag.* 8, 2; 1986;103-112.

25. Alessi (Dana L). Book jobbers-their yesterday: Here today, gone tomorrow. *Libr Acquis Prac Th.* 5; 1981; 25-29.

26. Eaglln (Audrey B).Publishers trade discount and public libraries. *Libr Acquis Prac Th.*15; 1991;95-97.

27. Lockman (E D).The resolution on trade publishing discount. *Libr Acquis Prac Th* .8; 1984; 68-71.

28. Bauman (Susan). An application of Davis model for vendor study. *Libr Acquis Prac Th .18*; 1994; 83-89.

29. Secor (John). The resolution on trade publishing discount. *Libr Acquis Prac Th* . 8; .1984; 71-74.

30. Somers (Sally). Vendor library relations: A perspective. *Libr Acquis Prac Th.* 19; 1997;135-139.

31. Lockman (E D).Op cit. P 66.

32. Hossan(Sarwar) and others. Problems and prospects of library collection in Bangladesh. *ILA Bull.* 26, 2;1990; 67-68.

33. Kaula(P N). Book trade and libraries. *In* SARDANA (J L), *Ed.* Libraries and the book trade. Seminar papers. 1982. ILA, Delhi. P 15.

34. Gandhi (R S). Collection development in special libraries. *In* Mangla(P B), *Ed.* Op cit. P 314-321.

35. Monhinder Singh . Problems in the acquisition of publications of state governments. *In* MANGLA(P B), *Ed.* Ibid. P 437-451.

36. Reidelbach (John H). Selecting an approval plan vendor II: Comparative vendor data. *Libr Acquis Prac Th* . 18; 1995; 157-203.

37. Lockman (E D). *Op cit.* p 67.

38. Bauman (Susan). *Op cit.* p 84.

39. Mastejulia (Robert). *Op cit.* p 141.

40. Schrift (Leonard). The Thor power tool decision and its impact on scholarly publishing. *Libr Acquis Prac Th* 12; 1988; 175-188.

41. Layman (Peter). Document delivery and on demand publishing: Implication for reference service. *Coll Res Libr News.* 53; 1992; 7-11

42. Secor (John). *Op cit.* p. 73.

43. Bhatt (R K).Book acquisition programme in libraries and information centres under the financial crunch. *Hr Lib Sc.* 34, 1-2; 1995; 20-6.

44. Alvi (Wajih). Escalating book prices: their impact on libraries. *ILA Bull.* 16, 1-2; 1980; 86-92.

45. Goil (N K). Impact of rising prices of reading materials on library developments. *ILA Bull.* 16, 1-2; 1980; 47-49.

46. Mohamed Ismail. Library collections and the effect of rising prices of books in India. *H Lib Sc.* 27, 3-4; 1988; 177-180.

47. Narender Kumar and Saini(Veena). Remainders. *ILA Bull.* 1; 1989; 53-56.

48. Patil (P K). Librarians, booksellers and the publishers: Need for triangular relationship. *In* Sardana(J L), *Ed.* Libraries and the book trade. Seminar Papers. 1982. IL A, Delhi. p 65.

49. Fiste (David). Practical aspect of collection development . *Libr Acquis Prac Th.* 13; 1989; 33-35.

50. Clack (Mary Elazebeth). Serial pricing: a dialogue between libraries and publishers. *Libr Acquis Prac Th.* 10; 1987; 3-10.

51. Markwith (Nicholas). The resolution on trade publishing discount. *Libr Acquis Prac Th* .8; 1985; 45-49.

52. Singh (S P). Role of subscription agents in serial collection building in university libraries: A case study . *In* MANGLA (P B), *Ed. Op.cit.* p 430-438.

53. Dey (P P). Collection development in specialized and research libraries. *In* Mangla(P B), *Ed. Ibid.* p 308-313.

54. Sylvia (M). What journals do psychology students need? A citation analysis of thesis reference. *Coll Res Libr.* 60, 4; 1999; 313-18.

55. McCarhy (P). Serial killers: Libraries respond to soaring costs. *Libr J.* 124, 11; 1999; 41-4.

56. Vaidya(M M). Problems in acquisition of periodicals and serials: Librarians view point. *In* Sardana(J L), *Ed. Op.cit.* p 28.

57. Puri (R P). Import of periodicals for libraries: Book trade view point. *In* Libraries and the book trade. *In* Sardana (J L), *Ed. Ibid.* p 37.

58. Reddy (Y N) and Suseela(V J).Periodical prices in relation to mailing charges, foreign exchange and inflation. *IASLIC Bull.* 40, 3; 1995; 107-116.

59. Reddy(Y N). Rising trends in periodical prices: need to develop national based periodical centres and networks. *Annals of Libr Sc Doc.* 41, 1; 1994; 23-32.

60. Anand(A K). Subscription to current periodicals in university libraries in India: A discussion of some problems. *ILA Bull.* 17, 3-4; 1981; 202-208.

61. Kapoor (A L).Acquisition of foreign periodicals in India: Some problems. *ILA Bull.* 15, 3-4; 1979; 67-76.

62. Secor (John). *Op cit.* P 72.

63. Bonk (Sharon C).Towards a methodology of evaluating serial vendors. *Libr Acquis Prac Th.* 16; 1993; 130-13.

64. Saxena (R K). Ethics of collection development in university libraries. *In* Mangla (P B), *Ed. Op. cit.* p 145-161.

65. Sridhar (M S). Problems of collection development in special libraries. 1992. Concept Publishing Company, New Delhi. p 68-72.

66. Cox(J E). Mega vendor: Threat or promise. *Ser Libr.* 28, 3-4; 1998; 117-119.

67. Marriman(J). Work of subscription agents. *Ser Libr.*30, 1; 1999. p 1-24.

68. Hodge (Stanley P). Future development by book publishers: Jobbers and networks; their impact on library collection development. *Libr Acquis Prac Th* . 5; 1981; 15-16.

69. Dole (Wanda V). Librarians, publishers and vendors: Looking for Mr. Good boy. *Libr Acquis Prac Th* . 21; 1997; 125-134.

70. Cine (J) and Sinhot (L). Librarians, publishers and vendors: The triangular relation. *Libr Acquis Prac Th* . 11; 1987; 25-34.

71. Dole (Wanda V). *Op cit.* p 128.

72. Grasse (Charles D).Book publishing in the future and show it will impact on libraries. *Libr Acquis Prac Th* . 5; 1981; 17-19.

73. Lockman (E D). *Op cit.* P 70.

74. Boissonnas (Christian M). The cost is more than that elegant dinner: Your ethics are at work. *Libr Acquis Prac Th.* 11; 1987; 154-152.

75. Secor (John). *Op cit.* p 72-74.

76. Schrift (Leonard). *Op cit.* p 177.

77. Flansburg (Craig).Panel presentation: Truth in vending. *Libr Acquis Prac Th.* 9; 1985; 65-78.

78. Sachdeva(Sunil). Import of books for libraries: Book trade viewpoint. *In* Sardna(J L), *Ed. Op cit.* P 55.

79. Damsi (M).From the (ivory) tower to the (cold) shower: A tongue-in-cheek comparison of academic versus commercial and trade publishing. *J Sch Pub.* 30, 2; 1999; 75-82.

80. Davidar (D). Cool bird in a hot climate: Penguin's part in the growth of Indian trade publishing. *Logos* 6, 3; 1995; 145-9.

81. Roy(A).English India: Realising the potential. *Bookseller.* 4788; 26 Sep. 1997; 28-30.

82. Altbach (Philip G) and Teferra (Damtew), *Ed.* Publishing and development: A book of readings. 1998. Vistaar Publications, New Delhi. p 7.

83. Datus (C Smith, Jr). The economics of book publishing. *In* Altbach (Philip G). and Taferra (Damtew), *Ed. Ibid.* p 31-46.

84. Graham (Gordon) Multinationals and third world publishing. *In* Altbach (Philip G). and Taferra (Damtew), *Ed. Ibid.* p 17.

85. Guedon (Jean Claude). Research libraries and electronic scholarly journals: Challenge or opportunities. *Ser Libr.* 26; 3-4. 1995; 1-20.

86. Clack(Mary Elazebeth). *Op cit.* p 5.

87. Brooke (Dixon). Subscription or information agency services in the electronic information era. *Ser Libr.* 29. 3-4; 1996; 57-65.

88. Brown (Linda A). Approaches to Internet based collection development models: Trades, and issues. *Libr Acquis Prac Th.* 21; 1997; 157-203.

89. Hunter (Kevil). Payment and subscription models for online publications. *Libr Acquis Prac Th* . 21; 1997; 157-203.

90. Gleason (Paul). International copyright. *In* Altbach (Philip G) and Teferra (Damtew), *Ed. Op.cit.* p 47-74.

91. Vishwanathan (T). Electronic publishing *In* Malhotra (D N), *Ed.* 50 years of book publishing in India since independence. 1998. Federation of Indian Publishers, New Delhi. p 215-218.

92. Jacso (P). CD-ROM collection dilemma. *Inf Today.* 12, 1; 1995; 22.

93. Rao(S S). CD-ROM databases services: A survey. *On-line CD-ROM Rev.* 23, 4; 1999; 230-6.

94. Knibbe(A). Subscription agent's role in electronic publishing. *J Elec Pub.* 4, 4; 1999; 43-47.

95. Baldwin(C).Electronic journal publishing: meeting user needs. *IFLA J.* 25, 4; 1999; 214-17.

96. Getz (M). Electronic publishing in academia: An economic perspective. *Ser Libr.* 36, 1-2; 1999; 263-300.

97. Kovacs(D K). Electronic publishing in libraries. *Acq Libr.* 20; 1998; 41-49

98. Scupola(A).The impact of electronic commerce on the publishing industry: Towards a business value complementarity framework of electronic publishing. *J Inf Sc.* 25, 2; 1999; 133-45.

99. Chakraborty (A K). Publishing on CD-ROM: Indian potential. Desidoc*Bul Inf Tech.17, 5; 1997; 23-30.*

100. Amudhavalli (A). Impact of electronic publishing on collection development. *DesidocBull Inf Tech.* 17, 1; 1997; 7-10.

101. Kane(George). Online acquisitions tools and prices. *Against the Grain.* 11, 2; 1999; 54.

102. Wilhite (M G). Acquisition of electronic access to information: More money, more records, more time. *Acq Libr.* 21; 1999; 37-49.

103. Kytomaki(P) and NORDINFO (Nytt). Information networks and collection development policy. *Inf Manag.* 4; 1996; 18-23.

104. Altbach (Philip G) and Teferra (Damtew), *Ed. Op cit.* p 159.

105. ZeLl (Hans M). Africa: The neglected continent. *In* Altbach (Philip G). *Ed.* Publishing and development in the third world. 1992. Vistaar, New Delhi. p 101-118.

106. Altbach (Philip G), *Ed. Ibid.* p 151- 168.

107. Graham (Gordon). Multinationals and third world publishing. *In* Altbach (Philip G). and Teferra (Damtew), *Ed. Op cit.* p 17-30.

108. Chakava (Henry). Kenyan publishing: Independence and dependence *In* Altbach (Philip G), *Ed. Op cit.* p 117-150.

109. Nwanko (Victor U). Publishing in Nigeria today. *In* Altbach (Philip G), *Ed. Op cit.* p 151- 168.

110. Hossain(Sarwar) and others. *Op cit.* p 59-72.

111. Arboleda (Amadia A). Distribution: The neglected link in the publishing chain *In* Altbach (Philip G). and Teferra (Demtew), *Ed. Op cit.* p 47-74.

112. *Ibid.*

113. Hasan (A). Promoting national strategies in Asia and the Pacific: Problems and prospectus. 1981. Unesco, New Delhi. p 19.

114. Moutchia (William). Interview in *Asian Bank Development Rev.* 13; 1982; 4.

115. Augsburger (A E). The Latin American book market: Problems and prospects. 1982. Unesco, Paris. p 60-61.

116. Aloke (Sitesh). Study of book industry: Small publishers. 1985. National Council for Applied Economic Research, New Delhi. P 88.

117. Tajeshwar Singh. Publishing in the third world: Learning do's and don'ts from India *In* Altbach (Philip G), *Ed. Op cit.* p 243-264.

118. Graham (Gordon). *Op. cit.* p 29.

119. Malhotra (D N), *Ed.* 50 years of book publishing in India since independence. 1998. Federation of Indian Publishers, New Delhi. p 323.

120. Gupta (Rajendra Kumar). College level publishing. *In* Malhotra (D.N), *Ed. Ibid.* p 210-214.

121. Ghai (S K). Marketing and distribution of books. *In* Malhotra (D N), *Ed. Ibid.* p 271-277.

122. Raghavan (D). Publishing in public sector. *In* Malhotra (D N), *Ed. Ibid.* p 250-254.

123. Koutchoumow (J A). India: At the threshold of new book vision. *In* Malhotra (D N), *Ed. Ibid.* p 315-320.

124. Narendra Kumar. India: 50 years of Independence: 1947-97 Status, growth and development. 1998. B.R. Publishing Corporation, New Delhi. p 161.

125. Lee (Marshal). Bookmaking. 1979. R.R.Bowker, New York. p 10.

126. Mastejulia (Robert). *Op cit.* p 143.

127. Lottman(H R). The distribution dilemma. *Pub weekly.* 1, 37; 1978; 15.

3

Research Design

Introduction

For conducting any research, planning of research is most important upon which the complete study depends. Such planning acts as a guideline to investigate the problem. Various research problems require that different strategies be employed which relates to the idea known as design or research design. According to Schvaneveldt, "A research design refers to a plan, blueprint, or guide for data collection and interpretation, sets of rules that enables the investigator to conceptualize and observe problems under study".[1]

The present study is an attempt to understand the acquisition of documents in special libraries in India and its linkages with Indian publishing industry. It aims to study collection development policies, acquisition of various kinds of documents, the linkages of collection development process with publishing industry and tries to identify various kind of problems which special libraries face in developing a need-based and quality collection.

Literature Survey

Prior to launching the study a survey of the related literature was undertaken. The purpose of this exercise was to understand the already existing trends, findings and problems so as to arrive at a right perspective. The research topic was divided into various sections and a search was made for related research material in various journals, books, reports, seminar/conference proceedings, etc. A bibliography was prepared of the most relevant and related research based articles. A detailed and in-depth study of these articles was done and findings noted down.

Data Gathering: Questionnaire Method

In survey research, questionnaire is widely used to gather data on a particular problem. Questionnaires are administered to a sample of population in order to know their opinion, experiences and attitudes. The primary advantage of this technique is that one can make broad generalisations from a relatively small number of responses. For gathering data about the present research, questionnaire and interview methods have been used.

"A questionnaire is a formulated series of questions especially for statistical study".[2] According to Krishan Kumar, "it is a written document, listing a series of questions pertaining to the problem under study, to which the investigator requires the answers".[3] For this study, four different sets of questionnaires, one for librarians/information officers/documentation officers and one each for publishers, distributors and vendors were designed.

Questionnaire for librarians was designed to get librarians view point on various issues related to collection development activities in special libraries. Questions have been included to collect information about library collection, its nature and budgetary allocation for each category. Similarly questionnaires related to publishers, distributors and vendors contain questions related publishing and supply of various kinds of documents.

While designing questionnaires an attempt is made to:

(i) know and analyse minutely the research problem,

(ii) formulate questions clearly to elicit maximum response and information,

(iii) request for information which can easily be provided and is not of confidential nature, and

(iv) formulate conceptually valid questions which promote understanding and accuracy and encourage respondents to participate in research.[4]

All the above pre-requisites were taken into consideration while designing questionnaires.

Designing of the Questionnaires

Before designing the questionnaire a through survey of literature was conducted related to the research topic so as to get a complete understanding of the problem. Objectives of the study and hypotheses of the research were formulated. On the basis of these objectives and hypotheses four different sets of questionnaires were designed. All the four questionnaires cater to four different but related constituents and aimed at comprehensive but accurate information related to investigation. A brief overview of the questionnaires is given as under:

Contents of Questionnaire for Librarians / Information Officers / Documentation Officers

The questionnaire (Appendix 1)is divided into eight sections. The first section deals with the profile of the library where information about various kinds of library collection has to be furnished. Section II contains questions about library budget for various kinds of library material, section III is about collection development policy, section IV deals with identification and selection of library materials. This section is followed by section V on acquisition of library materials and section VI on selection of vendors for the supply of such materials. Section VII contains questions related to vendors and their services .The last section deals with the questions related with the acquisition of periodical publications.

Contents of Questionnaire for Publishers

This questionnaire (Appendix 2) is divided into seven sections. Section I is related with the profile of the publishing house, section II deals with the type of publishing being undertaken while section III contains questions related with the pricing of publications. Section IV is about selection of manuscripts for publication. It is followed by Section V which contains questions on marketing of publications. Section VI deals with foreign publications whereas last section is about questions on relationship between publishers and librarians.

Contents of Questionnaire for Distributors

The questionnaire (Appendix 3) is divided into four sections. The section I contains questions about profile of firm, section II deals with the procurement of books. Section III contains questions regarding sale of books, discount rates, etc, while section IV looks into linkages between libraries and book trade.

Contents of Questionnaire for Vendors

The questionnaire (Appendix 4) is divided into five sections. Section I deals with profile of the firm while section II contains questions related to procurement and supply of books to libraries. This section has questions on aspects like type of material supplied and discount rates. Section III is related to payments and discount etc. It is followed by last section which contains questions on linkages between libraries and book suppliers.

Measuring Techniques

In this investigation basically survey research has been used to gather data. Most of the questions consist of multiple choices where respondents have been asked to tick mark (√) their answers. In addition following techniques have also been used.

Rank Order

In some cases rank-order procedure has also been used where respondents were asked to rank their answers as 1,2,3... in order of their choice. An example from questionnaire 1 is given below:

Q. 22. What is the main criteria taken into consideration for selecting the book suppliers?. Please rank your answer as 1, 2,3 in order of priority.

Discount ☐ Service ☐ Variety of stock ☐ Financial Capacity for accepting late payments ☐ Timely procurement of orders ☐ Office infrastructure ☐ Personal visits ☐ Regular communication and correspondence ☐

Category Rating Scale

This technique has also been used in case of some questions. The respondents have been asked to tick mark (√) one category out of several unnumbered categories with verbal description which least characterises the characteristic or behaviour of the person or a situation . An example from publishers' questionnaire is given below:

Q3. What criteria do you follow for accepting the manuscript for publication? Tick mark (√) the appropriate answer.

(i) Subject of the manuscript:

Always ☐ Mostly ☐ Sometimes ☐ Rarely ☐ Never ☐

(i) Quality of the manuscript:

Always ☐ Mostly ☐ Sometimes ☐ Rarely ☐ Never ☐

(ii) Reputation of the author:

Always ☐ Mostly ☐ Sometimes ☐ Rarely ☐ Never ☐

There are several questions in each questionnaire which have open-ended answers where respondents were asked to give their opinion or suggestions.

Summated Rating Scale

Summated rating scale has also been used for analysing some questions. Respondents were asked to select from a range of options like 'Always', 'Mostly'.... For example, librarians were asked to answer about the frequency of following the collection development policy in terms of 'Always', 'Mostly','Sometimes', 'Rarely', 'Never'. For the purpose of analysis, these options were weightage according to their use e.g. Always=5, Mostly,=4, Sometimes=3, Rarely=2, Never=1. The weighted index was created by multiplying the number of responses with the value assigned to each option in the scale. Scores of all items were summated and then divided by the total number of responses =

$$\frac{(4 \times 32 + 3 \times 15....)}{\text{Total No. of Responses}}$$

Weighted Index

The averages in all the variables in different scales were calculated according to weighted index and were re-arranged according to their ranks. An example from the chapter 9 is given below (Table 1.36).

Understanding of Library Requirements

Extent	*No. of Responses*	*Per cent*	*WI**	*Rank*
Always	19	14.1	0.70	2
Mostly	97	71.9	2.87	1
Sometimes	19	14.1	0.42	3
Rarely	0	0.0	0.0	4
Never	0	0.0	0.0	5
Total	135	100.0		

Note : *Weighted Index is calculated on a Five Point scale with weights assigned as follows : Always = 5; Mostly= 4; Sometimes= 3; Rerely= 2; Never= 1.

Pre-Testing of Questionnaires

To find the validity of questions, all the four questionnaires were pre-tested before finalizing the questionnaires. The main objective of pre-testing was to find out respondents' opinions, the language used, to rule out ambiguities and doubts, if any so as to get accurate responses and results. During this exercise several suggestions were received from librarians, publishers, distributors and vendors. In the light of these suggestions several questions were revised and some new questions were also added in the final draft. The librarians, publishers, distributors and vendors who participated in pre-testing exercises were not administered final questionnaires.

Administering the Questionnaires

As mentioned above, four different questionnaires have been designed. The first questionnaire is for librarians, Information Officers /Documentation Officers. This questionnaire was distributed personally. Details are given in Table 1. In addition, the questionnaires were also sent by post. Email has also been used for sending the questionnaire as attachment in Word format. The list of special libraries was obtained from Association of Special Libraries and Information Centres (IASLIC).[5] While selecting the libraries for sending the questionnaire, care was taken to include national level libraries located in major cities of India. Several other non-member libraries were also included in the survey on the basis of their importance and suggestions received from senior people in the profession.

Similarly list of publishers, distributors and vendors (library suppliers) have been taken from the book traders' latest directory.[6] Some other publishers, distributors and vendors were also included on the basis of discussion with senior librarians. A self- addressed envelope with requisite postal stamps was enclosed with questionnaires for receiving the duly filled in questionnaires. Data was also collected through personal visits from librarians, publishers, distributors and vendors located in Delhi. As a follow up measure, reminders were sent after a month to the individual respondents wherever necessary. In order to maximize the response rate, reminders were sent at regular intervals.

The distribution and collection of questionnaires took place during the following period.

Table 1

Questionnaires: Distribution and Collection Schedule

Questionnaires	*Distribution Period*	*Collection Period*
Librarians	January-June 2001	January-September 2001
Publishers	June-September 2001	June-December 2001
Distributors	August-October 2001	August-December 2001
Vendors	August-October 2001	August-December 2001

The number of questionnaires sent to various constituents of population and the number of responses received is given below in Table 2.

Table 2

Questionnaires: Response Rates

Questionnaires	*No. of Questionnaires Distributed*	*No.of Responses Received*	*Response Rate (%)*
Librarians	250	135	54.0
Publishers	150	70	46.6
Distributors	60	32	53.3
Vendors	80	55	68.7

The response rate for librarians' questionnaire is 54 per cent, for publishers it is 46.6 per cent. The response rate for distributors is 53.3 per cent while for vendors it is 68.7 per cent.

Data Gathering: Interview Method

For publishers and librarians, interview method has also been used to supplement the information wherever necessary. A schedule for interview was designed both for librarians and publishers (Appendix 5 and 6). According to Krishan Kumar, "In interview there is always a possibility to achieve an excellent communication between a respondent and a researcher. A researcher can personally explain and clarify the questions".[7] The purpose behind interview is both to fill the gaps in the information provided by the respondents in questionnaires and also to get additional information which normally people do not give in writing. One more purpose of personal interviews is that some times senior people do not have time to fill up the questionnaire. However during personal interactions, it is easy to get required information from such people. The interviews were conducted only with librarians and publishers. The distributors and vendors were excluded from interviews due to their relatively lesser importance as compared to librarians and publishers in the present study and also due to the fact that most of the information has already been collected from them through questionnaires.

Conducting of Interviews

As a first step towards conducting the interviews, a list of leading librarians and publishers was prepared. The list was prepared by interacting with selected librarians and publishers. Appointments were fixed on telephone before personally visiting their offices. The interviews were conducted on the basis of schedules (Appendix 5 and Appendix 6) designed for this purpose. During the course of interviews, the investigator has been able to get quite important information on various sensitive issues such as fixing of prices by the publishers, discount rates, etc. Details regarding conducting of interviews is given below in Table 3 along with the period during which interviews were conducted.

Table 3

Conduct of Interviews

	Category	*No*	*Period*
(i)	Librarians/ Information Officers/Documentation Officers	20	November-December 2001
(ii)	Publishers	12	November-December 2001

Data Analysis and Interpretation

After having received the responses from librarians, publishers, distributors and vendors, the task of data analysis and its interpretation was started. Data analysis is the process of bringing order, structure and meaning to the mass of collected data. All the data and information collected through questionnaire and interviews have been analysed to bring out the results. The analysis of textual data has been done by organising data into categories, themes and patterns.

For the analysis of data, all the questionnaires received back were coded with the help of the coding structure developed for the purpose of data processing. The entire data was fed to the computer using Statistical Package for Social Sciences (SPSS). All the variables were defined and values were assigned. SPSS offers a large number of statistical routines commonly used in social sciences. Frequency distribution tables have been produced for all the variables. On the basis of these tables, findings of the study have been derived.

Standard used for Bibliographical References

For providing the bibliographical references, ISI[8] standard number IS-2381-1978 with slight modification (size has been left out) was used in the study. The abbreviations for journals in library and information science have been used according to *Library Literature and Information Science.*[9] Examples are as follows:

(i) Simple Book

Sethi (A R). Information seeking behaviour of social scientists: An Indian conspectus. 1990. Hindustan Publishing, New Delhi. P. 212.

(ii) Ordinary Composite Book

Krishan Kumar. Information seeking behaviour of Sociologist. *In* Binwal (J C) and others, *Ed.* Social Science Information : Problems and prospects. 1990. Vikas Publishing House, New Delhi. P. 254.

(iii) Contribution in Conference Volume

Gandhi (R S). Collection development in special libraries . *In* MANGLA(P B), *Ed.* Building library collections and national policy for library and information services. Seminar papers. 1985. ILA, Delhi. P. 314-321.

(v) Title entry

Webester's Delux unabridged dictionary. Ed 2. 1979. Dorset and Baber, USA. P. 1313.

(v) Journal Article

Sethi (A R). Information seeking behaviour of area specialists. *ILA Bull*. 22,3-4;1987;154-55.

References

1. Schvaneveldt(Jay R). *Understanding research methods.* 1985. Longman, New York. p 103.

2. *Concise OXFORD dictionary*. 1977. Oxford University Press, Calcutta. p 1368.

3. Krishan Kumar. *Research methods in library and information science*. Rev. Ed 2. Har-Anand Publications. New Delhi. p 120.

4. Busha(Charles H) and Harter (Stephen H). *Research method in librarianship: Techniques and interpretation.* 1980. Academic Press, Orlando. p 64.

5. Indian Association of Special Libraries and Information Centres. List of members. 2000.Calcutta. p 40.

6. Directory of Indian publishers and distributors, 2000. 2001. Indian Bibliographic Centre, Varanasi. p 188.

7. Krishan Kumar. *Op cit.* p 185.

8. IS:2381-1978. Recommendations for bibliographical references. 1978. Indian Standard Institution, New Delhi.

9. Library literature and information science. 2000. *Abbreviations for titles of periodicals.* 2001.The W.H.Wilson Company, New York.

4
Collection Development

Introduction

With the emergence of complex and integrated societies, the human species has created a tremendous volume of information over the last few centuries. The traditional method of learning has been through the printed documents, even today with the changing scenario, it is so. The printed material, like books and other documents will always remain in the mainstream as a source of information in the libraries for a long time to come.

All libraries perform various functions and among those, collection development occupies the most vital position. "It is the document collection that gives library a character more so than either staff or building".[1] Unless a library possesses adequate recent documents supplemented with latest reference and bibliographical tools, it can not serve its clientele properly and meet the urge for mental food of its potential users.

The term "collection development" refers to the process of systematically building library collections to serve study, teaching, research, recreational, and other needs of library users. The process includes selection and deselection of current and retrospective materials, the planning of strategies for continuing acquisition, and evaluation of collections to determine how well they serve user needs. Overall, collection development encompasses many library operations ranging from the selection of individual titles for purchase to the withdrawal of expendable materials.

"Collection development", according to Magrill[2], "as a planning process, uses the methodology typically followed in planning: establishing mission and policy statement, describing present state of affairs, reviewing relative strengths and weaknesses, considering environmental influences and other current trends, setting goals, and designing strategies to reach these goals. Collection development operates within the constraints of certain conditions that vary from one place to another and from one time to another".

Collection development is a dynamic process that should involve both the information professionals and the service community. It must be responsive to the total community's needs, not just to those of current or most active users. "It should be geared primarily to identified needs, both long terms and short terms, rather than to abstract standards of quality".[3]

Under this process duties of acquisition librarian are : (a) to receive requests from members for purchases of titles; (b) to ascertain that such requests are not for titles/editions already in the library; (c) to verify that such titles actually exist; (d) to determine price and availability of a given title; (e) to place order for requested titles; and (f) to receive and pay for the ordered titles.

Factors Affecting Collection Development

Magrill[4] has categorised the local conditions that influence collection development which can be grouped under five broad headings:

The Community or Institution

The first group of variables cover the community and/ institution in which a library is located. Libraries within the organizations are influenced by several factors, but their primary concern is with the organisation they are designed to serve. The role of the library collection in an institution is to further the purpose and mission of the institution as a whole. Special libraries are designed to meet the needs of a specific agency or company.

Purpose of the Library

Closely related to the institution is the purpose of the organisation for which the special library established. The main purposes of the special library are:

(a) to provide advanced resources to specialists/ researchers for various on-going research projects;

(b) to acquire and provide need based information services on demand and in anticipation, using latest technological devices.

Clientele

A third group of variable that influences collection development is library's clientele, the real or potential users of its collection. The needs of the users, demonstrated and perceived, are seen by many libraries as the primary basis upon which collection is developed or various information services are provided.

Present Collection

How much the present collection will influence future developments depends upon preceding variables; the purpose of library and the ways it is used, as well as additional variables of size and age. The larger and older the present collection and more research oriented the library, the more influence the present collection may have on future collection development plans, because the tendency in such libraries is to build on strengths that already exist in collection. In special libraries, however, this factor becomes little less significant as the emphasis is on latest and up-to-date resources.

Collection Development Policy

A collection development policy is the written statement prepared for the guidance of the library. It is an important tool for guiding all activities related to planning, budgeting, selecting and acquiring the material in the library. Collection development policy helps in deciding what to purchase and what not, for the library. Effective collection development programme requires creating a plan to correct weaknesses of the present collection, and to further strengthen it.

Elaborating on collection development, Dowd[5] has stated that "a collection development policy should constitute three elements viz: a historical record of what has been done in the past; a description of parameters of the existing collection; a blueprint for the future of the collection".

Collection development policy is essentially a communication device, describing what the collection covers and what to cover in the future. Therefore, it is also an assessment of current resources before the need arises. It is a guide to consider about resource sharing; and it provides a common language to describe the collections. Librarian can use it to create a rationale for funding, to inform the researchers about the strengths and the weaknesses of the collection, and to establish a hierarchy of needs. A written policy helps to assure some continuity and consistency in the collection development programme even though there are changes in staff and funding.

According to Roben and George[6] a policy statement performs the following functions:

1. It informs everyone about the nature and scope of the collection.
2. It informs everyone of collection priorities.
3. It forces thinking about organisational goals to be met by the collection.
4. It generates some degree of commitment to meet the organizational goals.

5. It sets standards for inclusion and exclusion.
6. It reduces the influence of single selector and personal bias.
7. It helps to ensure a degree of consistency despite the changes of staff.
8. It guides staff in handling complaints.
9. It provides a public relation document.

Elements of Collection Development Policy

A written collection development policy should ideally consists of following elements so as to make it comprehensive and self explanatory:[7]

1. A brief general description of the community to be served.
2. Specific identification of the clientele to be served
3. A general statement regarding the parameters of collection such as the subject field covered, limitations set on the types of format that the library will acquire, etc.
4. A section on the general limitations and priorities that will determine how the collection will be developed. To what degree will the library collect retrospective materials or how many copies of a publication will library buy.
5. A discussion of the library's role in cooperative collection development programmes.The policy should make it clear as to whether the basic philosophy is one of self sufficiency or cooperation.
6. A subject wise, break down of the collection into its constituent subject areas, identification of each type of material to be collected.

One more important feature of collection development work in special libraries is that it is more specialized. The most important feature of the special libraries is that they tend to have a collection that is very current. Despite the heavy emphasis on current materials, the best known collection aids are of little value to the person(s) responsible for collection building in the special library. Most of the material acquired is very technical and of interest to only a small number of specialists. As a result, there is no real market for review services. According to Perkins, "recommendations of clients and knowledge of their information needs are the key elements in deciding what to buy".[8] Thus, special library's collection usually constitute new publications acquired for current use, not for use in distant future.

Conclusion

Overall, the collection development planning process, highlighted by the invaluable collection policy statement, provides a means by which the library selects and manages its collection of information resources. These guidelines are, in effect, a contract between the library and its community, supplying a framework within which complex decisions are made with consistency and reason. It can thus, be concluded that "while a special librarian's collection policy is most often governed by practical concerns more so than on collection development theory or criteria, the general consensus deems collection policies useful as librarians aim to describe their collections in terms of depth and extent of coverage, types of materials collected, exchange agreements, and the many other special considerations that special librarians tend to encounter".[9]

References

1. Ray (Ron L). The disintegrating library system: Effects of new technologies in acquisitions. *Libr Acquis Prac Th.* 17; 1993; 127-36.

2. Magrill (Rose M). *Acquisition management and collection development of libraries.* 1989. American Librarian Association., Chicago. p 51.

3. Barker (Joseph W) and Rebecca (A Rottman). Acquisitions for effectiveness, efficiency and the future. *Libr Acquis Prac Th.* 22 ;1998; 137-63.

4. Magrill (Rose M). *Op cit.* p 155.

5. Dowd (Sheila T). The formulation of a collection development policy statement. *Libr Acquis Prac Th.* 23 ;1999; 147-53.

6. Roben (D Stion) and George (B Miller), *Ed.* Collection development in libraries. 1980. Jai Press, Greenwich. p 67-87.

7. Evans (G Edward). *Developing library and information centre collections*. 1987. Libraries Unlimited, Littleton. p 146.

8. Perkins (P L), *Ed. Guidelines for collection development*. 1979. American Library Association, Chicago. p 20.

9. Collins (J) and Finer (R). *National acquisition policies and system*.1982. British Library, London. p 79.

5

Acquisition of Printed Documents

Introduction

The term 'special library' is used to denote the libraries specialising in a specific subject or group of subjects. As a generic term it has been used to include different kinds of libraries, such as libraries attached to industrial and commercial organisations, libraries of learned societies, government agencies and departments, etc. In fact emergence of special libraries is a post second world war phenomena. They emerged for meeting the specific localized information needs and research requirements of a specific clientele group. Such libraries are generally small in size supporting mainly research and development activities of the organisation and, necessitating greater selectivity in the collection. The range of subjects collected in a special library may be very restricted, but the variety of forms and types of materials can be of wider range.

Special libraries serve a limited and well-defined group of clientele, usually limited to its parent organisation. They often contain indepth working collections, to provide support for information services, the emphasis being on current and up-to-date information in its primary area of interest. A special library's acquisition department has to build a comprehensive, need-based, up-to-date and balanced collection required for independent research in a specific area. Such material may contain research findings, scientific experimental results, and other information useful for researchers.

Scope

Special library is mostly concerned with the acquisition of "micro-documents" that provides intensive and highly specialized information usually contained in primary documents, like proceedings, monographs, patents, standards, research reports, technical reports, periodicals, etc. including major indexing and abstracting services in the field. It may also include reference works like dictionaries, encyclopedias, bibliographic databases, bibliographies, handbooks. Pertinent foreign language sources are also included. Older material such as historical surveys are preserved and retained for historical research. A collection at this level supports doctoral and other original research. The collection in special libraries is frequently and systematically reviewed for currency of information. Printed documents include different types of documents which have been described below.

Books

Books despite the fast technological revolution and networking, still constitute the most important part of library collection. "It is the book and its many surrogates which are emblematic of stability in cultural transmission and it is the journal which represents, above all, the symbol of power, status, and achievement within the academic discipline".[1] The library still has a strong repository function and will continue to collect and house information in all media formats. Thus, collection development remains an immensely important yardstick in determining the nature and, to a considerable extent, the level of service which a library is able to provide. The three vital components of this process are selection, ordering and acquisition.

Evans[2] has suggested the following basic consideration to become a first rate book selector:

1. Do not forget that collection development is a dynamic series of inter-related activities.
2. Take time to learn about the basics of book trade.
3. Study the publishers who produce the best material for the library, examine their catalogues in detail, look for advertisements, learn the names of their editors.
4. Spend time reading reviews in a wide variety of sources.Scope.
5. Examine the trade and national bibliographies with great care, determine how accurately they report the materials that the library needs.
6. Knowledge of library's users is the foundation upon which to build its collection.
7. Be interested in what is going on in the world, and read a lot.

Thus, an ideal selector should have full and detailed information about these aspects. In addition, the selector should be intimately familiar with the aims of the organisation and its activities.

Selection Tools

There are many book selection aids which can assist the librarian to do a satisfactory job. They vary in the speed with which they cover current publishing, in the type of books listed, in the kind and amount of information given for each title, in the type of library for which they are intended, in format, frequency and usefulness.

Every one involved in collection development recognizes the importance of bibliographies and review sources in building up a good library collection, no matter how often such tools are used in a specific library setting. What the selection aids provide is, to some degree, a kind of overview of the output of publishers and media producers. Despite their shortcomings and limitations, these aids are time saving and essential, if libraries are to function with any degree of efficiency. For books, these selection aids can be divided into following six categories:

1. Current sources for in-print books;
2. Catalogues and announcements;
3. Current reviews;
4. National bibliographies;
5. Recommended, best, core collection lists; and
6. Subject lists.

Steps

The following steps are involved in this process.

Request Processing

The first step in acquisition work is to organize the requests received to acquire an item.

Pre-ordering Search

Pre-ordering work has to be done to process each request which consists of verification or searching of two elements. First is the establishment of the existence of a particular item by verification. Second is the establishment of the need for the item by the library searching. In verifying, the concern is with the correct author, title, publisher of the work, and other necessary ordering data. Searching is concerned with whether the library already owns the item, whether it needs a second copy or multiple copies or new edition of the same book, and whether the item already has been ordered but not received.

Before placing the order, there are several files to check in order to establish the library 's need for the selected book.

It is better to begin with the title because there are likely to be less variation and doubts. Special libraries acquire variety of material for which separate catalogues are maintained for different forms of documents, so these catalogues must be searched. In the technical service area also, several files must be checked to determine whether the item is already on order, acquired or being processed. Normally three files must be consulted, if the department has a manual system: the in-process file, the verified requests file (items waiting to be typed on order forms), and the standing order file.

Ordering and Acquisition

Acquisition work involves locating and acquiring the items, identified as appropriate for the collection. In small libraries same people are likely to be doing both selection and acquisition work. But in bigger libraries, the work is done by two separate, yet interrelated units.

Acquisition Methods

Five major methods are employed to acquire material for the library: firm order, standing order, approval plan, deposit or gift, and exchange. Each method has a useful role to play in developing a collection in an efficient and effective manner. Regardless of the method used to order material, the vendor must be given enough information to assure shipment of the correct material. The information may be about author, title, publisher, date of publication, price, edition (if there are various editions), number of copies, order number, and International Standard Book Number (ISBN).

Processing requests for materials involves a number of activities to ensure that the library acquires the needed items as quickly and inexpensively as possible. Time and money would be wasted if requests were simply forwarded to a publisher or vendor. Inaccurate information, duplicate requests, unavailable material, and other similar problems would generate unacceptable costs for both, the library and the supplier. Each acquisition department develops its own set of procedures to reduce problems of this type, and while there are hundreds of variations, the basic process is the same: Pre-ordering, ordering, receiving, fiscal managing, and record keeping. Acquisition departments also have internal goals. Four common goals are:

(i) to acquire material as quickly as possible;

(ii) to maintain a high level of accuracy in all work procedures;

(iii) to keep work processes simple, so as to achieve the lowest possible unit cost; and

(iv) to develop close and friendly working relationships, both with other library units and vendors.

Once a decision has been made to acquire a particular item for the library collection, due thought must be given to the means by which it is to be obtained. Although many items are ordered individually, a number of libraries, particularly the large ones attempt to minimize the time consuming procedure associated with item-by-item ordering by placing standing, blanket and approval orders with reliable vendors.

Reports

Reports constitute a very important source of information for special libraries. All special libraries collect various types of reports from several sources. Report can be defined as "a publication giving a formal or official record, as of the activities of a committee or corporate body, or of some special investigation, or the proceedings of a government body".[3] They are one of the primary source of getting information. It originally meant to carry back and it is this sense of a documents prepared for a known readership, rendering an account of work as required by an agreement, a contract or a specification, particularly in the fields of scientific and technical research and development. Reports representing the deliberations of committees, as for example those appointed by the government, and law reports, to feature in special libraries, but by far the largest category concerns research and development. Indeed it can be said that the research and development report is the document which marks the true special library, for not only do special libraries collect reports from around the world relevant to their interest, they also are responsible for storing and disseminating the reports issued by the organizations which they are specifically established to serve, as for instance research laboratories, technological centres, testing stations defence establishments, government departments and large industrial and commercial concerns.

The value of the report as the most rapid and effective means of disseminating the results of scientific and industrial research and development to clearly identified audiences is well realized. Reports are still used as the main means of imparting government and industrial information because amongst other reasons they offer speed of publication and controlled distribution. Speed is achieved because the decision to publish rests with the issuing organisation and is not subject to rigorous and delays imposed by the refereeing system in traditional publishing activities. But because of originator's absolute control over the contents and distribution of reports, accessibility often becomes difficult. It is one of the reasons why a consistent report acquisition policy becomes difficult.

Selection and Procurement

Most of the reports are acquired from their respective sponsoring bodies. There do not exist any selection or evaluation tool for the reports. Reports are also available from authorised agencies like Jain Book Agency in New Delhi or Bookwell publisher. In some cases reports are confidential and are not issued for public use. Librarians have to use various informal channels like personal contacts for the acquisition of reports.

The best way to keep a report collection in harmony with the needs of the library and its users its to select the reports felt to be relevant as and when they are announced and made available. Such a selection policy can be implemented by using the announcement journals of agencies serving major subject areas.

Patents

"A patent is a limited monopoly granted by the state to the owner of an invention to have the sole right to operate or work the invention for a certain number of years".[4] All such inventions must meet certain criterion of novelty, and must be capable of industrial application. Special libraries are mainly concerned with patents as sources of information and are not usually involved with the writing; filling, exploitation; licensing and contesting of patents, such specialized tasks being normally the concern of the inventor himself, the patents engineer, the patents examiner and the patents agent.

All major industrial countries operate a patents system because it has long been recognized that the protection obtained in return for the publication of technical information acts as a stimulus to the inventive spirit and so in the long run benefits the state by promoting technical progress in almost positive manner.

There are, of course, considerable differences between the patent laws of different countries and the manner in which information relating to patents is made available.

Patents As Sources of Information

The value of patents as sources of information is not always easy to assess. They often review and evaluate the prior art which led up to a particular invention and that taken collectively they can be indicative of major trends in research and development.

Types of Patents[5]

All There are four types of patents as given below:

(i) *Conventional Patents:* Ordinary certificate, granting the exclusive privilege to the patentee.

(ii) *Patents of Addition*: Patented invention further improved and modified either by the original inventor or someone else is protected by it.

(iii) *Secret Patents*: Invention relating to instruments and ammunitions of war is/are granted secret patents.

(iv) *Priority Patents*: These are granted under a reciprocal priority arrangements established between the home country and a few commonwealth countries.

Selection Tools

Patents offices bring out various publications to give information about the new patents registered with them. These sources of information are:

(i) *World Patent index* (WPI) *abstracts journal*. Dervent Publications, London. It is a weekly publication exclusively devoted to patents etc.

(ii) *World Patent index gazette section*. Dervent Publications, London. It contains four indexes. Many Patent Offices issue abridgement of patents granted.

A careful perusal of these sources of information needs to be carried out regularly for selection of patents.[6] Besides these sources of information, the reviews published in scientific and technical periodicals of the relevant fields, the indexing and abstracting journals, such as, the *Chemical Abstracts, Science Abstracts, Computer Abstracts, Desalination Abstracts*, etc, there are commercial and non-official abstracts also, such as, *Basic Abstracts, Airplane*

Patent Digest, etc., which are other patent selection sources. Then there are official abstracts which are useful selection tools, and some of these are : The *Abridgments* of British Patent Office, The *Abridgements* of Indian Patents, *Resumes in Bull de la Propriety Industrielle* of French Patent Office. List of additions of large libraries, publications of research and industrial organizations, and the check list of the Patent Offices and Patent Inspection Centres may also serve as useful selection tools for patent literature. Apart from these sources, there are several online databases which contain patent information. WPI is most important database which is available on-line through Dialog. INPADOC is another important database which is also available through Knight-Ridders (formerly Dialogue).[7]

Procurement of Patents

After finalisation of list of patents to be procured, Patents Offices of respective countries should be approached directly. Patents are mostly government documents and, therefore, their procurement is not possible through normal book trade channels. For retrospective patent literature, distributors or agents specialised in dealing with government publications should be approached. For older patents, the rare-book suppliers may also be contacted. When the interest of an organisation is well defined, it is advisable to place standing orders with the Patent Offices. For more comprehensive coverage, resource sharing may be resorted to. There is a continuous updating of patents through amendments and reissues. The librarian should keep a track of these and procure them as and when these an issued.

In India, Indian National Scientific Documentation Centre (INSDOC) has been designated as Patent Office. It brings out *Indian Patents Database on CD-ROM* and can also be requested for supplying a copy of a particular patent. Normally, a copy is supplied by the INSDOC in response to such requests. INSDOC provides *Patents Watch Service* (PWS). It renders assistance to inventors in the laboratories of the Council as well as those undertaking sponsored research, in drafting patent application and filing them both in India and abroad. It also maintains a patents' inspection centre.

Theses

"A thesis is a statement of investigation or research presenting the author's findings, and any conclusions reached, submitted by the author in support of his candidature for a higher degree, professional qualification or other award."[8] A narrower, dictionary definition is a proposition laid down or stated, especially as a theme to be discussed and proved. The terms thesis and dissertation are used interchangeably when referring to work carried out at universities, with a preference for thesis in the United Kingdom and dissertation in the United States. Theses are of value in special libraries because they often contain accounts of investigations of an advanced nature, reflecting a writer's attempts to extend the limits of knowledge in a particular subject area. Theses may therefore contain results not available elsewhere, but it must always be remembered that such results derive from a candidate's main concern of demonstrating to his tutors a grasp of a given subject, and the research methodology involved.

Selection Tools

A guide to theses which covers all subject fields or a specific area and the availability of the items which it lists varies from university to university. Often a copy of a thesis may be borrowed by applying directly to the University concerned, occasionally it can only be consulted at the university.

British Library Lending Division has been trying to increase the utilization of British doctoral theses by making them available, usually as microfilms, the theses of those universities which have agreed to participate in the building up of this collection. In the United States the principal source of reference is *Dissertation Abstracts International* (DAI).[9]

An aid to retrospective searches for United States theses is the *Comprehensive Dissertation Index*[10] (CDI), a work of thirty-seven volumes, covering the years 1861-1972, from the same publishers as DAI. Volumes 33-37 consist of an author index (available separately) and can be consulted with profit without having access to volumes 1-32. CDI is kept up to date by a series of supplements. In India this work is being done Indian Council of Social Science Research (ICSSR).[11] One of the main aim of ICSSR is to collect, organise and disseminate the information of unpublished research project reports which are generated through sponsorship of Social Science Research Programmes by ICSSR as well as other social science research institutes. It is also procuring (on payment basis) unpublished Ph.D. dissertations in social sciences accepted by Indian universities. So far, about 4800 Ph.D. theses and 2800 research project reports are available in National Social Science Documentation Centre (NASSDOC). These unpublished reports and dissertations have been processed and indexed. Identified concepts are translated into controlled vocabulary indexing language by using standard subject indexes and Library cf Congress Subject Headings.

Trade Literature

Trade literature is a book or pamphlet issued by the manufacturer, or dealer, or agent describing his goods and products and carries information on the production or modification of a product from its design to marketing stage. The contents of trade catalogue comprise of details of a product, design data, test results, operating instructions and price etc.

Trade literature is a vital component of any special library collection, yet its treatment can give rise to a number of problems related to its essential characteristics. Firstly there is the conflict which occurs because the librarian sees trade literature as an excellent source of up-to-date technical information to be integrated into the rest of his collection, whereas the publishers of trade literature sees its prime objective as the furtherance of business. Thus, trade literature takes on an ephemeral status, capable of modification in accordance with how the issuing organization sees the needs of the moment.

Selection and Acquisition

The traditional ways of obtaining trade literature are to consult general and specialized trade directories; to examine appropriate trade journals; and to ask various company representatives to send their literature. A ruthless policy of weeding and updating must be introduced, if the service is to be of any value. Certain commercial organizations have attempted to bring some sort of order to trade literature by offering manufactures' publications . The yearbook of United Nations Industrial Development Organisations (UNIDO)[12] gives a list of directories of the manufacturers of the industrial equipment. A visit to engineering or industrial exhibitions offers a wonderful opportunity for the selection of trade catalogues. The maintenance of a comprehensive and up-to-date directory of the manufacturers, dealers and agents of products in which the users of library are interested; and an efficient system of correspondence with each of them is helpful for procuring the trade literature.

Standards

'Standard' refers "to an agreed target for performance, an accepted format for the operation of a system etc."[13] Briefly stated the purpose of a standard specification is to simplify production and distribution, to ensure uniformity and reliability, and to eliminate wasteful variety. Standards are formal rules designed to cover such topics as testing, terminology, definitions and symbols, performance and construction, and codes of practice . They are also important in influencing and specifying degrees of quality and levels of safety. Often they take a long time to prepare because they rely on agreement being reached among the interested parties concerned.

Value of Standards

Standards are considered to be a difficult form of information. Problems frequently arise because enquirers misquote standards numbers, or persist in using old designations. Often, the knowledge of certain standards is mandatory if tenders for contractors are to succeed, for many organization insist that work is performed to a particular specification. Again, engineering drawings will require particular standards to be followed, standards which in some cases are unfamiliar both to the engineer and the librarian. Thus, it is vital that a special library keeps up-to-date with standards and the activities of standards organizations, and also makes itself familiar with the services of major national bodies.

Procurement

The procurement of standards is not much of a problem as they are available through selected government agencies and referred by code numbers. The Indian standards and standards belonging to other countries can be had from the office of Bureau of Indian Standard situated in New Delhi against advance payment. The standards are revised and amended quite frequently which requires librarians to remain in constant touch with issuing agencies.

Maps

Libraries of all types need reference materials that visually present the features of the earth and other celestial bodies. These materials include shed maps and atlases; globes; aeronautical, navigational, and celestial charts, aerial; satellite, and space photographs; etc. Because it is possible to illustrate the geographic position of so many different things by satellite photography and other large-scale, high-speed remote-sensing techniques, the number and types of maps available have greatly expanded. Maps may be physical, emphasizing natural features of the land; political, showing boundaries of governmental unit; or special topic, showing such information as historical events, manufacturing, crop production, weather patterns. Meteorological maps show the relation between the atmosphere and weather conditions. Most countries produce at least one topographic map serial. Not all libraries will need to collect all types of maps; in fact, small library are likely to limit their acquisition to carefully selected examples.

The collection development policies for the map collections identify the users who will be served by the collection, the types of maps a library will collect, the geographic areas to be covered, and the formats (sheets, bound, microform, etc.) in which the maps will be acquired. Special libraries may focus on the needs or interests of researchers in particular departments, anticipating how maps will be used by a particular clientele helps in narrowing the range of maps that should be acquired. Policies may also specify acquisition procedures for maps as sets of serials; some libraries buy only complete sets.

Because of the special acquisitions, storage, and reference requirement associated with individual sheet maps, large libraries tend to house them in special map collections. While order preparations, book-keeping, and ultimate approval of payments rest with the acquisitions unit in most libraries, selection, verification, and upon-receipt identification should be done by a person knowledgeable about maps. This may be a bibliographer in the acquisitions unit, but it will more likely be a member of the staff of the map collection.

Government Documents

Government documents constitute one of the most current and vital parts of a special library collection. A government document is an " informational matter published as an individual document at government expanses as required by law."[14]

Government publications can be divided into two categories; (1) Parliamentary documents which include proceedings, reports, etc. of legislative bodies, acts of various states and central government, (2) Non-parliamentary documents which consist of administrative reports, transactions, rules and regulations, codes, gazettes, budget estimates, reports of commissions and statistics.

All these publications contain useful information not only for statistical information but also for the account of legislature and administrative changes. They also contain policy matters and decisions relating to important sectors like, industry, labour, housing, science and technology, etc.

Procurement

Acquisition of government documents is a problematic area. Their identification is most difficult art as their bibliographical control is very poor and not up-to-date. Most of the time information about these documents is not made public which makes it difficult to procure them. These publications go out of print very soon and are not available after some time.

As these publications are low priced and are mostly sold at net price, booksellers usually avoid to supply them. They are also not available through any other usual channel except official agencies.

Acquisition Work: Linkages with Publishing Industry

The publishing trade is closely connected with library collection development programme as bulk of the purchases relate to published work only. A knowledge of book trade, to the librarian particularly distribution network is essential for developing the most cost-effective collection of information materials. Three types of purchasing agents may be utilized when the library acquisition unit decides to order an item: Vendors, wholesalers or publishers but vendors are the key source of getting books into the libraries.

Vendor Selection

Vendor selection process is the most important factor in acquisition of documents. "It may be characterised as a courtship and the resulting approval of relationship as marriage. Courting couples often start by exchanging the highlights of their past history and important information".[15]

The decision to choose one or more vendors for acquiring material in the library is a most critical function. The library may wish to concentrate its business with a single vendor when the budget is small. It is simply unrealistic to spread a small budget over several vendors, usually all of whom provide essentially the same type of service.

Selection of a vendor should be based on his capabilities, performance, financial stability, negotiation, and mutual expectations and responsibilities. The library's decision will have an economic impact, perhaps a significant one, on the selected vendors(s), so a judicious decision is needed. The library and the vendor enter into a relationship that will develop over a period of time and it is imperative that the decision be made on a rational basis with the expectation that the library's needs will be met effectively and efficiently within the available economic realities in this regard. "One does not establish himself with a wholesaler and move to another one immediately. The nature of the business is largely detailed, which takes a long time to do correctly. It is based on agreement and interpretation of that agreement."[16]

Discount

Discounting is a complex issue in any commercial activity, and it is highly complex in the book trade. Every publisher has a discount schedule that is slightly different, if not unique. Some items are no discount items; these are usually textbooks, scientific and technical titles or the items that have limited appeal but with more potential than the net titles. "Trade" discount items include the items that are normally high demand items, or high-risk popular fiction. The discount for these items range from 30 to 60 per cent or more. Vendors normally receive 30 to 40 per cent discount, primarily because of their high-volume orders.

Vendors usually encounter financial problems in the form of rising costs and declining sales. A number of publishers are requiring pre-payment or have placed vendors on a 'proforma' status, where pre-payment is required and credit extended on the basis of the current performance in payment of bills. Much of the credit/order fulfillment extended by publishers depends upon an almost personal relationship with a vendor. This means that for libraries the selection of a vendor must be made with utmost care. It is not inappropriate to check a prospective vendor's service performance with other libraries as well as their financial status.

Vendors: Their Role

Vendors provide a very important service to the library by saving a significant amount of time and money. Although vendors do not give high discounts, the time saved by placing order for 10 different titles, published by 10 different publishers, to one vendor is more economical than placing orders to 10 different publishers. It further adds to savings, which result from "batch effect" of unpacking only one box and authorizing only one payment. Most vendors also promise to provide fast and accurate service. It is true that a few publishers, if they accept single-copy orders, handle these orders more slowly than they do to large orders. But it is also true that the vendors do not always have a specific title when it is ordered, which also means that additional time must be allowed to secure the desired item.

Ordering for the titles brought out by the publishers, that the vendor cannot handle delays the matter. "In some cases the vendor report of failure, making the acquisition process even slower . Under such circumstances, buying directly from the publisher is the best approach to this problems, if one knows the exact publishers of the titles".[17]

Some vendors wait for placing orders with the publishers until they have received multiple requests before placing the final order as by placing a multiple-copy order they will receive a better discount. For the library, delay may be one to several months, because it may take long time for the vendor to accumulate enough individual requests for the title to make up an order of sufficient size. Vendors who do place single-copy orders for a customer usually offer a lower discount. Again the acquisition staff must weigh service and speed against discount. Occasionally, a vendor has a title in stock after the publisher has listed the item as being out of print. On occasion a vendor can supply out of print material, and a few vendors will even try to find out of print items for their best customers. "Beyond fast and accurate service, vendors provide personal service. A smooth working relationship with anyone, including a vendor, depends upon mutual understanding and respect". [18] When relationship is achieved, it is much easier to solve problems when they arise, even the difficult ones. The vendor, because of the smaller base of customers, normally can handle the problems more quickly than can a publisher's customer service department. Even the small account customer receives careful attention from a vendor, something that seldom happens with publishers, particularly the bigger ones.

One useful service that many large vendors offer is a periodic report about the status of all the library's orders. If the reporting system is properly organized, it can save lot of time both of librarian's and vendor's. The accuracy of these reports is quite important and the result can have an impact on collection development programme of the library. An item on order encumbers funds to pay for it when it is received. The precise cost of the item cannot be determined until it is received, and one hopes to set aside just slightly more than the total cost. Most libraries and information centres operate in a system where the funds not spent in a given year must be returned to the funding authority (not carried forward into the next year). "Having large sum of money tied up in outstanding orders that may not be delivered before the end of the fiscal year can mean a real loss for the collection, as a result the library loses twice as the item ordered is not received and the money is lost. If one is buying foreign books and the currency's value is fluctuating widely, losses can be large".[19] Producers can and raise their prices without notice, and in times of inflation one can count on regular price increases. So the less time funds are encumbered, the more purchasing power the library has.

Problems

Collection development and acquisitions, while not ordinarily perceived by the public as particularly demanding or exciting, contain elements that bring great personal satisfaction to those whose careers are spent in the library. There is distinct joy in knowing that one has contributed to the building up of a fine collection of library books. Little can excel the feeling that the librarian experiences when the material needed by a particular user can be placed immediately in his or her hand.

But the work related to collection development is not hassles free. Librarians have to encounter innumerable problems in their acquisition work. The variety of special problems that arise in purchasing library materials are so great that it almost defies categorization. A few of the common difficulties are mentioned below.

Publishers' Faulty Policies

Publisher's system of release of new titles has become much more conservative in recent years. Many publishers announce a title well in advance of its publication, and take the decision to publish the title when sufficient number of orders have been received.

In recent years, the librarians as well as wholesalers have become concerned at the tendency of some publishers to sell "direct only" to the library market, thereby eliminating an element of choice otherwise available to librarians. For the vendors, of course, this is a loss of business, and their ability to provide service to the library community is diminished. Likewise, librarians often are incensed to find that they are forced to purchase books directly from the publisher. This problem is compounded by the fact that not all publishers have a sufficient library or educational sales force in place. "The cost, efficiency of services and the products themselves, i.e documents, are influenced by a complex set of factors over which librarians have little or no control. As publishers are increasingly finding it difficult to store books for longer times, books are going out of print more quickly".[20] Speed and accuracy of delivery, willingness to handle wide range of publications, a proven track record with other libraries constitute important ingredients of a book supplier. Indian book trade is not well-organised. Most of the book sellers want easy money. They hardly believe in good service. They take interest to supply only those publications which are easily available and give them higher margin of profit. Due to this reason, only a small percentage of the titles on order are usually supplied. The book sellers are keen to sell those titles which are readily available in their stock of what they want to sell rather than the booksellers run small business with a low investment and maintain a small stock for counter sales only. Such book sellers are always keen to grab the orders, even though they may not be able to execute them. As a result the libraries are made to wait for a long time, compelling them to indulge in rush purchase at the end of the financial year for the fear of budget cuts in the forthcoming years. In the bargain, these booksellers are able to push the sale of their unsold books which were neither on order nor required for the library.

Another most crucial problem which occurs in building up a sound collection is lack of proper infrastructure. As a result, "the libraries located in metropolis and major cities are well served by bookshops while the libraries located in rural areas and even towns are not".[21] On top of that, bookshops tend to be very conservative in their stocking habits, preferring to sell international bestsellers or topical quickies or textbooks. Though Indian publishing industry ranks seventh in the world and third after USA and UK in the production of English titles, the industry still remains at developmental stage given the size of the population. Furthermore, Indian publishing industry, in the post-independence era has been beleaguered by the problems of an overall shaky economic base. The basic problems of all publishers are primarily the lack of capital, paucity of printing paper at reasonable price, lack of effective distribution channels, high postal rates, heavy railway freight charges, etc. "Most publishing houses in India have been set up or are owned by entrepreneurs. While well-meaning and genuinely interested in book business, they lack proper understanding of the intricacies of book publishing".[22] Timely distribution of books perhaps constitutes the real Achilles heel of Indian publishing industry. The logical and geographical dimensions are immensely vast in our country that extends over an area if 3,000 kilometres wide both north-south and east-west. Although there are quite a few importing wholesalers with any interest in Indian books, but retail outlets remain few and far between in urban areas and virtually non-existent in small towns.

Shrinking Budgets

Nowhere in the world, the library budget is keeping pace with the growth of literate and ever-increasing demands for it. Every year more books and other documents are published. The realisation of importance of information is also increasing. Consequently, there is a heavier demand for the sources of information, but the budget allocation to most of the libraries, however, remains static year after year. In some cases, the library budgets suffer a cut to save money for other priority items. Even if there is no such cut, the purchasing power with the allocated funds goes on dwindling due to inflation. The price of the books and other reading materials, are going up continuously. There is a cycle of conflicting forces like availability of more literature, along with the increasing demand for it, and inadequate money to purchase adequate literature to meet such ever-growing demands of their users are affecting libraries particularly in India. Although the problem of shirking budget is a universal one, but is quite serious in India. Though special libraries have sufficient funds at their disposal but the rising cost of foreign currency due to devaluation of Indian rupee has serious implications leading to financial constraints.

Foreign Books and Far Off Markets

The availability of books in the local markets has always been found helpful in collection development. For higher education and research, the Indian scholars and researchers mostly depend on foreign publications. Since foreign books are quite costly, the Indian booksellers for the representatives of the foreign publishers do not stock them adequately. Even most of the foreign publishers themselves do not stock them adequately. Most of the foreign publications are procured from abroad against orders. The final supply takes about three to six months in view of the distances involved and due to the import formalities. Moreover, all the foreign books ordered are not supplied. Distant book markets certainly stand in the way of collection development efforts of the librarians.

Book Markets in India

Whereas libraries are spread all over the country, the book markets in India are concentrated in metropolitan cities like Delhi, Mumbai, Chennai, Bangalore and Kolkata. "The libraries situated in these big cities are in an advantageous situation. But the libraries in other towns and cities located, far off from the book-markets, experience difficulties in developing their collections".[23]

Publications of Regional Language and Lesser Known Publishers

There is no difficulty in locating and procuring those publications which are brought out by the well-known publishers and are distributed through normal trade channels. But the major problems come regarding the publications which are brought out by upcoming publishers. The percentage of such publications is higher and remains unnoticed as they are brought out by small and newly emerging publishers or author-publishers in the unorganised sector. Due to this reason these publications, usually remain unknown and unprocured in spite of their value and usefulness. Similarly publications which are brought out by regional language publishers are difficult to acquire due to absence of any bibliographical control and far off locations.

Bibliographical Tools

The coverage of the Indian books in the bibliographical tools published from abroad is extremely poor. These are, therefore, not perfect tools to use for collection development. As regards the Indian bibliographical tools, there are few bibliographical sources of national importance but unfortunately these are neither up-to-date, nor comprehensive and also not regular. Indian National Bibliography (INB) covers Books published in various languages but it suffers from the above stated limitations. However situation has now started to improve and bibliography is now regularly being published. Other important national bibliography is *Indian Books in Print* which do not cover the Indian language books. For acquisition of government publications, theses, technical reports, and non-print materials, etc., hardly any dependable tool is available in India. One is supposed to use a number of available tools to arrive at a respectable coverage. However, the existing Indian bibliographical tools can only be useful in collection building after their quality is improved in terms of their coverage up-to-date-ness and regularity, etc.

Lack of Knowledge of Each Others' Systems

Librarians, publishers, and vendors all maintain that they are misunderstood. Librarians and vendors criticize publishers for churning out catalogues and flyers which do not contain the information needed for selection and acquisition. Librarians argue that catalogues should not only contain bibliographic information but should also contain details about editions and date of availability.

Quotation System

For acquiring documents, various systems are being followed by the libraries. However, the collection development process in a library suffers where quotation system is followed. Some unreliable book sellers quote the lower rates in order to get the orders. They on appointment, however, never supply most of the books ordered with them. They supply only those books which have remained unsold in their stock. The anxiety of library to purchase the books at the lowest quoted rates, deprives it the service of the efficient, established and reputed book sellers who are in position to supply most of the books on order. Therefore, the choice of right and well-established vendor is very important for any library in collection building because it is he who can execute the orders for books in full (as far as possible) and expeditiously.

Unstable Prices and Exchange Rates

The book sellers sometimes do not stick on to the prices quoted by them because publishers, particularly the foreign ones, frequently revise their prices upward. Some unscrupulous book sellers take undue advantage of this phenomenon. Because of the non-availability of the latest catalogues of the publishers, the library is unable to verify the charged rates as a result, the collection development programme suffers. Similarly the Good Offices Committee frequently revises the exchange rates due to devaluation of Indian rupee, upsetting the total procurement programme of the libraries in India. Unfortunately, for the last three years GOC has got split into two factions due to some differences between ILA and Publishers'Federation. Both the factions are fixing their own conversion rates which vary from each other substantially. The conversion rates fixed by ILA are comparatively low but information about these reaches very late in libraries. More over booksellers do not accept these conversion rates due to which libraries have to suffer financially.

Sale of Remainder Titles

Many book sellers in India specialise in acquiring remainder titles. For this purpose they visit foreign book markets and purchase in bulk the easily saleable remainder titles at throw away cost. These remainders, though purchased at much lower rates than their normal published prices are sold at higher cost. This allow the book sellers a heavy margin of profit. Such traders adopt all sorts of marketing techniques to promote and push their sale. Unsuspecting book selectors and librarians fall prey to the whole game and become a party in purchasing the out-of-date publications at exorbitant rates. Some unscrupulous librarians also join this racket knowingly and willingly for petty gains and flood their libraries with the remainder titles. Such uncalled for practices affect the development of worthy collection in the libraries.

Conclusion

Library collection development is not an easy task in India. There are many problems. There is always a paucity of funds to purchase even urgently needed publications. The markets for foreign books are far off. Production of Indian books is concentrated in Delhi, Mumbai, Kolkata and Chennai. Moreover, Indian book trade is unorganised, more interested in making easy money and less efficient in service. All the Indian publications are not brought out by the established publishers. Some of them remain unknown because they are published by small scale, new publishers. Publications of the publishers dealing in Indian languages, are available in their own regions only. Indian bibliographical tools are suffering with various limitations. Besides these, there are other problems concerning quotation system, advance payment, faulty import policy, ineffective distribution system, unstable prices and fluctuating exchange rates, paucity of suppliers of non-print materials, sale of remainders in the name of new and latest publications, etc. Libraries should be well aware of these problems. Inspite of all these constraints, librarians should have the skill and full knowledge of these problems to build-up a need-based, up-to-date, and balanced collection.

References

1. Young (Arthur P). Libraries and digital communication: Collision or convergence? *J Acquis Libr.* 22, 1995; 11-13.
2. Evans (G Edward). *Developing library and information centre collections.* 1987. Library Unlimited, Littleton. p 146.
3 Prytherch (Ray), *Ed. Harrod's librarians' glossary.* Ed 9. 2000. Gower Publishing Company Limited, England. p 625.
4. Webester's Deluxe unabridged dictionary. Ed. 2. 1979.Dorset and Baber, USA. p 1313.
5. Parasher (R G). *Developing library collection.* 1993. Medallion Press, Littleton.
6. *Ibid.* p 186-187.
7. *Patent Information and documentation handbook.* 1988. Wipo. Geneva.
8. Prytherch(Ray). *Op cit.* p 725.
9. *Dissertation Abstracts International.* 2000. Ann Arbor, Michigan.
10. *Comprehensive Dissertation Index, 1861-1972.* 1973. Ann Arbor, MI: Xerox University Microfilms.
11. Database of research project reports and Ph.D. dissertations .New Delhi. Indian Council for Social Science Research Centre.

12. UNIDO Inernational yearbook of industrial statistics. 2002. Unido, N.Y.
13. Prytherch (Ray). *Op cit.* p 695.
14. Galloway (Margret E). The expanding universe of special formats. *Coll Res Libr News.* 47. November 1986; 652.
15. Boissonnas (Christian M). The cost is more than that elegant dinner: Your ethics are at work. *Libr Acquis Prac Th* 11; 1987; 154-152.
16. Narendra Kumar. *India: 50 years of independence, 1947-97: status, growth and development.* 1988. B.R. Publishing, New Delhi. p 40.
17. Aloke (Sitesh). *Study of book industry: Small Publishers.* 1985. National Council for Applied Economic Research, New Delhi. p 88.
18. Tajeshwar Singh. Publishing in the third world: learning do's and don'ts from India *In* ALTBACH (Philip G), *Ed.* Publishing and development in the third world. 1992.Vistar, New Delhi. p 243-264.
19. Malhotra (D N), *Ed.* 50 years of book publishing in India since independence. 1998. Federation of Indian Publishers, New Delhi. p 323.
20. Gupta (Rajendra Kumar). College level publishing. *In* Malhotra (D N), *Ed. Ibid.* p 210-214
21. Ghai (S K). Marketing and distribution of books. *In* Malhotra (D N), *Ed. Ibid.* p 271-277.
22. Tajeshwar Singh. *Op cit.* p 245.
23. Koutchoumow (J A). India : At the threshold of new book vision. *In* Malhotra (D N), *Ed. Ibid.* p 315-320.

6
Acquisition of Periodical Publications

Introduction

Periodical publications constitute a significant part of the research collection in most of the special libraries and because of their continuous value in research programmes, considerable expenditure is involved in their purchase, handling, processing and storage, etc. These are viewed as highly important resources for current information, and in certain disciplines such as the physical sciences, life sciences, medicine, and engineering, etc. they are much more vital to research than are book materials.

The significance of periodical publications as a means of transmission of knowledge has increased manifold since World War II. The magnitude of their publications itself provide ample proof of their importance. The 2001 edition of *Ulrich's International Periodicals Directory*[1] covers 164,000 regularly 'and irregularly issued periodical publications arranged under 973 subjects, published by 80,000 publishers from 200 countries. Osborn[2] has also estimated that there will be 1.5 million periodical publications by the year 2000.

One of the basic necessity in this context is to define exactly what is included under the term "periodical publication". Although the library profession has put forward a generally accepted definition, the term may be interpreted slightly differently in various types of libraries, resulting in a need to identify the local definition before trying to understand the acquisition procedure in a particular setting.

In 1978, British, Canadian, and American librarians agreed upon the definition of a periodical as:

"A publication in any medium issued in successive parts bearing numeric or chronological designations and intended to be continued indefinitely. They include periodicals; newspapers; annuals (reports, yearbooks, etc.); the journals, memoirs, proceedings, transactions, etc. of societies; and numbered monographic series".[3]

According to Ranganathan[4] "Periodical publication is a documents with the following attributes:

1. *Periodicity.*-A volume or small group of volumes of it, is published or intended to be published or completed normally once in a year or at other regular intervals though irregularity in interval is not ruled out;
2. *Distinguishing Number.*-Each successive volume or periodical group of volumes, is usually distinguished by the year of publication and/or by a number belonging to a system of single or complex ordinal number usually called a volume number; and
3. *Continuity.*- The intention had been to continue the publication for ever and with the same title in all the volumes though not actually carried out."

Role of Periocical Publications

For the purpose of this study periodical publications have been taken up as generic term which includes journals, periodicals, annuals and proceedings, etc. These have a particularly important role to play in special libraries where they often merit a greater share of budget. They are somewhat costly in terms of their handling and permanent storage. For each subscription, particularly to periodicals, the library commits staff time to receiving and checking each issue, preparing claims for missing issues, recording, reporting holding to union lists, and generally dealing with the myriad small problems associated with keeping the current issues, and making necessary payment not only for these but for such associated items as title pages and indexes, supplements, and special issues.

A number of libraries have adopted procedure to discourage casual initiation of new periodical publications subscriptions. In some situations in which budgets have become particularly tight, a new subscription cannot be entered unless a title of equal cost is discontinued. Furthermore, in libraries that divide their budgets according to subject fields, the commitment to purchase it may permanently reduce future allocations for the purchase of monographs.

Selection Principles

Three primary factors are usually weighed when determining journal's worth: usage, relevance and availability of these journals in nearby libraries.

Usage may be estimated by gathering statistics on circulation outside the library, use in the library, photocopying, inter library loan requests from the library's clientele, and inter library loan requests from other libraries.

Relevance, the second major factor contributing to a journal's overall worth, is typically measured more subjectively. Sometimes as estimate of, relevance is based simply on the professional judgement of a librarian or a library user, relevance may also be determined by citation analysis. The number of times a journal title is retrieved in online bibliographic database searches and the number of times articles within a journal are cited by authors of other articles are useful indicators of possible relevance. Since frequency of citation of a journal may be related to the number of articles the journal contains, which may itself be related to the size or frequency of publication of a journal, raw citation statistics can be misleading.

Due to shrinking budgets and rising cost of periodicals, libraries often resort to resource sharing. If a particular journal is prohibitively costly and is available in nearby library, the subscribing library may omit it from its subscription list and borrow it from the neighbouring library.

Periodicals subscription constitutes the largest segment of budget of the special libraries the world over. Whereas the books are added annually in thousands, periodicals titles are subscribed at the rate of few hundred a year. In allocating the acquisition budget, the percentage to be expanded on periodical publications takes on special importance because the purchase of a periodical publications subscription commits the library to a long-term acquisition process, involving repeated payments over the years. In view of the cost and processing time associated with periodical publications, most libraries have in recent years tended to formalize their procedures for selecting and canceling periodical publications. Evidence of such formalization can be found in comprehensive statements of collection development policy related to periodical publications, committees charged with reviewing requests for all new periodical subscriptions, and empirical studies of how various groups such as students, researchers and specialists actually use periodical publications.

The general principles of periodicals selection do not vary much from those governing the selection of books. The factors governing the selection of periodicals depend on:

(i) The scope of the library,

(ii) Demands of the readers,

(iii) Whether the title is easily available elsewhere,

(iv) Periodicals already taken, and

(v) The financial resources of the library.

ASLIB[5] has recommended the following criteria for selecting the periodicals and serials for a special library:

(i) Recommendations by specialists;

(ii) Recommendation by members of the library staff;

(iii) Opinions of librarians of other institutions;

(iv) Announcements and reviews;

(v) Consultation of list of most cited periodicals;

Osborn[6] has recommended the following principles to decide whether or not a new periodicals title be added to the library:

1. Acquire the tools that open up the literature of a subject or a country;
2. Acquire titles that are analysed in standard indexing services;
3. Acquire the basic journals in the field of specialization of the organization;
4. Whenever possible and desirable, obtain sample copies to make the selection process more judicious;
5. In order to maintain a systematic programme of periodical selection, check new periodical titles each month;
6. Build-up periodical files on the basis of long runs, not broken files;
7. In research libraries, allocate a sum of money each year for the purchase of sets and backfiles. When hardcopy cannot be procured, acquire microforms;
8. Control duplicate subscription on the basis of relative values;

9. Always think of acquiring a title by gift or exchange in the area of interest of organisation;
10. Review each entry on the visible index every three years or so to see whether the title or extra copies are still worthwhile.

Core list of journals basic to a discipline, considered essential for a particular group of library users can be developed by using one or more of several criteria such as volume of past use of individual journal titles, subjective ratings of experts, frequency of citation of a journal in other journals, frequency of publications, number of pages or articles published in a year, number of places a journal is indexed or abstracted, and subscription cost can be taken into consideration instead of adopting published core list of journals, some libraries develop their own list, taking into account local use patterns and judgement of local experts, as well as the number of volumes of the journal owned by the library, and the availability of each journal of other nearby libraries.

Identifying Periodical Publications

Periodical publications employ a different bibliographic network than that used by monographs, very few of the selection aids for books provide their coverage.

There are several guides as well as specialized subject guides. Reviews of periodicals are few and far apart. In the past selection was not such a problem when publishers used to supply free sample copies of new periodicals for the library to examine and to subscribe. Today many publishers charge for such sample issues. Some important sources which help in identifying various periodicals are as follows:

Ulrich's International Periodicals Directory. Ed 37. 1998-99.Bowker, New Jersey.

World List of Social Science Periodicals.1986.UNESCO, Paris.

Union list of Social Science Periodicals.1992. ICSSR, New Delhi.

Susheel Kaur and Sapra (P). Directory of periodicals published in India. 1994. Sapra and Sapra, New Delhi.

All of the above, with the exception of *Ulrich's International Periodicals Directory* with *Ulrich's Quarterly,* are of limited value in identifying new titles because they are annuals, which means the information is at least several months old. As noted earlier, periodicals change in a variety of ways (titles, frequency, editorial policy, and so on), and keeping up with existing titles is enough of a problem without adding the need to identify newly created periodicals. The best source of information for periodicals acquired by American libraries is the Library of Congress's *New Serial Titles* (NST), which now reflects data in *Online Computer Library Center (*OCLC). If one can justify costs, online systems provide the most current information. Certainly OCLC is one source as arc British Record Society (BRS) and Knight-Ridder.(Formerly Dialog) The later services have information from Ulrich's.

There are several directories to periodical publications which arc available online. Some of the important directories are: *Online Guide to Serials*, available at http:// www.faxon.com/guide/default.html;*Publist,* available at<http://www.publist.com/>, an online directory of over 150,000 magazines, journals, newsletters and other periodicals published worldwide. *Ulrich's International Periodicals Directory,* has an advanced search option *Tradepub,* available at <http://www.tradepub.com/>, an aid to finding and subscribing to professional trade publications. *The Alternative Press Center's Online Directory,* available at <http://www.altpress.org/direct.html>, gateway to over 370 alternative press serials; *Docsource*, available at <http:// www4.infotrieve.com/ webdoc/search.html>, a searchable list of 65,000 journals.

Acquisition Sources of Peridocal Publications

Publishers

Most publishers accept direct subscription orders for their periodicals, although a few make their publications available only through agents or exclusively through a general purchase arrangement such as a standing order or a membership in the publisher's parent organization. Occasionally, a subscription, particularly for a periodical issued by an educational institution or a learned society, may be obtained solely as gift or exchange. In a few other cases, a periodical such as monograph periodical must be requested issue by issue, as no subscription is possible.

The complexity of keeping up with a variety of periodical subscriptions, even in small libraries that purchase no more then twenty or thirty titles, is often a complex task. If each periodical is ordered directly from its publisher, it is likely that the subscription expiration dates will be scattered over the year. The acquisitions staff has to remain careful not to let a renewal time slip by unnoticed, since it may be even harder to replace missed issues then to devise a system to anticipate renewals.

Some periodical publications that are not marketed through an agent must be ordered directly from the publisher. Typically, the periodicals issued by educational institutions and organizations and by scholarly societies that maintain a nonprofit status, have to be obtained by subscription directly from their publishers. Even then, exceptions exist. A few periodicals from nonprofit groups are available exclusively through agents, while others can be obtained only as a gift, on exchange, or through membership in the group. It is thus, imperative that the periodicals' acquisitions staff be aware of these variations and be prepared to accommodate whatever procedure is required by a publisher.

Subscriptions Agents

A more effective and reliable method of getting periodical publications is through a subscription agent than directly from the publisher. When orders are placed directly, the amount of work required to monitor expiration dates, place renewals, and approve payments over and over again for each title is too great. Therefore, if most orders are placed with an agent, this frees up time for other problem solving activities related to periodicals. Automatic renewal by a vendor saves library staff time, and when the invoice arrives there is still the opportunity to cancel titles no longer required. There may be multiple-year subscription rates that will save money. Information about discontinuation, mergers, changes in frequency, assistance provided in claiming missing and back issues and other alteration are the standard services provided by subscription agents.

The particular specifications drawn up by a library for its subscription agent should, reflect the needs of that library and the expectations of its users. As Harry Kuntz phrased it in his article on the selection and evaluation of periodicals agents, "The rapid placement of orders, speedy handling of claims, and prompt attention to renewals are basic to any periodical publication operations, large or small."[7] For example, agreement must be reached on the amount of lead time required by the agent for processing an order for a new subscription; once this is done, the library can expect either that issues of the new periodical will be arriving within a specified time period after order is placed, or that the agent will explain the reasons for delay.

Standing Orders

Some of the periodical publications can be acquired by the library through standing order which means automatic supply of the title by the publisher as and when the title get published. As in the case of subscriptions, certain publishers refuse to sell their output except through a standing order placed by the library directly with the issuing body.

Membership

In many ways, obtaining publications by taking out membership in the body that issues a publication or group of publications is similar to placing a standing order. Some groups will not sell their periodical publications except to members, while others give discounts or provide their publications as part of the membership perquisites, so that the cost of membership is clearly less than purchasing desired publications separately. Some subscription agents will undertake to handle standing orders and memberships for participating libraries, but the library will very likely encounter organizations that will not allow an agent to be involved in the transaction.

Gifts, Exchanges, Deposits

Periodical publications are also received on exchange basis or as gift under the auspices of academic institutions or scholarly groups. Such arrangements must be monitored carefully to ensure that an exchange is operating as initially established or that the gift subscription is arriving regularly and on time. Because of the special care required to keep the arrangements working properly, these subscriptions are not free; in fact, they may be more costly than if they were purchased.

In a number of cases, however, purchase in not an option, since, for various reasons, the titles may be available only through an exchange arrangement or by gift. In these instances, the acquisitions staff should be certain that the value of the materials outweighs the time required to negotiate and maintain the arrangement.

Deposits are much like gifts and exchanges, except that they may not be officially the property of the receiving library. It is important to know in detail the terms of a depository agreement before accepting it, especially for periodical publications. Libraries have upon occasion lost an extremely valuable periodical run because the organization that made the deposit decided to reclaim the material.

Another factor to consider accepting a depository arrangement for periodical publications is whether the library would be willing to pay for a subscription if the agreement is suddenly terminated. It is generally unwise to spend staff time on items that are of marginal importance to the collection, since it is probable that the entire set will eventually be discarded if the gift, exchange, or depository arrangement disappears.

The future status of a subscription is relatively unimportant if it is for a current-issues only title. Some periodical publications which have value for the topical and timely information need not be retained. These are ideal materials to be acquired by gift or exchange, since they do not have to be monitored to any great extent. It is unlikely that the library would want to accept such items on deposit, however, since without their clear ownership, the library would be unable to dispose of outdated issues with impunity.

Bid Contracts

This is another way of acquiring the periodical publications in a library. The purpose of bidding is to obtain for the library the best service at the least cost, although it is sometimes difficult to maximize both these aspects. Since, at present, a library is not likely to save money on the subscription price by working through an agent, it becomes imperative that the quality of the agent's service be high. Unfortunately, it is easier to measure discounts than good service; and the bidding process, if it results merely in award of a contract to the lowest bidder, it can cause more problems for the library then it solves. The library staff must be very careful in writing performance specifications and in monitoring that performance to identify ineffective subscription agencies to which contracts should not be awarded in the future.

Most librarians dislike the use of a bidding process to secure a subscription agent. Osborn[8] has noted, negotiating bid is both time consuming and generally financially unrewarding for the library and the agent.

In general, bid specifications for a subscription agent should include a description of the types of periodical publications to be acquired, such as whether they are all domestic publications of periodical type; the length of time given to the agent to place the subscription or report on its status; frequency and form of billing; and discount and service charges. Failure to live up to the terms of the contract should result in penalties, specified at the outset.

Through Government Agencies

In some countries government has assigned the job of procuring the periodical publications to its own agencies to eliminate agents. In our country, the job was assigned to State Trading Corporation(STC). Formed in 1956 to broaden the scope of Indian exports and to arrange essential imports, STC entered the field of book trade in 1974. The Government of India had earlier found that their libraries were facing various problems at the hands of private subscription agents who were also misusing the valuable foreign exchange provided to them for the import of books and periodicals. STC was therefore, asked to import foreign publications. A request was made to the universities through UGC to place their orders for the foreign periodicals with STC. There was mixed reactions, among the librarians over this decision. There was no risk to pay STC in advance the subscription of periodicals . As also STC could be expected to be service-minded rather then profit-minded like booksellers, these could be the advantages. However librarians had their own doubts. They thought that STC being a government undertaking may not be as efficient as a private agent; and secondly, it has no experience in book trade.[9] State Trading Corporation no longer provides this service.

Periodicals Subscription Problems

Subscription of periodicals poses several problems for a librarian. There is distinct lack of professional subscription agencies due to which libraries suffer a lot. Girja Kumar and

Tandon[10] have studied some important problems concerning procurement of periodicals in Indian context. This study is based on the information collected both from the librarian and the periodicals dealers in respect of : (1) Subscription procedure, (2) Refund for missing issues as also for complete volumes when not supplied, and (3) Exchange rates, and payment procedures. Many more problems being faced by the librarians are briefly stated as below:

Subscription Procedures

Generally, most of the libraries subscribe to the periodical publications through agents. In case the foreign publishes have appointed their sole agents, the orders are placed with them. The subscription agents are appointed by inviting quotations. This method has not been found to be successful because the experience of the librarians is that the agents who offer lower rates usually do not give efficient service. Only those agents who are ensured suitable remuneration provide better services. Most of the libraries do not invite quotations every year and they renew the subscriptions on the basis of pervious years' performance of the agent. A large number of libraries renew their subscription every year which results in the late placing of orders as also late payment of subscription. It is necessary that the process is rescheduled to avoid these delays. The other way can be that the libraries may consider the placing of standing orders which would help to avoid delays and to minimise routines.

Refund

It has been a common practice of the libraries to ask for the refund for the missing issues when lost in transit, etc. But when complete volumes are not supplied to the libraries, subscription is either adjusted or refunded invariably. It happens when the periodical has ceased its publication or when it is behind the publications schedule. In case the library discontinues its subscription, the recovery of dues becomes a problem. The agents do not like to refund the subscription unless they receive payment from the publishers. In all cases, getting the refund is a job, demanding regular persuasion from the library, involving a protracted correspondence stretching over a long period.

Exchange Rates and Payment Procedure

Almost all the libraries make advance payment to the agent; the advance however, varies from 80 to 100 per cent . Normally the exchange rates recommended by the Good Offices Committee (GOC) are accepted, but some libraries pay at the bank exchange rate also. While claiming payments the agents submit publishers' invoice or renewal notice and the certificate for exchange rate. Most of the librarians, however, believe that many agents do not forward their payments to the publishers immediately after these are made but they misuse the advance amount paid to them.

Periodicals Through Gift and Exchange

Gifts are rare as far as current periodicals are concerned. They are often possible for back files of periodicals from individuals, who have acquired them for one reason or another, or from institutions but valuable gifts or back files rarely come unsolicited. When it comes, it is most welcome. But very often the gift is made to shift the burden from one place to another and with grace. Unless the gift has a positive utility for the library, it should be politely refused. In a service library, only usable gift materials should be acquired or maintained.

The libraries attached to the organisations which have periodical publications of their own can procure a number of current periodicals in exchange with these publications. But only institutional publications are available on exchange, not the commercial ones. Exchange is not a bargain, it is a convenience and a method to get over some difficulties such as foreign exchange, cash remittances, accounting records, etc. Newly started periodicals are generally more easily available on exchange than the old and established ones.

Exchange of publications is a friendly relationship and, therefore, it must be handled with that spirit.[11]

Procurement of Back Files

The acquisition of the back volumes of periodicals is also part of the procurement programme. The cost of the back files of periodicals is usually very high and their acquisition is a slow and tedious process. Extreme precaution, therefore, is needed before a decision is taken to acquire the back files of a periodical. A newly established library needs the back volumes of periodicals to build-up periodicals collection. An old library may also require the back files of periodical when it is needed too frequently for some new project and inter-library-loan is not considered feasible. There are dealers who specialize in the supply of back files of journals. Purchase can be made by calling quotations from different dealers and by placing order with the one who is willing to supply at the lowest rates. While placing the order, it should also be seen that the rates quoted are for the bound volumes, each complete in all respect with its title-page and index. These back volumes are purchased like books and are paid when found all right after physical examination. For the periodicals which are infrequently used, inter-library-loan facilities from other libraries may be relied upon, or alternatively their acquisition in microforms may be considered. It will be still better if the acquisition of back files of periodicals is organised on cooperative basis among the local libraries whether to be acquired in original form or in microform.

Librarians should guard against going into the second-hand periodicals market to equip long range back files or back runs, for in the field of rare and out of print material the prices are many times more than the original. Unless it is backed up by lowest quotation, the librarian may come to trouble at the time of audit. Well-known and established back volumes dealers like the Today and Tomorrow, New Delhi; the Researchco, New Delhi; the Satish Serials, Delhi; the New India Books and Periodicals, Delhi (from India) and the

Dawson, UK; the Kraus Reprints, USA; the Faxon, Westwill, USA (from abroad) and many others may be approached for meeting the requirements of back volumes of periodicals depending upon their place of publication.

Missing Issues

Every library faces a problem of missing issues and incomplete volumes of periodicals, whether the journals are received from India or abroad, whether these are subscribed directly from the publishers or through subscription agents. The loss of issues in transit is usually because of two reasons : (i) Issues are not delivered due to some one's personal interest, or laziness of the postman, and (ii) Misdelivery due to the carelessness of the postal employees.

If claim for the missing issue is made promptly, depending upon the policy of the publisher the copy is usually replaced, provided it is in print. But the problem is that a periodical takes about five months in reaching India from the United States of America. However, some publishers also send micro edition of the missing issue if the original is out of print, others may extend the period of subscription in lieu of the issue, but most of the publishers do not agree to replace the missing issue free of cost as the complaints for missing issues are maximum from India and are recurring in nature. The only way to get the full supply of periodicals is either to get it by registered post or by air mail.

Other Problems in Periodical Management

Periodical work is entirely a problem area. By nature periodical publications are individual, erratic and unpredictable. Their selection, acquisition, check-in, cataloguing and even public service constitutes a difficult assignment. The routines involved are incessant, their price, title, publishers, frequency and scope are subject to change. Periodical publications merge or split, get suspended for varying lengths of time. Even periodical number is a fertile area for confusion and chaos.

Indian Subscription Agencies

Though several agencies are providing the services related to subscription and supply of journals to libraries e.g. M/s Central News Agency (CNA), New Delhi; Universal Subscription Agency, New Delhi; D.K. Agencies, New Delhi; Allied Publishers Subscription Agency, New Delhi; Globe Publications International subscription Agency, New Delhi; Living Media India Limited, New Delhi; India Book House, New Delhi; India Book House, Chennai; Creative Books & Periodicals, Mumbai. However, Central News Agency, New Delhi is one of the oldest and most popular subscription agency.

Services being Provided by CNA

CNA supplies journals to 9,500 subscribers and handles 25,000 orders. The number of publishers handled by CNA is 5,000.[12] CNA, besides having contacts with publishers and originating institutions all over the world, also have standing order arrangements for continuations of all kinds of journals. It generates new catalogue records for the newly introduced periodicals, showing the correct current title, place of publication, sponsor's/publisher's name, frequency, year of commencement (whenever available), and other details, incorporating the essential information about different volumes and their prices.

CNA offers subscription services both to Indian and overseas customers, helping them procure with speed and the highest measure of certainty, periodicals/serials: both regular and irregular, on all subject areas under science and technology, social sciences, and humanities. Some of the important features of subscription through Central News Agency have been stated as follows by the CNA management in a written statement:

- Has a completely automated subscription division, which has ready data for over 15,000 titles from over 5,000 publishers. Subscription rates are updated on a daily basis and the entire billing, ordering, dispatching and claims process is automatically done by our computers.

- Conventional mail channels used by overseas publishers are a constant irritant for Indian subscribers, because of delayed deliveries and missing issues. CNA has its own representatives in the UK and USA who take care of consolidating all issues for our clients and shipping them to New Delhi once every week. This ensures complete control of the issues and cuts down on transit delays and issues missed in the mail. All this comes to clients at no extra cost. All issues received by us are sent to our clients by registered post/courier/hand delivery.

- It has been observed that issues received from multiple sources tend to get misplaced or lost in a library. CNA has tried to eliminate this problem by consolidating all issues for large clients at their end and then dispatching them with a packing list, to the clients after proper check-in into our control system. This helps in maintaining a complete record of all issues sent to the client and also automatic follow-up in case of missing issues.

- Claims for titles received via exclusive airfreight service are generated automatically by its system after expiry of thirty days of the due date of receipt of an issue. This is done even before the subscriber sends in a claim to saving on valuable time and cutting down on the inconvenience caused by time barred claims.

- Proforma invoices quote the subscription rates available on the date of preparation of the invoice and at Good Offices Committee (GOC faction controlled by Federation of Booksellers Association) approved conversion rates. These conversion rates are valid for sixty days from the date of our proforma. Any revision in the basic subscription rates between the date of our proforma invoice and receipt of your payment and order, would be charged in our supplementary invoices.

- All claims for missing issues, whether received through airfreight service or otherwise, are forwarded to the publishers by the fastest possible means (email/fax/airmail). Copies of publishers' responses are also provided to the clients, whenever received.
- Deal with publishers directly and orders are always accompanied by advance payments.
- Guarantee the rates that are charged to clients and substantiate this with proof of rates from publishers, if required.
- Follow a very transparent system and provide clients with the subscription reference numbers allotted by the publishers. This serves a dual purpose; it guarantees that the subscription has been correctly paid by to the publisher on behalf of the client and also ensures online access to the subscriber, wherever available. All the information available in database is posted on our website periodically. Subscribers also get access to their order status and the issue receipt status on website.

Electronic Journals

Computer and telecommunication technologies, symbolised by the Internet have provided the opportunity to handle masses of information with speed and economy to publishers, leading to large scale electronic publishing. It increasingly offers the possibility of using computers and communication networks to create alternative electronic forms of the conventional paper journal. "This has led to the emergence of electronic journal available either online or on CD-ROMs".[13] In most cases, electronic journals are duplicates of paper journals in electronic form, typically available in HTML or PDF formats. Although there are some wholly electronic journals, i.e. those with no print counterpart, these are in the minority.

Special libraries are increasingly subscribing to journals in electronic formats. Vendors like CatchWord, Electronic Journals, EBSCO Online Electric Library Canada, JSTOR are providing full text databases of journals in electronic formats.

In India, EBSCO Publishing, a part of US based EBSCO Information Services Group is the largest vendor of online journals. Subscribers may now access full text e-journals via EBSCO Online or via EBSCO full text databases. It provides full text for 3,300 journals. Full text coverage is retrospective to 1965 for 205 titles and 1990 for many others.[14] Similarly M/s Edutech Services Pvt. Ltd.Chennai, are providing online access to 5400+ journals out of which 3,200 are full text.[15]

Yet another vendor, Informatics (India) Ltd. has set up, J-Gate, an Internet gateway and portal for integrating e-content and e-commerce for journal literature. It envisages to provide seamless access to journal articles at publishers' site, local sites of the libraries or at the J-gate archive, through a table of content and abstract database.[16]

One of the most serious limitations of all these databases is the absence of Indian journals. There is hardly any Indian journal included in any of these databases. The subscription cost are also quite high. The current annual subscription of EBSCO database is 10,000 dollars which many of the libraries find difficult to afford.

Advantages

The advantages of electronic journals are as given below:

(i) *Speed*: Articles can be put on the Web as soon as they are ready, without having to wait may be months for a space in a journal issue. The American Chemical Society put articles on their Web site "as soon as publishable" which can be up to 11 weeks before print.[17] This all means that the information is much more up-to-date than can be achieved with paper.

(ii) *Easily searchable:* Searchability is one of the core advantages of a digital format. Easier it is to find research materials, the fewer duplicated experiments there will be, resulting in less wasted time.

(iii) *Interactive:* The rapid turn around time means that articles can be read, commented on by the journal's readers, and amended much more quickly than can be done with print. The ease with which e-mail can be sent, or forms filled in means that there can be much greater feedback through the Web.

(iv) *Accessible:* For any researcher, availability from a desktop computer means a significant increase in accessibility, particularly for those who do not work within easy reach of the library. The fact that entire archives will be available, several people can read an issue simultaneously, and they cannot go missing. Also different layers of access can be given to different people with little extra effort, e.g. different levels of subscription, allowing access to abstracts only, or full multimedia.

(v) *Better Search facility:* Enables searching article contents by words and/or phrases.

(vi) *Eliminates problems of lost content:* Electronic subscription eliminates problems related to loss of content resulting from theft or destruction of library print material. E-journals currently are designed for access, not preservation. Few publishers, presently guarantee permanent access to their electronic journal websites and certainly, if the library cancels a subscription, there is no promise of continued access to those volumes to which the library did subscribe.

Disadvantages

The disadvantages of electronic journals are as given below:

(i) Readers' comfort level with electronic journals varies widely. This format does not enable browsing and quick scanning of a page or pages of text, as we are accustomed to doing with the print product.

(ii) Readers must learn how to "use" electronic journals, how to find them, how to connect, how to navigate through the publisher's website, how to install the software required to view full-text of articles (most often, this means installing the *Adobe Acrobat Viewer*).

(iii) Electronic journals are "resource-intensive" and almost invariably require a fast network connection and fairly good computer hardware.[18]

(iv) Journal websites move or are re-organized, resulting in unexpected and unannounced changes to URLs.

(v) There are substantial library staff costs in maintaining accurate lists of electronic journals, as vendors add or drop titles, offer and then withdraw free access, reorganize websites, etc.

(vi) The license agreements, access permissions, and technical requirements for each e-journal are different and must be handled one by one between the Library and the publisher.

(vii) In many cases, publishers only will provide electronic access (either free or subject to an extra fee) if the library agrees also to maintain a print subscription. As a result, there may be no gain to the library in terms of reduced book handling, binding costs, and shelf space.

The issue of subscribing to electronic journals is quite complex. Most of the libraries are in transitional stage and are subscribing journals in both the formats. The print journals can never be discarded completely. At least in core areas, libraries will have to maintain a sizeable subscription of print format. Further, negotiating favourable license agreements with publishers and vendors is required . Before switching over to a large scale electronic subscription, libraries will have to take the following facts into consideration : [19]

- collaboration with other institutions to implement cost-effective consortium cost-sharing arrangements,
- adequate workstation technology within institutions for optimal access to and use of electronic resources,
- subscription pricing that permits the elimination of print subscriptions in favor of electronic formats while retaining archival rights,
- recognition by respective institutions that the benefits of electronic delivery of information is not without a cost to the institution, and
- management of intellectual property and copyright requirements in the electronic environment, for network distribution, electronic reserves, and distance education.

Conclusion

Periodical publications are important part of special library's collection. Continued growth in the number of periodical publications and their spiraling costs are two issues of grave concern, especially in regard to scholarly journals. Areas of knowledge are being constantly divided into narrower areas of specialization and the number of persons interested in these decreases with each narrow division. Costs of producing a special interest journal rises, no matter how many or how few people are interested in reading about the subject. After a certain cost level is reached, the number of individual subscribers drops quickly. Usually any price increase to individual subscribers, designed to offset lost subscription revenue only makes the problem worse.

The exponential growth of periodical literature has immensely enhanced the need to evolve an effective and fool-proof serial control and management system. This need for establishing an impregnable control method becomes all the more necessary due to the prohibitively exorbitant prices of periodical publications. This is further multiplied by the fact that all serious scholars and users harbour a protective feeling towards them. The periodical librarian has always to be on his toes guarding against any possible discrepancy leading to the disruption in the system.

Electronic journals provide a solution to all these problems.Though subscription to electronic formats is slowly increasing but due to their high cost, a substantial number of libraries are not able to do so. A possible solution to reduce the subscription cost is consortia approach and minimum possible customization of number of journals keeping in mind the requirement of subscribing library.

References

1. Ulrich's International Periodicals Directory. Ed 39. 2001.Bowker, New Jersey. p. 1533.
2. Osborn (Andrew). Serial publications: Their price and treatment in libraries. 1980. American Library Association, Chicago. p. 25.
3. Anglo-American Cataloging Rules. 1988. American Library Association, Chicago. p. 622.

4 Rangaathan (S R). *Prolegomena to library classification.* Ed 3. 1967. Asia Publishing House, Bombay. p. 212.

5. Brown (Charles Harvey). *Scientific serials.* 1956. Association of College and Research Libraries, New York. p. 3.

6. Osborn (Andrew). Serial publications.Ed 3.1955. American Library Association, Chicago. p. 35.

7. Kuntz (Henry). Serials Agents : Selection and evaluation. *Ser Libr*, 2, Winter; 1977; 145.

8. Osborn (Andrew) *Op cit.* p. 114-116.

9. Kumar (PSG). Book acquisition and STC. *Her Libr Sci.* 13.1; 1974; 61-64.

10. Girja Kumar and Tandon (J C). Problems of periodical subscription in the Indian context. *In* Agrawal (S N) and others, *Ed.* Perspectives in library and information science. V. 2. 1982. Print House, Lucknow. p. 157-64.

11. Ketkar (N M). Acquisition of periodicals: Some observations. *Libr Her.* 8,1-2; July 1965; 109-10.

12. Information supplied by Mr. Sanjeev Puri, Director, Subscriptions, Central News Agency, New Delhi by Email.info@cna-india.com.

13. Schauder (Don).Electronic publishing of professional articles: Attitudes of academics and implications for the scholarly communication industry . *J Am Soc Inf Sci.* 45,1; 1994; 73-100.

14. www.epnet.com

15. www.edutechindia.com

16. http://j-gate.inforindia.co.in

17. Huber (Charles F). Electronic journal publishers: A reference librarian's guide. *J Electron Publishing.* 6, 3; 2001; 67-69.

18. Amiran (Eyal) and John (Unsworth). Postmodern culture: Publishing in the electronic medium. *Public Access Comput Sys Rev.* 1; 1991; 67-76.

19. Hickey (Thomas B) and Terry (Noreault). The development of a graphical user interface for the online journal of current clinical trials. *Public Access Comput Sys Rev.* 3, 2; 1992; 4-12.

7

Acquisition of Non-print Documents

Introduction

A special feature of collection of special libraries has been the emphasis on non-print material. Non-print materials are defined as library materials that require some form of media enhancement to be used. A common character of these special formats is their dependence upon equipment for access.[1] During the last three decades, there has been growing importance of such items as films, videos and audio recordings, microfilms and microfiches. As video and audio cassettes have become widely used to package a wide variety of research material, special libraries have begun to include statements on audio-visual material in their collection development policy. This increased acquisition of such materials has brought with it a general concern with problem of selecting the non-print forms, sources of information about and method of acquisition of various types, and problems of handling them once they are acquired. Bibliographic and evaluative information on these materials appear in a wide variety of sources. In addition, many are distributed in ways entirely distinct from the system used for books and serials. In addition to the general principles applied in selecting all library materials, other matters are to be considered for some of these formats: technical matters involved in their production, the extraordinary expense of some and the need to preview before purchase and the requirement for expensive, well maintained equipment for using them.

Some important special formats which special libraries acquire are discussed in succeeding pages.

Audio-Visual Materials

Films, filmstrips, slides, video and sound recordings, although composed of various combinations of film, plastic, and magnetic tape, are usually categorized as audio-visual materials.[2] They are both important sources of information as well as storage media. Keeping up with new technology, new equipment, and new producers of audio-visual materials is difficult; the procedures and distributors form a complex pattern. As with monographs, commercially oriented producers for most of these media tend to focus on either the mass market or the education market. Audio-visual materials can be divided in the following categories.

Films

Film were among the first audio-visual materials to be incorporated into library collections, and in spite of the rising popularity of the video recordings, films continue to be collected by libraries. The 16 mm film was the first motion picture format to become popular for educational purposes. Later when the 8 mm and super- 8mm appeared, material in these formats also began to be added by libraries.

Motion pictures in the 16 mm film format are popular for large group viewing because of their sharp image and good sound. It also has an advantage over certain others in equipment compatibility and can be shown on any 16 mm projector.

A major problem with acquiring films is the high cost. In fact, the cost of 16mm films has forced most libraries in Europe and USA into systems of cooperative ownership or rental.

Although large libraries and library systems purchase films, most small and medium-sized libraries depend upon centralized collections of 16mm films. Sometimes a library uses a combinations of these sources. When an individual library does purchase films, its staff has ordinarily previewed each item, before making a final decision to purchase. Fortunately, most films are available on a preview basis.

Selection of films is governed by the general criteria for evaluating any library material; suitability of content to the intended audience, possible uses, physical features, comparative merits, and cost. With this format, however, more emphasis may be placed on evaluation of technical aspects, such as the quality of photography, sound, lighting, editing, narration, etc. A major consideration will be whether film is actually the most effective medium for presentation of the particular content.

The sources of information, their production, distributors and printed evaluation do not present as neat a pattern as the sources about books and their publishers.

Filmstrips

Another film format, consisting of lengths of 35 mm film containing a series of still pictures are popular in some libraries. While they do not provide the motion which makes 16 mm and 8 mm films so attractive, filmstrips may be designed to suggest motion and may be accompanied by sound. Relatively low cost and ease of viewing are among the factors that have made filmstrips particularly popular. In general, selection criteria for filmstrips are similar to those for other non-print materials, but, as with other audio-visual format, technical quality particularly visual images and sound (where included) should be high. Since filmstrips, like films are restricted to a predetermined sequencing, the organisation of material presented in the filmstrip is very important. The educational objectives to be met by the filmstrip should be clearly evident to the one who selects it and effectively presented to the viewer.

Slides

These are single frames of 35mm films secured in a 2"×2", 2.25"×2.25", or 3.25"×4" mounting. They are relatively inexpensive and their projection equipment is easy to operate. In addition, they offer flexibility of sequence and pacing. Multimedia screen presentations, with sound and specially treated slides, can hold an audience's attention as well as fast-paced motion picture. For educational purposes, colour, resolution, and focus of the visual image in the slide are important selection considerations.[3]

Audio and Video Recording

As video and audio cassettes have become widely used to package a large variety of instructional and research information, special libraries have begun to include statements on audio-visual materials in their collection development policies.

Audio recordings come on either disk or tape. The popular form of audio recording is the magnetic tape. The material available on sound recordings encompass a wide scope. Predominant in terms of bulk is music, anthologies and languages, video recording include videotapes, videocassettes, and videodiscs, any form in which visual images have been recorded magnetically or by laser and can be viewed through a television . It may contain digital, motion, audio, or still images, and is read by a laser. Videotapes, most often distributed in cassette form, are strips of polyester with magnetic signals. Videocassette have been produced and sold to the public in 3/4-inch U-matic, 1/2-inch Beta, 1/2-inch VHS, and 8mm formats. Each requires different playback equipment. The videodisc, which require still another type of player, is superior to video-tape in picture and sound quality, in durability, and in access to specific parts of the recorded content. It can also store a greater range of signals (digital, motion, still, etc.). At the present time, however, the variety of content available on video-cassettes is much greater than that available on video-discs.

Library collection of video recording may contain locally recorded events and productions, as well as those produced commercially. Videotapes, particularly the locally produced variety, have been common in libraries for some time; but now that video cassettes are widely available for the home market, many libraries collect and lend these cassettes to users as they do the more traditional formats. The collection development policy for video recording should specify, in addition to goals of the collection and general selection criteria, which types of materials the library will collect and how these will be judged.

Acquisition Problems

The purchase of video formats presents complications not common in the acquisition of other special materials. The technology of video recording is developing rapidly which makes selection of particular formats and related equipment unusually difficult. Initial high cost and possible obsolescence are two of the problems the librarian faces. The ease with which video recording can be copied raises a host of legal questions, and also means that free preview of video recording so far more limited than for films. In spite of the collection development difficulties, video recording are replacing films in some libraries.

The same bibliographic tools may not list materials for both market. Many audio-visual materials are also produced by institutions, associations, and other non-commercial organizations. In addition, most audio-visual producers distribute their own materials, This diversity of producers and distributors makes it very difficult for librarians to identify what exists. Bibliographic control of most types of audio-visual materials is still less complete than the coverage of print materials. There is no general in-print list for audio-visual materials. For this reason, libraries usually maintain collections of producers/distributors catalogue.

Microforms

Microforms come in three basic formats microfilm, microfiche, and micro-opaque, each of which has several variations. Microfilm is produced from high-contrast photographic film, 16mm or 35mm, usually in black and white, although some materials are available in colour. Microfiche resembles microfilm in that it contains a series of micro images on film, but instead of the images that appear in row on a tool of film, they are arranged in a grid pattern on sheet of film.

Microforms have been hailed as the most cost-effective solution to conserving shelf space and reducing binding cost in libraries. Many periodical titles, as well as monographic sets, are available for purchase. Microforms also serve a preservation function, rare and out-of-print materials can be more widely available. The great drawback to making microform purchases a major part of collection development is user resistance. Microforms must be viewed in the library, on the proper machine, and in appropriate lighting conditions. User's objections can, however, often be overcome with careful planning. Harrington identifies the following factors as contributing to successful use of microforms in a library; establishment of centralized microform collection, provision of a comfortable and pleasant study environment, well-maintained readers and reader-printers, adequate bibliographic control, and enthusiastic, well-trained staff.[4]

Microform Publishing

Micro publishing, or the production of microforms, is often an on demand publishing process that is, duplicate microfiches or rolls of microfilm are produced from the master microform when there is a specific request. It is therefore a particularly appropriate form of publication for material with limited demand, and there are three major types: (1) reprinting or preservation of works that were originally published in a paper format, (2) publication of original works, such as dissertations or research reports, and (3) simultaneous publications of certain work in both subscriptions and backfiles of journals, working copies of rare books manuscripts, and government or international agency documents are the examples of the type of materials most often acquired in microform.

Apart from commercial publishers, libraries are the main source of microfilms. They are not usually purveyors of macro publications, but holders of negative films that another library may want copied or, more often, holders of original materials that purchaser wants copied. If the owning library has a copying laboratory, the purchaser may prefer to have the materials copied there. Also, the owning library may require that the materials be copied in its premises. A method of acquisition of microforms is the exchange of backfiles of serial sets for microform copies from commercial firms. Such exchanges may be legitimate but libraries should be sure that the value to be received is equal to or greater than value of the materials to be released.

Electronic Formats

• The development of electronic data storage and transmission technology has provided libraries with rapid access to information and opportunities for new services. Not only it has provided new ways to store information compactly and cheaply but also a new mechanism to manipulate, scan and store and exchange data. A host of library collection is now available in electronic format, both online and offline. Traditional special formats available in microforms are now being digitised and made available in electronic formats. These development have far reaching impact on the acquisition practices of special libraries which are now increasingly subscribing to full text journals available online. In India online subscription is not really taking place at a large scale. It is confined to big libraries located in metropolitan cities only.

Important Selection Tools

Selection of electronic formats such as floppy disks and CD-ROMs ought to proceed on the basis of a library's collection and service goals. As the number of these products increases, some librarians are recognizing the need for collection development statements to establish guidelines and criteria specifically regarding suitability of the contents for the library users, time span covered by an index, whether or not a print or online version exits, compatibility with equipment already owned by the library, reliability and services offered by the vendor, existence of licensing restrictions, searching capabilities, and cost.

Decisions about which electronic formats to provide to user most often arise in connection with reference material, because this is where information is more likely to be available both in print and electronically. Printed reference sources are less up-to-date than electronically delivered material and online databases.

Optical disks, specially in the form of CD-ROMs have become increasingly important as a medium for the storage and dissemination of information during the 1990s. CD ROM products offer the advantage of predictable costs and more currency than printed sources.

CD-ROM publishing is a relatively easy market to enter, and consequently there are large number of CD-ROM publishers. Most publishers are not prolific and many have only a single product. They may be engaged in various other aspects of the information industry.

Some of the important selection tools for electronic products are given below:

(i) CD-ROMs in Print: An international guide to CD-ROMs, Multimedia, Laser discs and Electronic products.2000. Gale Group, USA.

(ii) Directory of online databases. 1999.Gale Group. Santa Monica, California.

(iii) Elsevier Association Database Directory. 1985. Knowledge Industry, White plains. N.Y.

(iv) Union Catalogue of CD-ROM Databases in Social Sciences : Indo-Dutch Programme on Alternatives Development Exchange of Literature, Documents & Data/edited by Nutan Johry. 2000. Indian Council of Social Science Research, New Delhi.

The databases available on CD-ROMs are equally various. They can be categorised as bibliographic, quick reference, statistical and multimedia databases.

Because CD-ROM is a newer media in the market the bibliographic and evaluative sources for it are not yet as extensive. *CD-ROMs Review*; *the Magazine of Optical Publishing* (Bi-monthly, CW Communications) and *CD-ROM Librarian* (Monthly, Meckler) provide some guidance in this area.

Acquisition Criteria

According to Rowley[5] the following factors should be taken into consideration while acquiring databases on CD ROM:

(i) *Databases contents*: Coverage, and whether illustration and other details are included in a full text database.

(ii) *Currency*:Time period covered by the database. How up-to-date is the information, and how frequently are updates issued.

(iii) *Backfiles*: The availability of backfiles is an important issue in subscribing a database. It is an added advantage as it saves a lot of space.

(iv) *Retrieval software and indexing*: Retrieval software must be user friendly, efficient and effective. It must offer a full range of retrieval facilities, and must be able to support both the novice end -user and experienced searcher.Indexing must be appropriate and index terms should represent the document well.

(v) *Cost:* Price strategies for CD-ROMs are designed to reflect the extent of use of database. There are usually different prices for stand - alone users, single network users, other size user groups and site licenses. Decision should be carefully taken while going for the subscription.

(vi) *Standardization:* Standards for CD-ROMs were initially a serious problem, and difficulties can still arise if a number of discs from different suppliers are being run on one workstation network. It is important to check that all hardware and software components work satisfactorily with one another.

Problems

New technologies, however, for recording and delivering information also present problems to collection development librarians. One of the problem is the speed with which electronic technologies and the equipment required to use them have been developed, improved, and abandoned (in some cases). Not only librarians must struggle to keep up with what is new, but they must also decide when and where to incorporate electronic delivery into their library's services, knowing that the wrong decision may mean spending a great deal of money for equipment that will soon be obsolete.

The problems involved in the acquisition of non-print documents are further increased by cumbersome administrative procedures involved. According to Futas "many librarians have bogged at the tasks involved in checking films for damage, keeping motion picture projectors in order. The problems involved in cataloguing, storing, and preserving recordings in decent condition have weakened the resolve of some librarians in their acquisition of this medium".[6] Limited financial resources also cause some libraries to hesitate about extensive acquisition of non-print media. Some of these media are very expensive and require the purchase and maintenance of costly equipments if they are to be properly used.

The publishing pattern of these material is also more diverse. It is impossible to impose a coherent structure in this area. Most of the producers of this material distribute on their own which causes problems. There is no equivalent in this field to the bookshops.

In India the problem is further compounded by the absence of reliable vendors and agencies for procuring this material.

Recently the non-print material has become an important part of the library collection. For the supply of books and periodicals, several reliable and well-established booksellers are available in India, but there are very few suppliers who deal in non-print materials. Moreover, the lack of comprehensive and up-to-date selection tools for non-print materials further adds to the problems of the libraries.

Conclusion

Usually the audio-visual materials and microfilms are produced by the agencies specialising in the teaching aids. Machine readable materials are similarly produced by large publishers specialising in them. Indian agencies have not taken up the production of non-print materials so far. A majority of non-print materials per force is to be imported, bringing in the problems of its selection and procurement. Hewitt has concluded that "the increased acquisition of such material has brought with it a great concern with problems of selecting the non-book forms, sources of information about the methods of acquisition of the various types, and problem of handling them once they are acquired".[7]

Non-print material is an essential part of special libraries. According to Hawks "the developments that brought most of the non-print materials into existence occurred in the past hundred years, a period of rapid technological innovation that witnessed the introduction of the motion pictures, radio, television and the computer. Each medium embodies a certain technology that is the subject of continuous improvement and enhancement over the years". [8]

Selection and acquisition of non-print materials is generally considered to be more difficult and time consuming than selecting and acquiring print materials. This is due in part to the scarcity of selection and acquisition aids and in part to market volatility.

References

1. Mitchell (Whichard). Collection development and non-print materials. *Libr Trends.* 34; Summer 1985; 37-54.
2. Pemberton (Michael). *Policies of audiovisual producers and distributors: A handbook for acquisition personnel.* 1994. Scare Crow Press, N.J.
3. Magrill (Rose Marry). and Corbin (John). Acquisitions management and collection development in libraries. 1989. American Library Association, Chicago. p 165-194.
4. Harrington (Sue Anne). The development and management of a university microform collection.*Collect Manage.* 9; Winter 1987; 57-58.
5. Rowley (Jennifer). *The Electronic library.* 1998. Library Association Publishing, London. p 236-244.
6. Futas (Elizabeth), *Ed. Library collection development policies and procedures.* 1994. Phoenix, Ariz.: Oryx Press. P360.
7. Hewitt (Joe A). On the nature of acquisitions. *Libr Resour Tech Serv.* 32; 1989; 105-22.
8. Hawks (Carol Pitts). Building and managing an acquisitions program. *Libr Acquis Prac Th.* 18 ; 1994; 297-308.

8
Indian Publishing Industry

Introduction

The publishing trade is closely connected with library collection development programmes as bulk of the purchases relate to published works only. If publishers do not feel a responsibility to produce quality materials, a librarian will not be able to select quality material. Hence, the policies and procedures followed by publishers have a direct bearing on the acquisition process in libraries by way of affecting the numbers of orders fulfilled, time taken, and the cost involved. "The status of librarian's order and the amount of effort needed beyond the initial order, to get material into the library are again directly related with the publishing industry and its distribution network."[1]

Book publishing industry in India is one of the top ten in the World. Indian publishers publish books in 14 major languages, including English and the total number of titles published on an production consists of literature, followed by politics and economics (about 14 per cent) while natural sciences and medical sciences account for less than 5 per cent and more than one per cent respectively.[2] However, publishing in English is the largest, followed by Hindi and Bengali.

These figures may sound quite impressive but it is not so, keeping in mind the population of India. Though India publishes about 20,000 titles every year, it is still one of the lowest in terms of books per million of population at the rate of around 30 books per million as against 735 in Europe. There are about 14,000 publishers in India. The largest number among them is in Hindi followed by English and Bengali.[3]

Over the last few years the annual figure has ranged around 18,000, which in the previous years, has reached 22,000 and has fallen as low as 16,500.[4]

Though the book industry has been in existence for many years, there has been no systematic attempt to enumerate Indian publishers. A survey carried out for the Ministry of Education of the Government of India by the National Council of Applied Economics Research, New Delhi in 1973, had estimated that there were some 3000 active publishers in India of which the large majority were small-scale publishers (issuing 5-12 titles a year); 300 medium sized (issuing 12- 50 titles); and 100 large (issuing 50 or more titles a year). According to a recent study there are around 11000 publishers, of which nearly 1,000 belong to the corporate sector.[5]

Pre-Independence Period

Publishing and printing in India has a long history, dating back to sixteenth century. The origin of printing and publishing in India can be traced to a Jesuit Missionary who was Doctrine Christian.[6] Interestingly fifty nine years after the landing of Vasco De Gama, the first printing press was established in 1556. Within a hundred years of printing of Gutenberg's Bible in Germany, India initiated its groping towards fashioning of types for the many Indian languages.

The 200 years of colonial rule had a profound impact on education and publishing. The British imported both their language and their educational institutions into India. Their purpose was limited to provide British education for their children and to train a sufficient number of Indians to staff the lower echelons of bureaucracy. Indigenous educational institutions stultified during this period, and by the time the Britishers left, they were completely moribund leading to the establishment of English as the most important language. Publishers namely, Oxford University Press, Macmillan, Blackie's and Orient Longmans Green had set up their offices in India by the beginning of twentieth century. Their only activity then was to ensure that their publications were used as text books in the schools and colleges. Overtime and with the growth of printing industry they began to reprint some of their books in India, but they never adapted them for local conditions and did virtually nothing to encourage indigenous scholarship. The printing industry was also a slow starter. Printing press were imported into India either by the government or by Christian missionaries and hence were not available for general use. Most of Indian firms could not afford the high cost of importing presses and had to do with treadle machines. All the paper required by British government and by missionary establishment was imported.[7]

Post-Independence Period

When the Britishers left in 1947, the publishing industry was still in the womb. Aside from the major four British publishers, there were no publishers worth mentioning.[8] The freedom movement did spawn a few publishers, but most of them were geared to printing political tracts and pamphlets and only a tiny handful had ventured into book publishing. Educational publishing was dominated by the above mentioned four British publishers. Since they were mainly reprints, they had no need to develop a cadre of trained editors and publishing professionals. There were few printing presses and virtually no paper mills. As the main book activity was textbook oriented, retail book shops existed only in urban centres and served the needs of the colonialists and the English speaking Indians. In short none of the essential conditions for a successful publishing industry existed at the time India gained Independence.

Thus, before independence, publishing in India, with few exceptions, has mainly been a joint venture with British and American publishers. Beginning as sales representatives at the turn of century, they ventured into indigenous publishing sometimes in the mid-50s, first by reprinting standard British and American textbooks and later by striking out their own.

During the period between the World wars and just prior to independence, Indian publishing may be said to have emerged from a period of gainful experience.[9] Though much that was published during these years was political pamphleteering, it helped a great deal in clarifying the issues and mobilising public opinion.

Most of the early Indian publishers did not last long. Misrepresentation of the market due to largely political motivation of the publishing houses, harassment by British authorities, lack of professional and business expertise and experience and inadequate financial resources came in the way of success of the publishing houses. These pioneers did prove, however, that indigenous publishing of serious nature was possible and this helped to stimulate efforts made by the post-Independence publishers. [10]

Indian publishing blossomed only after India attained independence. The spread of education and increase in literacy rate, opening of new universities and colleges, phenomenal increase in number of students, created an unprecedented demand for books. Asia Publishing House, which was founded in 1943, dominated the Indian publishing scene for almost two decades after Independence. With a number of years of experience behind and with a powerful and expanding organisation for promotion and sale of its agency publications and with wider and valuable contacts in learned institutions, Asia Publishing House grew rapidly as an independent Indian publishing house of national standing that soon gained international status. By 1973 it had published more than 4300 titles. But its significance in Indian publishing is not by the number of titles, but the standards it set in Indian publishing which made Indian books representative of editorial strength and production standards in international publishing.[11]

Government's policy of providing free and compulsory primary education led to the setting up of schools as a result of which Indian textbook publishers began to make some headway. National Council for Educational Research and Training (NCERT), set up in 1961 developed model textbooks for adaptation and publication by the state text book boards. This had a very serious impact on publishing industry. Because of the numbers involved, the ability to arrive at a precise print order and comparative ease of distribution, publishing school text books is a profitable business. If left to commercial publishers, this business would have injected a very healthy and necessary amount of finance into the industry. At about the time NCERT came into existence, a number of American publishers set up companies in India. A major reason for the entrance of American publishers was the PL-480 book programme.

Subsidy Schemes

While Indian publishers were gradually building up their lists, there came a major development which had far reaching effect on the Indian publishing scene. This came in the shape of foreign subsidy schemes for providing low priced text books to Indian students. First among those was English Language Book Society (ELBS) of the British Government followed by Joint Indo-US Text book Programme under which 1500 titles were printed and published in India and were made available to students at a price which was almost 1/5th of the original American edition.[12] A similar Indo-Soviet Joint Textbook Programme was also launched in 1965. These schemes had their blessings and blights. A local book industry is needed, no matter how great the availability of books from abroad. This is necessary for cultural enrichment, for self expression by the nation's thinkers, writers and artists for development of sense of national unity as well as of a sense of historic traditions. Foreign books may be useful in many ways for some readers. But for most of the book readers in most countries, the books must grow out of local soil.

The college text book publishing has suffered from a number of problems, the most serious of these has been the availability of very low priced reprints of American and British text books. The Indian publishers' major advantage was that they could publish textbooks that were geared to Indian syllabi and conditions. However, due to declining educational standards and heavy reliance on crammers, cribs and question-answer type books, few publishers have been able to develop a strong list of college text books.

The single largest segment of Indian publishing scene is educational publishing which includes text books, reference books and other supplementary reading materials at school and college level. According to the latest Universities Handbook, there are 273 Universities, including 52 deemed to be universities and 11 institutions of national importance and 11,831 colleges affiliate to various universities.[13] The student population at all stages in schools in India is approximately 114 million. The figure underlines the importance which school text book publishing occupies in India. It is an accepted fact that publication of school text books provides the much needed constant fund flow to the publishers which also provides the base for supporting those books which the society needs but may not be financially sustainable. Primary, secondary and higher secondary text books have been nationalised and are being published by the agencies of the government. At national level NCERT is playing an important role of producing and distributing the school text books. In some states the departments of education and textbook boards look after this activity. The nationalisation scheme has certain inherent defects. According to an estimate more than 200 million textbooks are produced by different state publishing agencies, making it difficult to reach out to students in time. Authors have been deprived of freedom of expression. Politicisation has acted counter to the objective of uniform education and national interest. Export potential of textbooks is not fully exploited.[14]

Thus, two major areas open to Indian publishers are scholarly and general books. Sage Publications, New Delhi, Vikas Publishing House, New Delhi, Oxford University Press, New Delhi and Allied Publishers, Delhi, are some of the major publishers who have sustained and, on the whole had successful publishing programmes in this area. In addition, there are a number of small to medium size publishers who bring out small number of scholarly books a year. According to one estimate, as much as 60 to 80% of total turnover of books is accounted for by schools, college and university libraries, educational and research institutions, and public libraries. Library purchase rather than individual buying, constitute lion's share of the book market.[15]

Despite these favourable indicators, this area of publishing has not been without problems.

Problems

Almost Fifty six years after independence, Indian publishing stands at the crossroads. "In this relatively brief period of time, Indian publishing has been through its infancy, gone booming through its adolescence, suffered a series of rude shocks and now is looking at future with a mixture of uncertainty and apprehension" [16] What are the ills which have inflicted the book trade and what are the possible remedies?

The basic problems faced by publishers are primarily the lack of capital, paucity of paper at reasonable prices, the lack of effective distribution channels, high postal rates, heavy railway freight charges, delayed payments for books purchased by libraries, delay in the clearance of copy rights, lack of good designing and printing facilities. Opening up of the field of school text books to private publishers will do lot of good to Indian publishing. Some of the specific problems are as follows:

Ownership

Most publishing houses in India have been set up or are owned by entrepreneurs. While well-meaning and genuinely interested in the book business, they lack a proper understanding of the intricacies of book publishing. The absence of trained professionals further compounds this problem as does the fact that few manuscripts are critically evaluated. The net effect of this has been indiscriminate publishing due to which better scholars became dissatisfied with Indian publishers and began increasingly to seek foreign publishers for their books.

Price of Paper

The growth of an industry depends largely on the availability of raw material at reasonable price. Unfortunately, there has been shortage of paper for the last one decade, resulting in sharp increase in the price of paper which gets reflected in the selling price of the books. Publishing fraternity is extremely concerned over the continuous hike in the paper price and have been finding themselves in a difficult situation. If they fix higher mark up, the chances are they are not able to sell enough number of copies to register any respectable profit and if they don't, they find it difficult to break even. From Rs. 9/- per kg. in 1981 the price has gone up to Rs. 42/- per kg in year 2000. In 2002 alone the price has been increased twice. The rising prices coupled with non-availability of paper is constantly on the agenda of the Federation of Indian Publishers.

Lack of Funds

The biggest challenge before the Indian publishers is to mobilise funds required to develop a modestly original list in any of the fields. Apart from paper and printing costs, there are several initiation costs like advances to authors, fees paid to outside experts for a critical assessment of the work, artist's fee, design expenses and so on. Not many publishers would be prepared to take the risk, given the limits of the internal market and the competition that comes from the foreign publishers. They find it difficult to obtain credit and the discount structures for publishing does not permit adequate profits. The publishing enterprise needs to be protected and recognized as an industry to get loan from banks. Another proposal put forward by booksellers has been to establish a book finance corporation which can offer loans to publishers at low rates of interests without demanding tangible collateral guarantees.

Book Import

In keeping with the sprit of free flow of information, there has been no censorship or custom duty on the import of books. With effect from 1977-78, the import of educational, scientific and technical books was brought on the Open General License while other categories of publications such as fiction and children's books have been subjected to licensing. Thus, there are virtually no restrictions on book import. Indian publishers, in the face of decreasing library budgets have been pressing very strongly, but unsuccessfully, for a curb on the import of books. The in-flow of remaindered books is used as an argument for import restrictions.

Piracy

Piracy has been another worrisome aspect of publishing industry. As there is no effective law to curb piracy, pirates often invent new titles for best selling authors and reprint them. In 1983, the Copyright Amendment Bill was passed by the Parliament enshrining the main provisions of the Paris Convention compulsory licensing. But there is still no permanent relief to the publishing industry due to lack of effective execution. There should be a penal provision against the people, institutions and libraries who are either possessing or patronising copies of pirated editions.

Exports

In the matter of exports, Indian books reach out to over 100 countries, the largest buyers of our books are the United Kingdom, USA, Singapore, Malaysia, Bangladesh and Nepal and some Arab and Gulf countries. There are about 220 exporters of books and magazines registered with the book panel. Indian publishers have thus ventured into export business quite successfully catering to markets in several countries. However, enlarging the export market for Indian-tertiary-level, textbooks is an exercise of limited value. Just as India has weaned itself from British and American text, African and Asian countries will in time develop their own books. Participation in International book fairs, organisation of special book exhibitions, release of publicity material and market surveys are the steps in this direction. Africa is a big export market which can be developed as we have had a similar colonial history and common language i.e. English to communicate and do business. The community of Indian settlers in Africa can bridge the gap in promoting Indian book trade.

Distribution

Perhaps the real Achilles heel of Indian publishing is the distribution network. The logistical and geographical dimensions are immensely vast in a country that is over 3,000 kilometre wide both north-south and east-west. At the time of partition there were no real wholesalers but major retailers-cum-wholesalers. In the early 60s, UBS Publishers and Distributors (P) Ltd. came on the scene. In 1974, D.K. Publishers Distributors (P) Ltd. was established with the aim of distributing Indian books. Apart from these two there are no major wholesalers. Although there are quite a few importing wholesalers with, an interest in Indian books, but retail outlets remain few and far between in urban centres and virtually non existent in towns. It appears by estimates that Indian publishers and booksellers are nct effectively reaching and serving even 50 per cent of the market for the books in the country. With improving economic conditions, official efforts and general awareness, literacy levels are beginning to rise rapidly, with a corresponding demand for reading material. The future of Indian book business lies almost entirely in devising ways of reaching this market.

Training

The unprecedented advances in printing technology have made book publishing both an art and a science. In order to keep abreast of latest technological innovations and their applicability, it has been realised that for an industry which has more than 14,000 units working and employing lakhs of people in various operations of publishing process no systematic training programme has been available to provide trained human resources for the Industry. The Federation of Publishers' & Booksellers' Association of India (FPBAI). and other professional organisations have been organising occasional training programmes. A unique step in this regard was taken by University of Delhi to relate education to the growing social and economic needs of the society. With the help of the publishing industry and professional organisations, a course was drafted and introduced at undergraduate level, keeping in view the middle level requirements of the industry. The College of Vocational Studies (University of Delhi) started in 1972, has taken the responsibility of conducting the course in book publishing, leading to B.A. degree. The areas in which teaching and training is provided include editing, publishing management, production techniques, book design, distribution and marketing. It is also serving as centre for information and textbook material on publishing. Government should start more such courses keeping in mind the development of publishing activities in the country.

Electronic Challenge

One of the exciting development of the twenty-first century is the publication of documents in electronic forms.

The electronic media is providing many possibilities and opportunities for faster and quicker access to information at global level through communication networks. It has the potential to store large quantities of information with the advantage of accessing and transferring it to any place and from anywhere. Libraries are now increasingly subscribing to material in electronic formats especially scholarly journals and reference material. This poses a serious challenge before the Indian publishing industry. The publishers must gear themselves up to meet the challenge of new information environment. In the words of Vishwanath, the celebrated Indian publisher, "Indian publishing has survived through rough weathers and stormy seas because of the fighting will of committed and dedicated publishers who have strong instinct for survival in them. The future of publishing is bright for those who have the initiative and imagination" [17] The fear that the printed word might become obsolete in the electronic age is unfounded.

Book Trade and Libraries: Linkages

The publishing trade is closely connected with library collection development programme. The book industry and libraries not only compliment each other but are also mutually dependent for survival. Thus, publishers, vendors and libraries depend upon, and are directly affected by the products, requirements or services of one another.

The availability of good books largely depends upon continuous production of a variety of books by good publishers and their proper distribution at affordable prices. It is simply not possible to build a good library collection until and unless such material is easily and readily available. "The degree of proficiency and service conscientiousness of the publisher will greatly determine the degree of positive or negative influence on the acquisition activities of the libraries".[18] Thus, any study relating to the collection development programmes will not be complete without looking into the book trade, its problems and functioning and its linkages with library world.

Publishers, distributors and vendors form a partnership in practice and act as an extension of the library's acquisition process. For a successful collection development programme, it is necessary that these three function in close co-operation with the library. The library must be concerned with total services; the publisher, distributor and vendor must be concerned with providing these services while maintaining the fiscal responsibilities inherent in a business setting.

Librarians think of library collection in the long term; they build collections not only to meet today's needs; but also to serve as resources for future generation of scholars. Present and anticipated use is one of the criteria employed in the selection of a specific title. Librarians and faculty think of the informational value of the work, not of its format or the type of publisher who produced it or the method of distribution by which it must be obtained.

Publishers, on the other hand, are in the for-profit environment. Their goal is to produce materials that will sell and make a profit for the company. In contrast to librarians and sometimes vendors who like to ascribe lofty motives to their work, publishers are for the most part refreshingly honest about their being motivated by profit.

A common understanding of the processes involved in the publishing of books, journals and their distribution is essential to improve publisher/dealer/library relations. For example, it is necessary to know the distance a journal travels between its publication and its final arrival at library.

To an outsider, obtaining the journal would appear to involve a simple process. The library sends an order, the publisher receives and processes the order; and the issue gets into the mail, arriving promptly at the library. Just a quick look reveals a complicated process involving many links in this chain of transfer, where a break in any link can bring the process to an abrupt halt. Both libraries and publishers, faced with the tightening monies, need to look at the entire chain of transfers, asking which of the links can be eliminated in order to shorten the chain. Publishers for example, are examining the policies regarding over printing and the maintenance of back issues stock, as well as the labour associated with handling correspondence of creating additional labels for delivery of back issues of journals. Some of the publishers have given up the policy of holding back issues beyond the claiming policy period and that they will be available only from certain back issues dealers. In the library environment, processing costs of all kinds are suspect. Expenditure must be trimmed with services, and acquisition must remain the same or improve. None of the structures, changes and developments taking place in the publishing industry were possible without consulting the libraries, without learning their present and future circumstances, requirements and demands. The close connection between the customer and the agency can be a valuable stimulus for developing an individual and yet standardized and hence cost effective services. The exchange of information during personal visits and at conferences and symposia is a very important factor in this relationship, as is the cooperation with library associations and societies. Quality is becoming the most important factor in competition within the service sector to which publishing agencies, vendors and other subscription agencies belong. Next to favourable terms, the range of services offered by the supplier is increasingly becoming a deciding factor in purchasing decisions. For the smooth functioning of the acquisition department of a library, the vendor should have the ability to provide the flexibility required to accommodate each library's special situation and must actively maintain an up-to-date liaison with publishers, abiding by their term of sales, communicating with the customer service department to guarantee earliest possible delivery of out-of-stock titles. Sometimes of primary importance for a library is the timely delivery of every order regardless of the profit and terms of the sales.

The acquisition librarian must develop a basic understanding of nuances and language of publishing world for successful acquisition programme. Quite often a title will be available from a publisher in several editions, each offering a different discount to the vendor, and, therefore, a different discount to the library, while library ethics dictate that they should receive same discounts from different vendors.

Publishers's release of new titles has become much more conservative in recent years. Many publishers announce their titles well in advance of their publication and only make the decision to publish when sufficient numbers of orders have been received. "The most significant change is the rather dramatic decrease in number of copies of a new title. Twenty-five years ago, when the successful title had sold some 75% of its print run, this would have prompted the publisher to reprint additional copies. Today, when the initial print run is sold out, there is a very good chance it will not be reprinted and ultimately will be declared out of print'.[19] Order placement, thus, is dependent upon an ongoing evaluation of source of supply against library's objectives in placement of standing orders.

All too often, publishers and vendors treat librarians as business naivete and librarians tend to view the vendor as a big bookstore in the sky-browsing collections to whimsically order from and return to "Librarians most often have to put up with less than professional representation from a vendor who arrives with luggage in one hand and is too often too hurried to say anything of substance".[20] The librarians, as professionals in their own right have the right to demand that all vendors send only the right type of representative who is aware of company services, industry trends and their needs.

Just as there are numerous differences in publishers, the characteristics of vendors also differ greatly. The strength of a vendor's service centres around where he has chosen to concentrate, his financial resources, emphasis on large inventory, or approval plans, or firm-order. An understanding of trade's characteristics such as who determines the price of an item, how products are distributed, and what services can one expect all improve understanding and communication between librarians and book suppliers. It helps in identifying the most likely sources of information that is, which ones among thousands of producers are most likely to have what is needed. Second, by keeping up-to-date with what is happening in publishing industry, one can anticipate changes in quality and format. Third, librarians may be able to influence decisions about what is published, provided that the publishers know that the librarian is knowledgeable about what is involved in developing profitable books.

Without good knowledge of acquisition work, it is entirely possible that orders may continue to be sent to a firm offering attractive terms but whose pattern of delivery is slow, who does not stay on top of problems or who promises more than can be delivered either in the area of service or in the publication themselves. As a way of getting orders, some booksellers may promise a large discount; however, a discount is meaningless if the book is never delivered. Though publishers are trying to improve the organization and methods of book distribution. Despite the more use of computers and centralized warehouses, it still takes too long to get books to libraries.

Each type of publisher approaches the book buyer with such a different marketing strategy that delivery rates, out-of-stock reports, and cancellation of orders lack consistency. Publishers invest their capital to achieve their own desired results, from selling what is in stock today with little regard to out-of-stock titles, to actively accumulating back orders to justify reprinting. To make the acquisition policy effective and successful the librarian in his role as a professional purchasing agent is required to develop a working knowledge beyond the limits of his or her own department. Understanding the different classification of books, as well as knowing the difference between trade publishers, technical publishers, university presses, reprint houses, or text book publisher would prove very useful for the librarian.

Non-Print Publishing

The publishing pattern of non-print materials is extremely diverse and does not have a coherent structure. There are a number of organisations, professional associations, commercial companies who produce such materials. Many of these producers themselves distribute their materials which causes problems for the librarians used to dealing with one or two library suppliers.

As most of the non-print material is not available on approval basis, libraries used to obtaining books on approval find it difficult to acquire such material. The dishonesty of some librarians, who copy the material and return the original, has resulted in some distributors refusing to supply material on approval.

The diversity of production and distribution agencies also creates problems for the librarian in identifying available material and this is further aggravated by the absence of any bibliographical tool to cater for all the current output. Information about these materials is dependent upon the publishers' own publicity system. While there is an excellent bibliographical system for published books and a well tried distribution network, there is no system for NPM, merely hundreds of separate publishers' catalogues and lists.[21]

Conclusion

Without a thriving publishing industry, no library can develop a need-based collection. Image of cultural heritage of any country can be best preserved by its own publishers and that books should emanate from and reflect the country in which they are used. The soul of a country can be manifested only in the writings of its own language. In order to give encouragement to Indian language publishing, government should play a vital role by reducing postal and freight rates on transportation of books, publicise Indian languages, provide low interest long term loans, make paper available at reasonable price and build library movement.

Rererences

1. Gedin (Per). *Cultural Pride: The necessity of indigenous publishing.* (Paper presented for Obor workshop on third world publishing. February 1991).

2. Narender Kumar, *India: 50 years of independence, 1947-97.* Publishing: status. growth and development. 1998. B. R. Publishing, New Delhi. p, 3.

3. Jolly (G S). Book publishing: Theory and practice. 1999. Har-Anand Publications, New Delhi. p. 14-15.

4. *Ibid.*

5. Narender Kumar, *op cit*. p. 22.

6. Tajeshwar Singh. Publishing in India: crisis and opportunity *In* Altbach(Philip G), Ed. *Publishing in the third world: knowledge and development,* 1985. Heinemann, Portsmouth. p. 111.

7. *Ibid.* p. 113.

8. *Ibid. p.* 115.

9. *Ibid. p.* 116

10. *Ibid. p.* 118.

11. Jolly (G S), *op cit*. p. 18.

12. Narender Kumar, *op cit*. p. 56.

13. Universities Handbook. Ed 29. 2002. Association of Indian Universities, New Delhi. p. XIII.

14. Tajeshwar Singh, *op cit*. p. 115.

15. Malhotra(D.N.), *Ed. 50 years of Independence: 1947-97.* Publishing: Status. growth and development. 1998. B. R. Publishing Corporation, New Delhi. P 22.

16. Israe;(Samuel).The colonial heritage in Indian publishing. *Libr Trends.* 26 Spring 1978; 539-52.

17. Malhotra(D N), *Ed. Op cit.* p. 316.

18. Cox(JE) Mega Vendor: Threat or promise. *Sr Libr.* 28, 3-4; 1998; 117-119.

19. Schrift(Leonard). The Thor power tool decision and its impact on scholarly publishing. *Libr Acquis Prac Th.* 12; 1988; 175-188.

20. Whaley(John H). Approaches to collection development evaluation: Use and user studies. *Libr Acquis Prac Th.* 8; 1984;54-55.

21. Fothrgill (Richard) and Butchart (IAN). Non-book materials in libraries: A practical guide.1997.Clive Bingley, London. P158-162.

9

Analysis and Interpretation of Data

Collection development in libraries encompasses selection and acquisition of library materials. For this purpose libraries rely heavily on publishers, distributors and vendors as they are the suppliers of library's resources. They are in fact part of separate but intersecting systems. They depend upon and are affected by the products, requirements and services of one another.

For collecting the needful data on various aspects of collection development, four separate sets of questionnaires were designed and these were circulated among librarians.information officers/documentation officers (Appendix 1), publishers (Appendix 2), distributors (Appendix 3) and vendors (Appendix 4) to elicit their views on various issues regarding acquisition of library material and related problems.

To get additional information and supplement the information received through questionnaire is interview schedules (Appendix 5 and 6) were designed for librarians/ information officers/documentation officers and publishers. Interview was conducted with the respective group and analysis of such data was added at the respective place with the analysis of questionnaire.

The data collected from the questionnaires and interview schedules is analysed and interpreted below in four separate parts.

PART-1

Analysis of Responses Received From Librarians/ Information Officers/ Documentation Officers

To understand the problems related to collection development activities in libraries and information centres, a questionnaire was developed for the librarians/information officers/documentation officers to elicit their views on various aspects of collection development in special libraries. The questionnaire is divided in 9 sections. The questionnaires were distributed among 250 librarians. For administering the questionnaire, personal contacts were made. In addition, these were also sent through post and email. The Library directory brought out by Indian Association of Special Libraries and Information Centres (IASLIC) was used to identify the libraries for this purpose . Out of these 250 questionnaires distributed, 135(54.%) responses were received. The data obtained from these questionnaires has been analysed below.

Profile of Library

The first question was asked to find the year of establishment of these libraries. Responses received from these 135 libraries were grouped in seven groups on the basis of their year of establishment (Table 1.1).

Table 1.1
Period of Establishment

Period	*No. of Responses*	*Per cent*
Pre-independence	3	2.2
1947-50	7	5.3
1951-60	12	8.8
1961-70	27	20.0
1971-80	39	28.9
1981-90	17	12.6
1991-2000	30	22.2
Total	135	100.0

Table 1.1 (Diagram 1) shows that highest percentage of libraries i.e. 28.9 (39)were established during 1971-80 followed by 22.2 and 20 per cent (30 and 27) libraries established during 1961-70 and 1991-2000 respectively. The development of special libraries in India has been a result of scientific and technological progress made during the period of 1971-80 which has led to a spurt in establishing of various libraries. Similarly establishment of All India Council for Technical Education (AICTE) in 1987 for regulating technical education and mushroom growth of private management and engineering institutes in 1990s has also led to establishment of scores of good special libraries during 1991-2000.

Libraries :
Period of Establishment

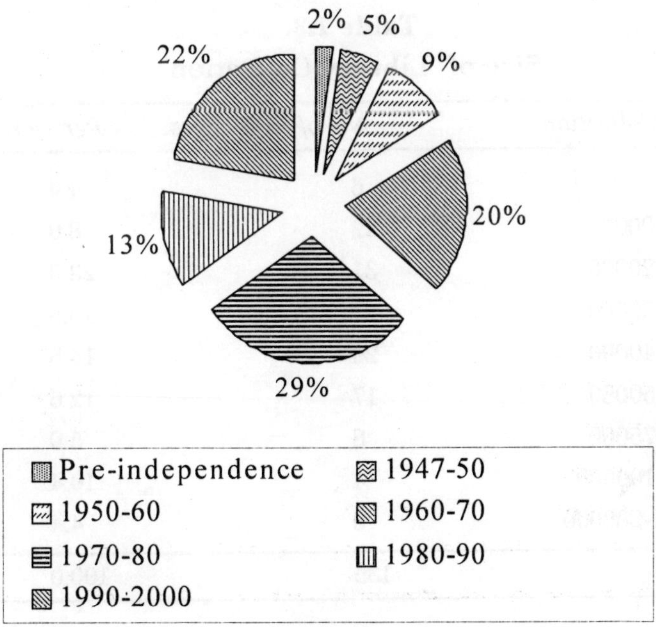

Diagram 1

Table 1.2
Affiliation Status of Libraries

Type of Institute	*No. of Responses*	*Per cent*
Educational Institute	74	54.8
Research Centre	24	17.8
Technical Board/Body	31	23.0
Business/Industrial	6	4.4
Total	135	100.0

Out of 135 librarians who responded, it has been found that highest percentage i.e. 54.8% (74) libraries are attached to educational institutes, followed by 23 per cent (31) libraries attached to technical bodies like AICTE. Most of these libraries belong to private engineering and technical institutes. However, 17.8 per cent (24) libraries are affiliated to research centres.

Table 1.3
Size of Library Collection

Total Collection	*No. of Responses*	*Per cent*
<5000	6	4.4
5001-10000	12	8.9
10001-20000	31	23.0
20001-30000	21	15.6
30001-40000	20	14.8
40001-50000	17	12.6
50001-75000	8	5.9
75001-100000	4	10.4
100001-200000	6	4.4
Total	135	100.0

Table 1.3 (Diagram 2) reveals that highest percentage, i.e. 23 per cent (31) Llibraries have a collection, ranging from 10,000 to 20,000, followed by 15.6 per cent (21) libraries, with 20,000 to 30,000 documents, 14.8 and 12.6 per cent libraries with 30,000 to 40,000 and 40,000 to 50,000 documents respectively.There are only 4.4 per cent libraries which have a collection ranging between 1 to 2 lakh.The size of collection in special libraries is generally not large, as emphasis is more on core collection in a narrow area to provide need-based services. Moreover, they tend to place more emphasis on quality rather than on quantity. The data in this table includes all type of documents such as books, journals, reports, CD-ROMs and audio-visual material.

Table 1.4

Collection of Books

Size	*No. of Responses*	*Per cent*
<5000	11	8.1
5000-7500	17	12.6
7501-10000	29	21.5
10001-20000	19	14.1
20001-30000	19	14.1
30001-40000	16	11.9
40001-50000	8	5.9
50001-75000	10	7.4
75001-100000	4	3.0
100001-200000	2	1.4
Total	135	100.0

Table 1.4 shows size of collection of books. There are 8.1 per cent (11) libraries where collection is less than 5000. These

are mainly newly established private management and engineering institutes. There are 1.4 per cent (2) libraries where collection of books exceeds 1 lakh but is less than 2 lakhs. The highest percentage (21.5%) of responding libraries are having a moderate collection of books ranging between 7,5001 to 10,000.

Table 1.5
Bound Volumes of Periodical Publications

Number	*No. of Responses*	*Per cent*
1-100	7	5.2
101-200	11	8.1
201-500	23	17.1
501-1000	21	15.5
1001-3000	42	31.0
3001-5000	23	17.1
5001-10,000	2	1.5
10001-20000	2	1.5
>20000	4	3.0
Total	135	100.0

The data in Table 1.5 related to bound volumes of periodicals reveals that largest percentage (31%) (42) of libraries have between 1001-3000 periodicals followed by 17.1 per cent (23) libraries having 30001-5000 bound volumes. There are only 3 per cent (4) libraries with more than 20,000 volumes. Being special in nature, these libraries focus on narrower areas and subscribe specialised periodicals in their areas.

Size of Library Collection

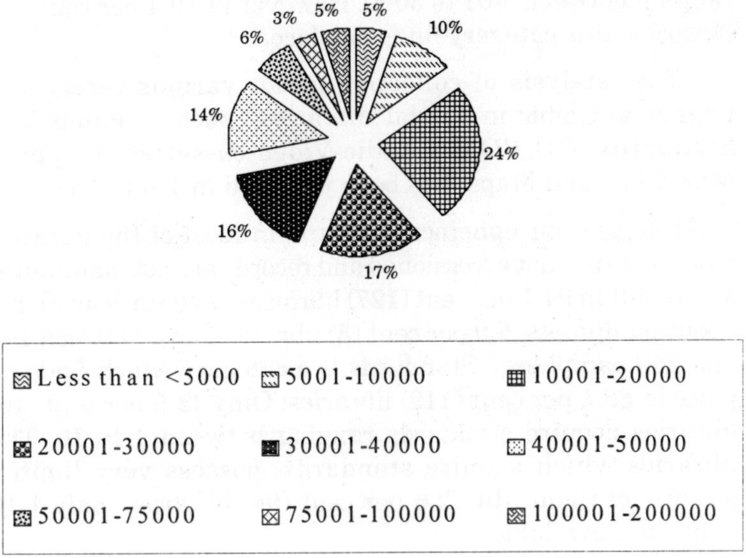

Diagram 2

Table 1.6
Size of Research Reports

Number	*No. of Responses*	*Per cent*
100-200	51	37.8
201-300	30	22.2
301-400	32	23.7
401-500	5	3.7
501-600	1	.7
2001-3000	2	1.5
Nil	14	10.4
Total	135	100.0

The analysis of report collection in Table 1.6 reveals that 83.7% libraries numbering 113 are having 100-400 research reports, followed by 5.9% libraries (8) having reports collection ranging between 401 to 3000. However in 10.4 per cent (14) libraries, this category finds no place.

The analysis of collection under various categories, usually available in special libraries, such as Pamphlets, Standards, CD ROMs, Audio-Video cassettes, Floppies, Microfilms and Maps has been provided in Table 1.7.

Due to their ephemeral nature, in most of the libraries pamphlets are not accessioned and records are not maintained as a result in 94.1 per cent (127) libraries, no data is available about pamphlets. 5.9 per cent (8) libraries have between 101 and 200 pamphlets. Standards is a category which finds no place in 88.1 per cent (119) libraries. Only 11.9 per cent (16) libraries acquire standards ranging between 1 to 10. The libraries which acquire standards, possess very limited number of them. In 72.6 per cent (98) libraries only 1-10 maps are available.

We are witnessing a substantial shift towards the adoption of electronic formats in special libraries, as a result more than 86 per cent (117) libraries are having CD-ROMs and 7.4 per cent (10) libraries are having more than 500 CD-ROMs. Given the fact that it is relatively a newer storage medium, CD-ROM format is gaining fast acceptability in special libraries.

Audio and video cassettes are available in 80 per cent (108) of the special libraries. However 20 per cent (27) libraries do not have audio-video collection.

Microforms (Microfilms, Microfiche etc.) are used basically for reports and back volumes of journals. In 29.6 per cent (40) libraries, there is no microform collection. Microforms are in fact being replaced by electronic formats such as floppies and CD-ROMs.

Table 1.7

Collection of Pamphlets, Standards, CD-ROMs, Audio-Video Cassettes, Floppies, Microfilms and Maps

Number	*Pamphlets* *No(%)*	*Standards* *No(%)*	*CD-Roms* *No(%)*	*A-V Casettes* *No(%)*	*Floppies* *No(%)*	*Microforms* *No(%)*	*Maps* *No(%)*
Nil	127(94.1)	119(88.1)	18(13.3)	27(20.0)	13(9.6)	40(29.6)	7(27.4)
1-10	-	16(11.9)	10(7.4)	11(8.1)	-	-	98(72.6)
11-20	-	-	1 (.7)	12(8.9)1	6(11.9)	9(6.7)	8(5.9)
21-30	-	-	15(11.1)	22(16.3)	28(20.7)	26(19.3)	15(11.1)
31-40	-	-	7(5.2)	12(8.9)	29(21.5)	25(18.5)	19(14.1)
41-50	-	-	5(3.7)	21(15.6)	20(14.8)	25(18.5)	11(8.1)
51-75	-	-	15(11.1)	8(5.9)	10(7.4)	13(9.6)	15(11.1)
76-100	-	-	14(10.4)	5(3.7)	2(1.5)	33(24.7)	-
101-150	5(3.7)	-	14(10.4)	5(3.7)	-	4(3.0)	-
151-200	3(2.2)	-	16(11.9)	12(8.9)	-	-	9(6.7)
201-300	-	-	9(6.7)	-	7(5.2)	-	2(1.5)
301-500	-	-	1(.7)	-	10(7.4)	-	1(.7)
>500	-	-	10(7.4)	-	-	-	-
Total	135	100.0					

*AV Cassettes: Audio-Video Cassettes

Computer floppies have emerged as an important library material. Several databases, both full text and bibliographical are available on computer disks. The collection of floppies ranges between 10 to 100 in 77.8 per cent (105), whereas in 9.6 per cent (13) there is no floppy collection. However in 12.6 per cent (17) libraries the number of floppies ranges between 200 to 400.

Budget

Table 1.8

Institutes' Budget (2000-2001)

Budget(Rs.)	*No. of Responses*	*Per cent*
Not Mentioned	80	59.3
1000000-2000000	10	7.4
2000001-3000000	-	-
3000001-4000000	1	.7
4000001-5000000	11	8.1
5000001-7500000	11	8.1
7500001-1 crore	8	5.9
1 crore - 2 crores	7	5.2
2 crores- 3 crores	2	1.5
Not fixed	5	3.7
Total	135	100.0

The idea behind knowing the budget of Institutes (Table 1.8) was to establish co-relation between the resources of organisation and the allocation made to libraries. About 59.3 per cent institutes (80) have not responded to the question.16.2 per cent institutions have a budget varying from Rs. 40 lakhs to 75 lakhs while 6.7 per cent institutes (9) have yearly allocation ranging between 2 to 3 crores. In 3.7 per cent (5) institutes there is no limitation of funds and yearly allocation is marked as "unlimited"

Table 1.9

Library Budget (2001-2001)

Budget (Rs.)	*No. of Responses*	*Per cent*
300000-400000	4	3.0
400001-500000	8	5.9
500001-700000	12	8.9
700001-800000	14	10.4
800001-900000	24	17.8
900001-1000000	20	14.8
1000001-1200000	12	8.9
1200001-1400000	18	13.3
1400001-1700000	12	8.9
1700001-2000000	2	1.5
>5000000	9	6.7
Total	135	100.0

Data in Table 1.9 reveals that in maximum percentage i.e. 17.8 (24) libraries, the allocation ranges between Rs.8 and 9 lakhs. The minimum allocation of Rs. 3 to 4 lakhs is in 3 per cent (4) libraries. 6.7 per cent (9) libraries have an allocation of more than Rs. 50 lakh as library budget. The data about library budget shows a large variance.The lowest category is of 3 per cent (4) libraries having a maximum budget of Rs. 3 to 4 lakh, followed by 5.9 per cent (8) libraries with 4 to 5 lakh . These libraries vary in size and collection leading to lot of variation, shown in budgetary allocation also.

Table 1.10
Budget for Books (2000-2001)

Budget (Rs.)	*No. of Responses*	*Per cent*
100000-200000	13	9.6
400001-500000	10	7.4
500001-700000	21	15.6
700001-800000	4	3.0
800001-900000	6	4.4
900001-1000000	16	11.9
1000001-1200000	16	11.9
1200001-1400000	10	7.4
1400001-1700000	5	3.7
1700001-2000000	10	7.4
2000001-2500000	13	9.6
2500001-5000000	6	4.4
>5000000	5	3.7
Total	135	100.0

The library budget for books (Table 1.10) ranges between Rs.1 lakh to 50 lakhs. Maximum percentage of libraries i.e. 15.6 per cent (21) have a moderate budget for books ranging between Rs. 5 to 7 lakhs followed by 11.9 per cent (16) libraries getting Rs. 9-10 lakhs and another 11.9 per cent (16) libraries with Rs. 10-12 lakhs. However, only 3.7 libraries (5) have a budget which exceeds Rs. 50 lakhs. In 17 per cent (23) libraries the budget for books is between Rs. 17 to 25 lakh per year.

Data in Table 1.11 pertaining to current periodicals depicts a wide range of allocation. 25 per cent (34) libraries have budget upto Rs. 1 lakh, followed by 13.3 per cent (18) libraries having 1 lakh to 2 lakh. The budget of 3 per cent (4)libraries exceeds Rs. 50 lakhs.

Table 1.11

Budget for Journals (2000-2001)

Budget (Rs.)	*No. of Responses*	*Per cent*
Upto 100000	34	25.0
100001-200000	18	13.3
200001-300000	6	4.4
300001-400000	4	3.0
400001-500000	7	5.2
500001-750000	5	3.7
750001-1000000	12	8.9
1000001-1500000	8	5.9
2000001-2500000	1	.7
2500001-3000000	0	0
3000001-4000000	8	5.9
4000001-5000000	7	5.2
>5000000	4	3.0
Total	135	100.0

The analysis of responses shows that there is no separate budgetary provision for research publications in any of the libraries as no response has been received for the question related to it.

Survey reveals that for online databases, libraries are making separate provision in their budgets for their subscriptions. 7.4 per cent (10) libraries have a budgetary allocation of Rs. 50,000 to 75,000 followed by 17 per cent (23) libraries which have an allocation of Rs 75,000 to 1 lakh. 17.8 per cent libraries (24) spend a sum which ranges between 3 lakhs to 5 lakhs. However, due to lack of infrastructural support 47.4% (64) libraries are still not having separate budget for it.

Table 1.12

Budget for Floppies /CD-ROMs and Online Databases etc. (2000-2001)

Budget (Rs.)	*Floppies / CD-ROMs / Online Databases*		*Audio-Video Cassettes*	
	No. of Responses	*Per cent*	*No. of Responses*	*Per cent*
Nil	64	47.4	82	60.7
15001-25000	0	0	6	4.4
25001-50000	0	0	17	12.6
50001-75000	10	7.4	12	8.9
75001-100000	23	17.0	9	6.7
150001-200000	2	1.5	9	6.7
200001-250000	5	3.7	0	0
250001-300000	6	4.4	0	0
300001-500000	24	17.8	0	0
700001-100000	1	0.7	0	0
Total	135	100	135	100.0

Audio-visual cassettes are emerging as an alternate medium of instruction quite fast and separate provisions are being made for these while allocating budgets. However, still more than 60% libraries do not make separate budgetary provision, whereas 12.6 per cent libraries (17) have a budget of ranging between Rs. 25,000 to Rs. 50,000. The highest allocation is by 6.7 per cent (9) libraries each in the group of Rs. 75000 to 1 lakh and Rs. 1 lakh to 1.5 lakh.

There is no separate budgetary provision for maps and atlases also. These are usually covered under the budget for books. Similarly, in no library there is separate budgetary provision for standards and patents as no responses have been received under this category.

The data given by librarians reveal that budget allocation in 100 per cent cases is revised from time to time. Contrary to general trend of reduced budgets, many of the special libraries are not short of funds. This is particularly true in cases of upcoming institutions.

Regarding the sufficiency of allocated funds, librarians were asked a question to find the adequacy of funds to meet users' requirements and it was found that 55.6 per cent (75) libraries find their budget allocation as adequate whereas, 44.4 per cent (60) libraries are not able to meet users' needs with their existing allocation. It has been observed that budget allocation in terms of amount of money is sizeable, it is the rising cost of library material which leads to its insufficiency. If sufficient funds are not available to meet users' requirements, then how librarians can meet their users' requirements. Therefore, a question was asked on this aspect and the analysis of the same has been provided in Table 1.13.

During the personal interaction with the librarians, a question was asked about the formula being followed in their library for fixing the library budget for various categories of documents. A majority of librarians informed that allocations are made on the basis of available resources in the organisation. They do not follow any formula in this regard. While allocating the budget to various library materials, users requirement are taken into consideration.

Table 1.13

Meeting of Users' Requirements

Method	*No. of Responses*	*Per cent*
Through inter-library loan	45	75.0
Refer users to other libraries	15	25
Ignore Users' requirements	0	0
Total	60	100.0

Out of 60 librarians/information officers/documentation officers who stated that their library budget is not sufficient to meet users' requirements, 75 per cent (45) have reported that they resort to inter-library loan for meeting user's requirements whereas remaining 25 per cent (15) refer users to other libraries. No library ignores users' requirements as providing them information is the priority in any special library.

Collection Development Policy

For developing need-based and balanced collection, it is desirable to have a written collection development policy. Therefore, questions were asked on this aspect. The response received have been analysed and presented in Tables 1.14-1.21.

Table 1.14

Written Collection Development Policy

Policy	*No. of Responses*	*Per cent*
Yes	97	71.9
No	38	28.1
Total	135	100.0

Written Collection Development Policy

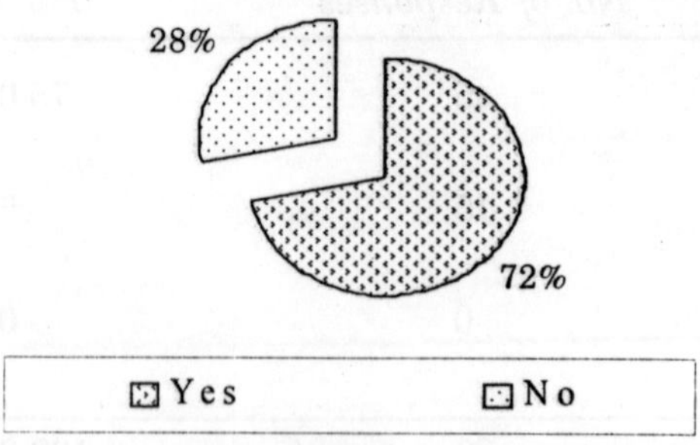

Diagram 3

Table 1.14 (Diagram 3) reveals that majority of the libraries, i.e. 71.9 per cent (97) have a written collection development policy as a tool to guide them while developing their library collection. However, 28.1 per cent (38) libraries do not have formal collection development policy.

Table 1.15

Authorities Responsible for Formulating Collection Development Policy

Authorities	*No. of Responses*	*Per cent*
Director	15	11.1
Library Committee	67	49.6
Librarian	26	19.3
Any other	27	20.0
Total	135	100.0

Though there are only 97 libraries (71.9%) which have a written collection development policy but all responding 135 libraries do follow some policy informally in their collection building programme.

The question pertaining to authorities who are involved in formulating the collection development policy has a mixed response. In about 50 per cent cases, it is library committee which takes care of formulating the collection development Policy. Librarians occupy second position contributing to 19.3 per cent while 20 per cent respondents have chosen the "Any other" category which is a mix of several authorities such as governing council, academic council and head of the organisation, a special committee of faculty members or heads of particular departments.

Table 1.16

Revision of Collection Development Policy

Revision	*No. of Responses*	*Per cent*
Yes	78	80.4
No Response	19	19.6
Total	97	100.0

Data on revision of policy as given in Table 1.16 reveals that more than 80.4 per cent (78) libraries revise their collection development policy and thus, relate it with the changing information needs of the users. It shows that a majority of libraries give due attention to the changing contours of user requirements and do fix their priorities from time to time afresh. However, 19.6 per cent (19) libraries have not responded to the question.

Table 1.17

Frequency of Revision of Collection Development Policy

Frequency	*No. of Responses*	*Per cent*
Annually	21	27.00
Biannually	0	0.0
Once in 5 years	0	0.0
Not Fixed	57	73.00
Total	78	100.0

However out of the 78 libraries which revise their collection development policy, only 27 per cent (21) revise their policy annually, whereas 73 per cent (57) libraries do not have any fixed periodicity of revision. No library follows bi-annual or 5 yearly plan of revision.

The reasons for revision in collection development policy present a mix scenario. Prime factors for revision in policy as shown in Table 1.18 are changes in management (33 per cent) (26) and changes in organizational profiles (31 per cent) (24) of libraries. Revision in curriculum is another important factor accounted by 14 per cent (11) libraries. Formation of new library committee is a factor reported by 19 per cent (15) librarians. 3 per cent (2) librarians have cited introduction of new programmes or new research areas as factors for revision of collection development policy under 'any other reasons'.

Table 1.18

Reasons for Revision of Policy

Reasons	*No. of Responses*	*Per cent*
Change in management	26	33.00
Changes in the organisational profile	24	31.00
Revision of curriculum	11	14.00
Formation of new Library Committee	15	19.00
Any other reason	2	3.00
Total	78	100.00

Table 1.19

Following of Collection Development Policy

Extent	*No. of Responses*	*Per cent*	*WI**	*Rank*
Always	35	36.00	1.80	2
Mostly	60	62.00	2.47	1
Sometimes	1	1.00	0.03	3
Rarely	1	1.00	0.02	4
Never	0	0.0	0.0	5
Total	97	100.0		

Note: *Weighted Index is calculated on a Five Point scale with weights assigned as: Always = 5; Mostly= 4; Sometimes= 3; Rerely= 2; Never= 1.

Data analysis (Table 1.19) regarding consistency in following the prescribed collection development policy reveals that 62 per cent libraries (60) 'Mostly' (rank 1)stick to it whereas 36 per cent libraries (35) 'Always' (rank 2) follow their prescribed policy. Remaining 1 per cent (1 each) follow policy 'Rarely' (rank 4) or 'Sometimes' (rank 3) only. There are no respondents in the 'Never' category.

There are certain criteria which are usually kept in mind while selecting the books for the library. Therefore, librarians were asked a question on this aspect and the same has been analysed and presented in Table 1.22.

The above findings have also been established on the basis of personal interviews and interaction with the librarians.

Table 1.20

Preferences in Selection

Preference	*Yes*	*No.*	*% (yes only)*	*Rank*
Well known authors	116	19	85.9	1
Faculty recommendations	103	32	76.3	2
Well known publishers	99	36	73.3	3
Scholarly publications	98	37	72.6	4
Foreign authors	74	61	54.8	5
Indian authors	62	73	45.9	6

The data about preference in selection (Table 1.20) reveals that 45.9 per cent (62) of total respondents give preference to Indian authors. But as special libraries mostly acquire foreign materials due to the very specialized nature of their requirements, the preference for foreign authors is 54.8 per cent in comparison to preference for Indian authors.

Well known authors in their respective areas find an overwhelming preference of 85.9 per cent (rank 1) respondents as against the new authors. Any book by Philip Kotler on Marketing Management has the potential of instantaneous approval as compared to any other author in management area. Similarly books by authors belonging to well known academic institutions such as Harvard Business School, Boston, USA, Massachusetts Institute of Technology, Massachusattes, USA, Kellogg Business School, Evanston, USA and Indian Institute of Management in India are selected without any rigorous scrutiny.

Well known publishers such as Prentice-Hall, McGraw Hill, Oxford University Press and Sage Publication, etc, also get a preference (73.3%) in selection process.This establishes that a well known author or a reputed publishing house can wield enormous influence in the process of book selection even without any serious examination of the contents of book.

Scholarly publications (publications based on research) brought by reputed research and development organisations account for 72.6% of respondents' choice. It includes publications usually based on case study method and applied research.

Faculty recommendations account for second top priority in terms of ranking as 76.3 per cent (103) librarians acquire books on faculty recommendations irrespective of authorship or publishing company or place of publication as they are the direct consumers. However aggressive marketing by publishers plays an important role in influencing faculty's recommendation of library material.

Thus, the findings reveal that well known authors have top most priority in terms of ranking, followed by faculty recommendations. Well known publishers are third in ranking while scholarly publications have got 4th rank. The 5th and 6th ranks have been received by foreign and Indian authors respectively.

Table 1.21
Format Preference

Format	*No. of Responses*	*Per cent*
Paper form	130	96.3
Electronic Form	5	3.7
Microform	0	0.0
Total	135	100.0

With the explosion of knowledge, documents are coming in variety of forms. Therefore, a question was asked about users' preference about various formats.

Data in Table 1.21 reveals that despite the fact that electronic formats are gaining fast acceptability in the market and library, paper format still constitutes the preferred choice in 96.3 per cent(130) libraries. There are only 3.7 per cent (5) librarians who have opted for electronic format as their first choice. No preference has been given for microforms. It clearly establishes the precedence of hard copy over soft copy version or electronic format. Probably lesser acceptance of electronic formats is on account of lack of awareness among users about their use, availability of inadequate infrastructure facilities and portability of paper form are the factors affecting acceptability of electronic formats.

Sources Used for Identification and Selection of Library Materials

Selection of right material is an important responsibility of a librarian for which different sources are used by librarians. These sources have been listed in the questionnaire to get response from librarians about the use of these sources. The response received from participating libraries are analysed in this section.

Table 1.22

Sources Used for Identification of Library Materials

Sources	*Yes*	*No*	*%(Yes)*	*Rank*
Faculty recommendations	135	0	100	1
Approval books	116	9	85.9	2
Booksellers' list	99	36	73.3	3
Internet online databases	79	56	58.5	4
Standard bibliographies	77	58	57.0	5
Publishers catalogue	68	67	50.5	6
Book reviews	36	99	26.7	7

The data in Table 1.22 reveals that Publishers' catalogues as a source for identifying, acquiring and building library collection are used by more than 50 per cent (68) libraries. Booksellers send the select list of books to libraries to promote their sale. 73.3 per cent (99) libraries use these lists for identifying books. Standard bibliographies are used by 57 per cent libraries. Although book reviews are considered highly valuable sources for identifying the quality books but only 26.7 per cent (36) libraries refer to book reviews for selecting library books. Usually the time lag between release of a title and publication of its review has a wide gap, therefore the response for this category seems low. Almost all libraries receive books on approval basis which provides an opportunity to see and scan the books physically. Therefore, it is regarded as most popular way of selecting books by 85.9 per cent (116) libraries.

Faculty members in special libraries tend to send their recommendations for library material regularly providing a help to develop need-based collection. Therefore, their recommendations for selecting library material are regarded to be the most valuable in this regard. All the 135 responding libraries use this medium for identification and selection of material in the libraries.

Various Internet sites related to books such amazon.com, firstandsecond.com are being increasingly used as a book selection tool and 58.5 per cent libraries (79) libraries access this medium.

The ranking order of the sources used for book identification and selection of library material thus reveals that faculty members recommendations have highest ranking followed by books received on approval basis. Booksellers' list and online databases have 3rd and 4th rankings respectively. Standard bibliographies, publishers catalogues and book reviews have lower ranks in order.

Table 1.23
Purchasing from Online Vendors

Purchase	*No. of Responses*	*Per cent*
Yes	40	29.6
No	95	70.4
Total	135	100.0

Nowadays, with the introduction of technology in the library house keeping jobs, librarians were asked a question if they purchase books from online vendors. Data received on this aspect was analysed and presented in Table 1.23. The data reveals that only 29.6 per cent (40) libraries purchase library material from online vendors like amozon.com, fabmart.com or firstandsecond.com. The medium of online ordering has really failed to take off in majority of the libraries. It has been observed that online vendors mainly cater to bulk orders and do not have any system of selling books on approval basis. Secondly most of them accept payment through credit cards or demand immediate payments after delivery for which many of libraries are not ready or willing.

Table 1.24

Extent of Purchase from Online Vendors

Extent	*No. of Responses*	*Per cent*	*WI**	*Rank*
Always	0	0.0	0.0	4
Mostly	9	23.0	0.37	2
Sometimes	20	50.0	0.61	1
Rarely	11	27.0	0.22	3
Never	0	0.0	0.0	4
Total	40	100.0		

Note: *Weighted Index is calculated on a Five Point scale with weights assigned as : Always = 5; Mostly= 4; Sometimes= 3; Rerely= 2; Never= 1.

The data (Table 1.24) reveals that 23 per cent (9) libraries are in the category which purchase 'Mostly' from online vendors while 50 per cent libraries (20) purchase only sometimes, while 27 per cent libraries purchase only 'Rarely'.

Table 1.25

Reasons for Not Using Online Vendors for Purchase

Reasons	*No. of Responses*	*Per cent*
Online access not available	12	12.6
Service not available for other publications	60	63.2
Payment procedures cumbersome	23	24.2
Response is not satisfactory	0	0.0
Total	95	100.0

The biggest problem expressed by 63.2 per cent librarians with online vendors is of not providing service to them for other types of publications. According to 12.6 per cent (12) libraries they do not have access to online vendors in their libraries, whereas 24.22 per cent (23) libraries report that payment procedures are cumbersome.

Table 1.26

Selection Authority/Authorities

Authorities	*No. of Responses*	*Per cent*
Library committee	22	16.3
Book selection committee	12	8.9
Head of the organisation	17	12.6
Concerned faculty	33	24.4
All the above	51	37.8
Total	135	100.0

The data pertaining to selection process given in Table 1.26 presents a mixed picture. The highest percentage (37.8%), goes to the group, consisting of library committee, book selection committee, head of the organization and concerned faculty members, whereas second largest response (24.4%) has gone to concerned faculty members, followed by library committee (16.3%). According to 12.6 per cent (17) libraries, selection authority is vested with head of the organisation while according to 8.9 per cent (12)libraries, book selection committee selects the books.

Table 1.27

Librarian's Role in Book Selection

Role	*Yes*	*No.*	*%(Yes)*	*Rank*
Preliminary selection	92	43	68.1	2
Forwarding agent	99	36	73.3	1
Recommendatory(Based on User's Requirement)	78	57	57.8	3

Data in Table 1.27 about the role of librarian, reveals that in 73.3 per cent (99) libraries (rank 1) their role is that of a forwarding agent who merely retains books received from the suppliers to forward them for approval to the approving authorities leaving no role for himself in actually selecting library materials. However, an almost equal percentage of librarians, 68.1 per cent(92) (rank 2)have stated that preliminary selection is done by librarian himself. Another 57.8 per cent (78) librarians (rank 3) have indicated that as librarians they recommend books based on users' requirements, though final approval lies with other authorities.

Librarians were asked when they make recommendations for acquisitions, how do authorities take their views for which, all librarians have expressed that recommendations made by them to acquire titles are approved by the authorities to varying extent. It shows that authorities consider the role of librarians to be quite important in the book selection process.

Table 1.28

Consideration of Librarian's Recommendations by Authorities

Response	*No. of Responses*	*Per cent*
Yes	135	100
Total	135	100.0

Table 1.29

Extent of Consideration of Librarians' Recommendations

Extent	*No. of Responses*	*Per cent*	*WI*	*Rank*
Always	35	25.9	1.29	3
Mostly	60	44.4	2.22	1
Sometimes	40	29.7	1.48	2
Rarely	0	0.0	0.0	4
Never	0	0.0	0.0	4
Total	135	100.0		

Note: *Weighted Index is calculated on a Five Point scale with weights assigned as: Always = 5; Mostly= 4; Sometimes= 3; Rarely= 2; Never= 1.

As far as the extent of acceptance of librarians' recommendation by management is concerned, 25.9 per cent(35) librarians have stated that their recommendations are 'Always' (rank 3) accepted while 44.4 (60)librarians have said that their recommendations are 'Mostly' (rank 1) accepted. In case of 29.7 per cent (40) librarians' recommendations are accepted only 'Sometimes' (rank 3). There are no responses in the remaining two categories of 'Rarely' and 'Never'.

The above findings have also been reinforced by the information provided by librarians during personal interaction. Librarians enjoy lot of informal authority in the matter of selection of library material. This is due to the fact that librarians know the exact requirements of users due to their day to day interaction with the users and practical experience.

Acquisition of Library Materials

After identifying the requisite library material, the process of its actual acquisition in library begins. Ordering and acquisition of documents brings libraries into direct contact with publishers and other library suppliers. Various questions on these aspects were asked in the questionnaire and the responses to the questions have been analysed below:

Table 1.30

System for Acquiring Library Materials

Systems	*No. of Responses*	*Per cent*
Approval system	80	55.5
Confirmed order system	38	31.9
No fixed pattern	17	12.6
Total	135	100.0

Majority of libraries i.e. 55.5 per cent (80) prefer receiving books on approval basis. This method gives them liberty to examine books physically and to select according to their respective requirements. 31.9 per cent (38) librarians have indicated that they acquire materials against confirmed orders, whereas in 12.6 per cent (17) libraries there is no fixed pattern for acquiring the library material.

Non-print material is not available on approval basis, as a result, identifying non-print materials has been a problem area. Various methods being usually adopted by the librarians have been listed in the questionnaire and they have been asked a question on identifying such materials. Responses received have been analysed and presented in Table 1.31.

Table 1.31

Identification of Non-print Materials

Methods	*No. of Responses*	*Per cent*
Enlisting name with NPM vendors	76	56.3
Through publishers' catalogues	40	29.6
By getting information from other libraries	19	14.1
By visits to fairs and exhibitions	0	0.0
Through institutional membership	0	0.0
Any other	0	0.0
Total	135	100.0

Information about such vendors is also not easily available, librarians have to do a lot of running around to get information on such materials. 76 libraries constituting 56.3 per cent (76) librarians enlist their names with the suppliers of non-print material, whereas 29.6 per cent (40) libraries get information through publishers' catalogues. 14.1 per cent libraries (19) rely on other libraries for this information. There are no responses in other remaining categories.

Selection of Book Suppliers

The criteria on the basis of which libraries select book suppliers is an important factor in the collection development process. Therefore, librarians were asked several questions related to selection of book suppliers. The responses have been analysed and presented in Table 1.32.

Table 1.32
Channels for Acquiring Library Books
(Total Responses 135)

Channels	*Yes*	*No*	*%(Yes)*	*Rank*
Vendors	116	19	85.9	1
Publishers	93	42	68.9	2
Distributors	58	77	43.0	3
No fixed pattern	0	0	0.0	0

Booksellers (vendors) are the prime source (rank 1)of actual acquisition of books as revealed by 85.9 per cent (116) libraries, whereas in 14.1 per cent (19) cases they are not. For 68.9 per cent (42) libraries, publishers are second choice for acquiring library books. 43 per cent (58) libraries have ranked distributors as third choice for supplying library books.

Table 1.33
Criteria for Selection of Book Suppliers

Criteria	*Yes*	*No.*	*%*	*Rank*
Discount	78	57	57.7	4
Service	116	19	85.0	1
Variety of stock	77	58	57.0	5
Capacity for accepting late payment	59	76	43.7	7
Timely procurement	113	22	83.7	2
Office infrastructure	51	84	37.8	8
Personal visits	60	75	44.4	6
Regular communication	90	45	66.6	3

Criteria for Selection of Book Suppliers

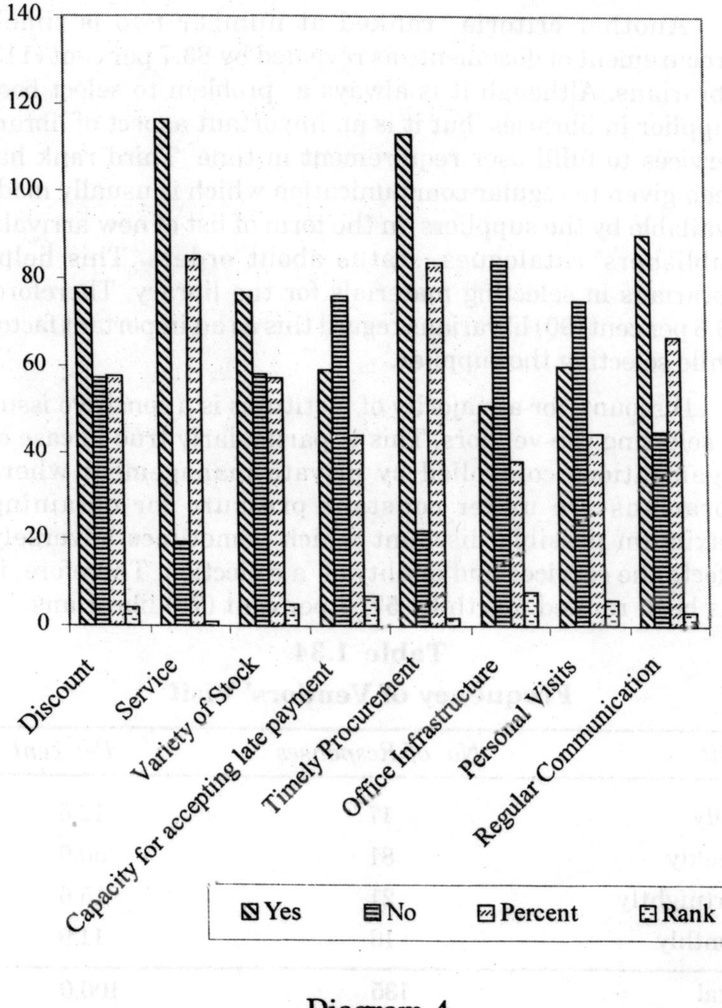

Diagram 4

Data in Table 1.33 (Diagram 4) reveals that service is the most important criteria which goes into selection of supplier of library material as majority of librarians i.e. 85 per cent (116) have ranked this to be number one for giving preference to any supplier over other factors.

Another criteria ranked at number two is timely procurement of documents as revealed by 83.7 per cent (113) librarians. Although it is always a problem to select book supplier in libraries but it is an important aspect of library services to fulfil user requirement in time. Third rank has been given to regular communication which is usually made available by the suppliers in the form of list of new arrivals, publishers' catalogues, status about orders. This helps librarians in selecting materials for the library. Therefore, 66.6 per cent (90) librarians regard this as an important factor while selecting the supplier.

Discount for a majority of institutes is a sensitive issue in selecting the vendors. This is particularly true in case of organisations controlled by private management where librarians are under constant pressure for obtaining maximum possible discount which sometimes adversely affects the services and quality of a collection. Therefore, it has been ranked fourth by 57. 7 per cent (78) librarians.

Table 1.34

Frequency of Vendors' Visit

Visit	*No. of Responses*	*Per cent*
Daily	17	12.6
Weekly	81	60.0
Fortnightly	21	15.6
Monthly	16	11.9
Total	135	100.0

Variety of stock as a criteria for selecting the supplier

has been ranked fifth by 57 per cent (77) librarians, followed by personal visits (sixth rank), capacity to accept late payments (seventh rank) and office infrastructure (eight rank) as revealed by 44.4 per cent (60), 43.7 per cent (59) and 37.8 per cent (51) librarians, respectively.

Therefore, the findings reveal that according to majority of librarians, service, timely procurement and regular communication are the first three most important factors. A majority of librarians i.e. 71.1 per cent (96) prefer their frequent visits, rather than having a fixed schedule of their visit.

As far as frequency of library visits by vendors is concerned, Table 1.34 reveals that highest percentage of librarians i.e. 60 per cent (81) prefer their weekly visits, followed by fortnightly (15.6%), and daily (12.6%). Only the lowest number of librarians opted for their monthly visits.

Vendors (Book Suppliers) and Services

It is important for libraries that they receive the ordered material in time so as to serve their users well. Therefore, libraries have to depend upon service provided by vendors for the timely acquisition of library materials. The data received on these aspects is analysed and presented in Tables 1.35-1.55.

Table 1.35

Vendors' Knowledge of Book Trade

Knowledge	*No. of Responses*	*Per cent*
Yes	120	88.9
No	15	11.1
Total	135	100.0

For supplying right kind of material, it is necessary on the part of vendors to have sufficient knowledge of book trade. On this aspect, data reveals that according to majority of the respondents (88.9%), vendors have sufficient knowledge of the book trade while 11.1 per cent librarians mentioned that they do not have sufficient knowledge.

Table 1.36
Understanding of Library Requirements

Extent	*No. of Responses*	*Per cent*	*WI**	*Rank*
Always	19	14.1	0.70	2
Mostly	97	71.9	2.87	1
Sometimes	19	14.1	0.42	3
Rarely	0	0.0	0.0	4
Never	0	0.0	0.0	4
Total	135	100.0		

Note: *Weighted Index is calculated on a Five Point scale with weights assigned as: Always = 5; Mostly= 4; Sometimes= 3; Rerely= 2; Never= 1.

Table 1.36 on understanding of library requirements reveals that 71.9 per cent (97) librarians have indicated that vendors 'Mostly' understand their requirements. There is an equal percentage (14.1%) of librarians who mentioned that vendors 'Always' or 'Sometimes'understand library requirements.

Table 1.37
Budgetary Division among Vendors for Books

Division	*No. of Responses*	*Per cent*
Proportionate	2	1.5
Minor variations	32	23.7
Substantial variations	70	52.0
No such division	31	22.8
Total	135	100.0

Table 1.38
Direct Orders to Publishers for Books

Order Status	Indian Books				Foreign Books			
	No. of Responses	Per cent	WI*	Rank	No. of Responses	Per cent	WI*	Rank
Always	19	14.1	0.70	3	0	0.0	0.0	4
Mostly	9	8.1	0.26	4	0	0.0	0.0	4
Sometimes	59	43.7	1.31	1	17	13.4	0.37	3
Rarely	48	34.1	0.71	2	57	42.2	0.84	1
Never	0	0.0	0	5	61	44.4	0.45	2
Total	135	100.0			135	100.0		

Note: *Weighted Index is calculated on a Five Point scale with weights as igned as: Always = 5; Mostly= 4; Sometimes= 3; Rerely= 2; Never= 1.

According to 52 per cent (70) librarians, their library budgets is not divided proportionately among various suppliers. Only in 1.5 per cent libraries (2), the budget is proportionately divided among various vendors while in 23. 7 per cent (32) libraries, there is minor variation. However, in remaining 22.8 per cent (31) libraries, there is no such division of budget among vendors.

Thus, the findings reveal that as vendors vary in terms of their perform ance and service, therefore, it is not desirable to maintain equality of budgetary allocation among various suppliers while placing orders.

The data in Table 1.38 reveals that 14.1 per cent (19)libraries place direct orders to publishers 'Always' for supplying Indian books while there are nil response for foreign books in this category because it involves a lot of paper work as well as expenditure. High percentage of libraries i.e. 43.7 per cent (59) place direct orders 'Sometimes' while the figure for foreign books in this category is 13.4 per cent (17). 34.1 per cent (48) libraries place direct orders for Indian books are in 'rare' category.For foreign books percentage of libraries in this category is 42.2 per cent (57). Since dealing directly with the publishers involves a lot of paper work, therefore, most of the libraries usually prefer to operate trough vendors only.

Table 1.39

Reasons for Placing Direct Orders with Foreign Publishers

Reasons	*No. of Responses*	*Per cent*
Response is better	0	0.0
Price charged are correct	0	0.0
Higher discount	0	0.0
Complimentary copies are provided	0	0.0
Non-available elsewhere	74	100.0
Total	74	100.0

All the 74 librarians, who are placing direct orders with foreign publishers have stated that such action is taken when required material is not available through local vendors.

Table 1.40

Reasons for Not Placing Order with Publishers

Reasons	*No. of Responses*	*Per cent*
Publishers do not supply	22	36.1
Publishers offer less discount	13	21.3
More paper work is involved	26	42.6
Supply their own publications	0	0.0
Total	61	100.0

Out of 45 per cent librarians (61) who have stated that they do not place direct order with publishers for foreign books, 36.1 per cent (22) librarians have stated that publishers do not supply directly to libraries, while according to 21.3 per cent libraries (13), they do not place direct orders because publishers give less discount as compared to vendors. According to 42.6 per cent librarians (26), placing direct order involves more paper work as individual orders have to be made.

According to data in Table 1.41 (Diagram 5), 53.5 per cent (72) librarians have stated that orders for Indian documents are fulfilled in upto 1 week's time, whereas according to 19.2 per cent (26), it takes upto 2 weeks' time. Maximum time taken for Indian documents is four weeks by 12.5 per cent (17) librarians. The time taken in fulfilling the orders in respect of foreign documents has been mentioned as 1 week by 11.8 per cent (16) librarians, upto 2 weeks by 17.7 per cent (24), upto 3 weeks by 9 per cent (13) librarians and upto 4 weeks by 21 per cent (29) librarians. (Diagram 6).

Table 1.41

Average Time Taken in Fulfilling the Orders and Percentage of Not Fulfilled Orders

Time Taken	*Indian Documents*		*Foreign Documents*		*Not Fulfilled Orders*		
	No. of Responses	*%*	*No. of Responses*	*%*	*Per cent of Orders*	*No. of Responses*	*%*
Upto 1 week	72	53.5	16	11.8	Upto 5%	0	0
Upto 2 weeks	26	19.2	24	17.7	Upto 10%	79	58.51
Upto 3 weeks	20	14.8	13	9.6	Upto 15%	42	31.11
Upto 4 weeks	17	12.5	29	21.4	Upto 20%	14	10.38
Upto 6 weeks	0	0	23	17.0	Upto 25%	0	0
Upto 8 weeks	0	0	20	14.9	Upto 50%	0	0
Upto 12 weeks	0	0	10	7.4	> 50%	0	0
> 12 weeks	0	0	0	0		0	
Total	135	100	135	100		135	100

Average Time Taken in Fulfilling Library Orders (Indian Documents)

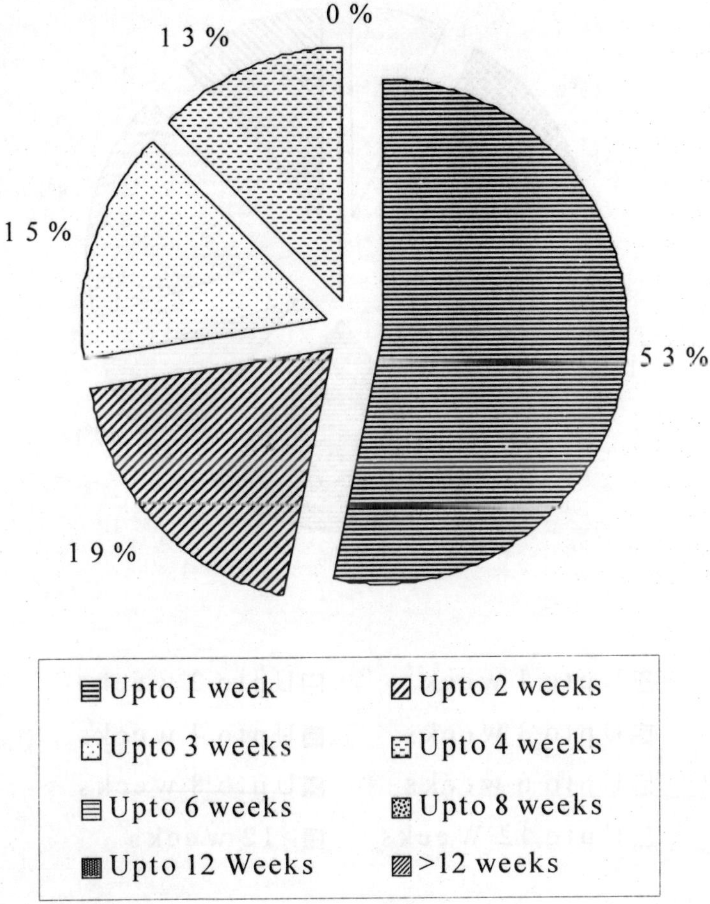

Diagram 5

Average Time Taken in Fulfilling Library Orders (Foreign Documents)

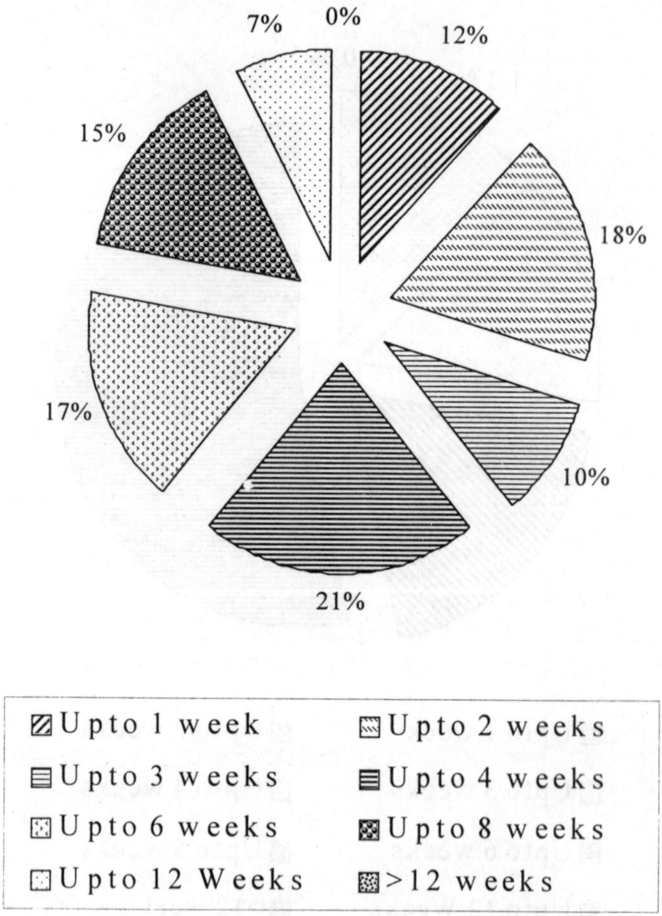

Diagram 6

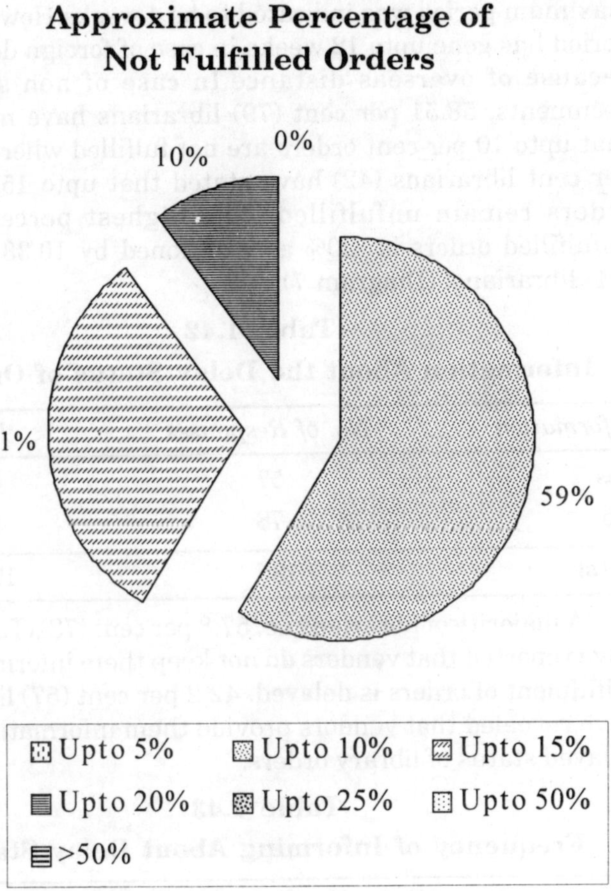
Approximate Percentage of
Not Fulfilled Orders
0%
10%
31%
59%
Upto 5%
Upto 10%
Upto 15%
Upto 20%
Upto 25%
Upto 50%
>50%

Diagram 7

The maximum period has been mentioned as 12 weeks by 7.4 per cent (10) librarians. In case of Indian publications, maximum period was indicated to be 4 weeks.However, this period has gone upto 12 weeks in case of foreign documents because of overseas distance.In case of non supply of documents, 58.51 per cent (79) librarians have mentioned that upto 10 per cent orders are not fulfilled whereas 31.11 per cent librarians (42) have stated that upto 15 per cent orders remain unfulfilled. The highest percentage of unfulfilled orders is 20% as mentioned by 10.38 per cent (14) librarians. (Diagram 7).

Table 1.42

Information About the Delay Status of Orders

Information	*No. of Responses*	*Per cent*
Yes	57	42.2
No	78	57.8
Total	135	100.0

A majority of librarians i.e. 57.8 per cent (78) (Table 1.42) have reported that vendors do not keep them informed if the fulfillment of orders is delayed. 42.2 per cent (57) librarians have revealed that vendors provide them information about delayed status of library orders.

Table 1.43

Frequency of Informing About Delay Status

Response	*No. of Responses*	*Per cent*	*WI**	*Rank*
Always	26	45.6	2.28	1
Mostly	12	21.2	0.84	3
Sometimes	19	33.2	1	2
Rarely	0	0.0	0.0	4
Never	0	0.0	0.0	4
Total	57	100.0		

Note: *Weighted Index is calculated on a Five Point scale with weights assigned as : Always = 5; Mostly= 4; Sometimes= 3; Rerely= 2; Never= 1.

Only 45.6 per cent (26) librarians (Table 1.43) have indicated that vendors always inform about delay status, whereas 21.2 per cent (12) librarians have reported that they are 'mostly' informed. According to 33.2 per cent librarians (19) they are informed about delay status of orders only 'sometimes'. Regarding compliance of orders, 79 librarians (58.5%) have stated that booksellers do not fulfil all orders. These 79 responses have been analysed in Table 1.44.

Table 1.44

Reasons for Non-Compliance of Orders

Reasons	*No. of Responses*	*Per cent*
Short discount titles	0	0.0
Order is too small	36	45.6
Orders are spread over several publishers	0	0.0
Ordered Material does not have high margin	0	0.0
Orders are for old editions	20	25.3
Titles are out of stock	23	29.1
Titles are not yet published	0	0.0
Titles are out of print	0	0.0
Total	79	100.0

The data in Table 1.44 (Diagram 8) reveals that according to 45.6 per cent (36) librarians non-compliance in fulfilling orders takes place if order is too small in terms of number of books. This particularly happens in cases when supplier has to obtain book from out of the way. According to 25.3 per cent (20) librarians, suppliers also fail to fulfill orders if the orders are for old publications. 29.1 per cent (23) of librarians have mentioned that orders are not complied with as books are out of stock.

Table 1.45

Sending Booksellers to Contact Faculty/Users for Approval of Books

Sending	*No. of Responses*	*Per cent*
Yes	93	68.9
No	42	31.1
Total	135	100.0

According to 68.9 per cent (93)librarians they allow the booksellers to contact faculty members/users for selecting books. Suppliers take books to faculty members directly and get their recommendations. (Table 1.45)

Table 1.46

Reasons for Allowing Booksellers to Contact Faculty Members

Reasons	*No. of Responses*	*Per cent*
Saves the time of library	58	62.3
Can explain contents	20	21.5
Faculty can give its recommendations on the spot	15	16.1
Total	93	100.0

According to 62.3 per cent (58) librarians (Table 1.46) it saves the time of libraries as booksellers themselves show the books to faculty members. According to 21.5 per cent (20) librarians the other reason for sending vendors to faculty members directly is that booksellers can themselves explain the contents of books while according to 16.1 per cent (15) librarians, the decision can be made on the spot.

Reasons for Non-compliance of Library Orders

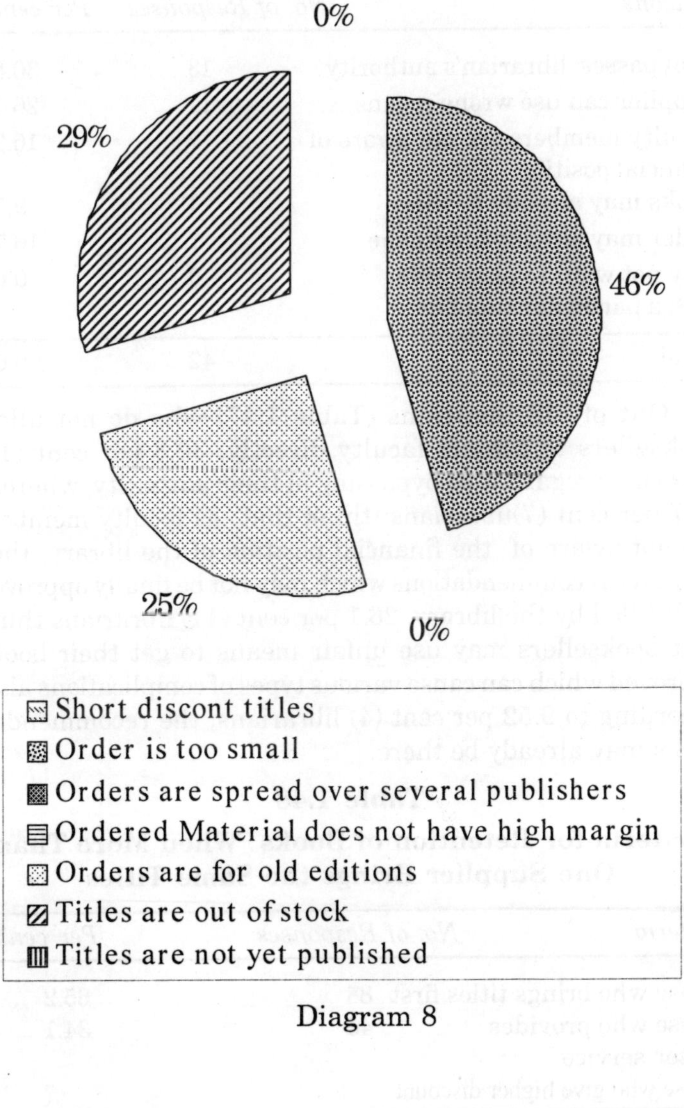

Diagram 8

Table 1.47

Reasons for Not Allowing Booksellers to Contact Faculty

Reasons	*No. of Responses*	*Per cent*
It bypasses librarian's authority	13	30.8
Supplier can use wrong means	11	26.1
Faculty members are not aware of financial position	7	16.7
Books may already be there	4	9.52
Order may already have gone	7	16.7
May not want to place order with a particular supplier	0	0.0
Total	42	100.0

Out of 42 librarians (Table 1.47) who do not allow booksellers to contact faculty directly, 30.8 per cent (13) librarians regard it as bypassing of their authority, whereas 16.7 per cent (7)librarians think that as faculty members are not aware of the financial position of the library, they may give recommendations which may not be finally approved or fulfilled by the library. 26.1 per cent (11) librarians think that booksellers may use unfair means to get their books approved which can cause various types of complications also. According to 9.52 per cent (4) librarians, the recommended books may already be there.

Table 1.48

Criteria for Retention of Books When More Than One Supplier Brings the Same Titles

Criteria	*No. of Responses*	*Per cent*
Those who brings titles first	88	65.2
Those who provides better service	46	34.1
Those who give higher discount	1	.7
Total	135	100.0

According to data analysed in Table 1.48, 65.2 per cent (88) librarians, they retain the books of those suppliers who bring them first, whereas 34.1 per cent (46) librarians, they give weightage to those who provide them better service. Only 1 librarian uses higher discount factor to retain a book, when the same title is brought by more than one supplier.

Table 1.49

Type of Books Brought by Suppliers

Type	*No. of Responses*	*Per cent*
Mostly newly released	99	73.3
Mix of new and old	36	26.7
Mostly old ones	0	0.0
Total	135	100.0

The data in Table 1.49 shows that according to 73.3 per cent (99)librarians, suppliers normally bring new books for approval, whereas 26.7 per cent (36)librarians have stated that they bring a mix of old and new books. It shows that the tendency to sell remainder titles is quite rampant which has adverse implications for collection development activities.

Table 1.50

Tendency in Booksellers to Push High Margin Books

Tendency	*No. of Responses*	*Per cent*
Yes	70	51.9
No	65	48.1
Total	135	100.0

According to data (Table 1.50), 51.9 per cent (70) librarians have stated that there is a tendency among booksellers to sell only high profit books. This tendency quite often deprives library of books which are cheap but good.

Table 1.51
Frequency of Pushing High Margin Books

Category	*No. of Responses*	*Per cent*	*WI**	*Rank*
Always	0	0	0.0	4
Mostly	34	48.5	2.42	1
Sometimes	26	37.1	1.48	2
Rarely	10	7.4	0.42	3
Never	0	0	0	4
Total	70	100.0		

Note: *Weighted Index is calculated on a Five Point scale with weights assigned as: Always = 5; Mostly= 4; Sometimes= 3; Rerely= 2; Never= 1.

According to data in Table 1.51, 48.5 per cent (34) librarians have stated that this tendency of pushing through high profit books is found 'Mostly' (Rank 1) while according to 37.1 per cent (26) librarians this tendency is noticed 'Sometimes' (Rank 2) while 7.4 per cent (10) libraries have stated that this tendency of selling only high profit books is 'Rare' (Rank 3).

Table 1.52
Committing of Errors by Booksellers

Types of Errors	*No. of Responses*	*Per cent*
Excess claim	13	14.1
Not supplying the exact titles	19	20.6
Supplying damaged books	6	6.21
Tempering with price proof	28	30.4
Sending double bills	0	0.0
Pasting high price stickers	0	0.0
Claiming mailing and handling charges	26	28.26
Total	92	100.0

Only 92 librarians have stated that booksellers commit errors. Out of them 14.1 per cent (13) have stated that suppliers claim excess payment. 30.4 per cent librarians (28) have stated that suppliers temper with price proofs. These cases take place in case of foreign publications where prices are not printed on covers and librarians have to rely on price proofs furnished by respective suppliers. According to 28.26 per cent librarians (26), book suppliers demand handling and mailing charges while 6.21 per cent librarians (6) have indicated that bookseller supply damaged books.

The above findings have also been duly established by several librarians while personal interaction. Librarians informed the researcher that there exists lot of corruption and business of remainder also thrives on the basis of corruption. Book sellers not only oblige librarians by various means but often librarians also insist on cut backs. Regarding the menace of remainders, some of the librarians told that it is not difficult to tackle it if librarians are sufficiently alert and co-operate with each other. The prices of books can be checked from several sources and one way of curbing this menace is to insist on original invoice as price proof while furnishing the bills. The librarians also agreed that a lot of sub standard material is coming from Western countries and United States in the form of remainders. The librarians suggested that GOC should also tackle this matter and disqualify the suppliers found indulging in selling remainders. It should regularly publish a list of such titles so that librarians become alert.

Regarding the role of GOC, most of the librarians expressed their disappointment with its functioning particularly with regard to fixing of foreign exchange rates. Some librarians did not rule out the possibility of corruption in these matters. They stated that Indian Library Association has failed miserably in its duty to fix conversion rates due to which booksellers are charging higher rates.

Table 1.53

Are the Errors Intentional

Intentional	*No. of Responses*	*Per cent*
Yes	62	67.3
No	30	22.7
Total	92	100.0

According to majority of librarians (6.3 per cent) (62), the errors committed by booksellers are intentional. This is particularly true in case of price proofs which are deliberately tempered to sell remainder titles. However 22.7 per cent (30) librarians have stated that errors do not take place intentionally.

Table 1.54

Action Taken Against Erring Booksellers

Action	*No. of Responses*	*Per cent*
Blacklist the supplier	9	16.7
Warn the supplier	38	67.6
Deduct extra payment	0	0.0
Correct the bills	9	16.7
Any other	0	0.0
Total	56	100.0

The data in Table 1.54 reveals that 67.5 per cent (38) librarians warn the suppliers not to indulge in such activities.But in 16.7 per cent (9) cases, supplier indulging in undesirable means has been barred from supplying books to library. Another16.7 per cent (9) librarians indicated that they correct the bills and rectify the errors.

Acquisition of Journals

Special libraries acquire sizeable number of both Indian and foreign journals. Journals are very important and also complex part of a library collection. Librarians were asked several question related to acquisition of journals. Their responses are analysed and interpreted in Tables 1.55-1.64.

Table 1.55
Number of Journals Subscribed

Number of Journals	*No. of Responses*		*Per cent*	
	Indian	*Foreign*	*Indian*	*Foreign*
1-25	7	12	5.2	8.9
26-50	15	22	11.1	16.3
51-75	5	20	3.7	14.8
76-100	42	31	31.1	22.9
101-150	28	19	20.7	14.07
151-200	32	14	23.7	10.37
201-300	2	2	1.5	1.5
301-400	1	8	.7	5.92
>500	3	6	2.2	4.4
Total		135	100.0	

Table 1.55 shows that highest i.e. 31.1 per cent (42) libraries subscribe 76-100 Indian journals, whereas 23.7 per cent (32)libraries subscribe journals in the range of 151-200. More than 500 journals are subscribed in only 2.2 per cent (3) libraries. As far as foreign journals are concerned, highest percentage (22.9) of (31) libraries are subscribing between 76 and 100 Journals followed by 14.07 per cent (19) and 10.37 per cent (14) libraries subscribing 101-150 and 151-200 journals respectively. There are 5.92 per cent (8) libraries as against .7 per cent (1) library subscribing to

301-400 foreign journals another 4.4 per cent (6) libraries are subscribing more than 500 foreign journals as compared to 2.2 per cent (3) libraries for Indian journals. The data pertaining to subscription of journals reveals that special libraries subscribe more foreign journals as compared to Indian journals.

Table 1.56

System for Acquisition of Journals

System of Acquisition	*Yes*	*No.*	*%*	*Rank*
Through subscription agencies	135	0	100.0	1
Direct from publishers	57	78	42.2	2
Through online vendors	15	120	11.1	3
Through exchange	43	88	31.8	4
Through membership and gifts	18	117	13.3	5

According to data in Table 1.56, 100 per cent (135)librarians' first choice for subscribing journals is through subscription agencies, while according to 42.2 per cent (57) librarians the second choice is to subscribe directly from publishers. Only 11.1 per cent(15) librarians prefer subscription through online vendors like EBSCO. 31.8 per cent (43) libraries acquire journal on exchange basis while 13.3 per cent (18) libraries receive journals as gifts and membership of learned societies.

In response to question No 44, 100 per cent (135) librarians have stated that they think it is better to subscribe through subscription agencies.

Table 1.57

Reasons for Subscribing through Subscription Agencies

Reasons	*No. of Responses*	*Per cent*	*Rank*
Single order can be made	112	83.0	2
Foreign exchange not involved	59	43.7	4
Sending reminders to one agency	60	44.4	3
Renewal is easy	114	84.4	1
Record keeping is easy	0	0.0	5

As per data in Table 1.57, 83 per cent (112) libraries (rank 2) subscribe through subscription agencies because a single order can be made, while 84.4 per cent (114) (rank 1) have stated that renewal is easy. 44.4 per cent (60) librarians (rank 3) prefer to subscribe through subscription agencies because they have to send reminders to only one agency whereas 43.7 per cent (59) libraries (rank 4) think that it is useful to subscribe through agencies as it does not involve making payments in foreign exchange.

Table 1.58

Problems of Subscription Through Subscription Agencies

Problems	*No. of Responses*	*Per cent*
More missing issues	38	28.1
No refunds for missing issues	62	45.9
Back issues not supplied	18	13.3
No response to reminders	17	12.6
Frequent exchange rate variation	0	0.0
Any other	0	0.0
Total	135	100.0

According to 28.1 per cent (38) librarians (Table 1.58) (Diagram 9), there is a problem of missing issues, whereas 45.9 per cent (62) librarians have said that payments are not adjusted for missing issues. According to 12.6 per cent (17) librarians, there are no response to reminders. This is a serious situation and affects the library services greatly.

Table 1.59

Changing the Subscription Agency

Response	*No. of Responses*	*Per cent*
Yes	59	43.7
No	76	56.3
Total	135	100.0

Data in Table 1.59 reveals that despite several problems 56.3 per cent (76) librarians have never changed their subscription agent. The most probable reason for not changing the subscription agent is that subscribing of journals is a long terms commitment and a majority of librarians do not want to disturb existing arrangement as subscription related problems are universal in nature and no subscription agency is exempted from these ills. However, 43.7 per cent (59) librarians have changed their subscription agents.

Table 1.60

Reasons for Not Changing Subscription Agency

Reasons	*No. of Responses*	*Per cent*
No other good agency available	14	23.8
Changing will not solve problem	30	50.9
Permission not granted by management	15	25.3
Total	59	100.0

According to highest i.e. 50.9 per cent (30) librarians (Table 1.60) the problems related with subscription of journals can not be solved by changing the subscription agent, while 25.3 (15) librarians have reported that management did not grant permission to change the subscription agency. According to 23.8 per cent (14) librarians, they did not change subscription agency as no other good agencies are available.

Changing the Subscription Agency

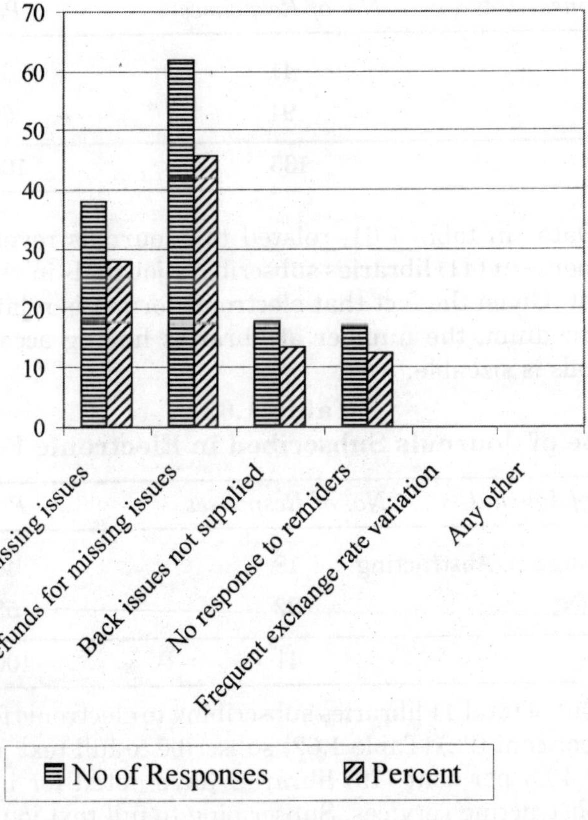

Diagram 9

Electronic Journals (E-Journals)

This section deals with electronic journals which are being fast accepted in special libraries. Several electronic databases containing both full text and abstract form of journal articles are now available for subscription. Special libraries are increasingly opting for electronic access though number of such libraries is still very low. The data obtained from librarians on electronic journals is analysed in Tables 1.61-1.64.

Table 1.61
Subscription of Journals in Electronic Format

Response	*No. of Responses*	*Per cent*
Yes	41	30.4
No	94	69.6
Total	135	100.0

Data in table 1.61, related to e-journals reveals that 30.4 per cent (41) libraries subscribe to journals in electronic format. Given the fact that electronic format is relatively a new medium, the number of libraries having access to e-journals is sizeable.

Table 1.62
Type of Journals Subscribed in Electronic Format

Type of Journal	*No. of Responses*	*Per cent*
Indexing and Abstracting	19	46.3
Full text	22	53.7
Total	41	100.0

Out of total 41 libraries subscribing to electronic formats, 53.7 per cent (22) (Table 1.62) subscribe to full text journals while 46.3 per cent (19) libraries have opted for indexing and abstracting services. Subscribing to full text journals is still a costly affair and beyond the reach of medium size libraries.

Table 1.63

Reasons for Acquiring Journals in Electronic Format

Reasons	*No. of Responses*	*Per cent*
Economical to acquire	0	0.0
Solves the problem of theft and mutilation	0	0.0
Provides networking facility	8	9.6
Easy to maintain	33	80.4
Total	41	100.0

According to 80.4 per cent (33) librarians (Table 1.63) they acquire journals in electronic forms as they are easy to maintain while 19.6 per cent (8) librarians have stated that electronic journals provide networking facility. Users can access electronic journals from their own desks.

Table 1.64

Reasons for Not Subscribing Journals in Electronic-Format

Reasons	*No. of Responses*	*Per cent*
Initial expenditure on infrastructure is high	0	0.0
Staff unwilling to handle	19	20.2
Readers resist the use	19	20.2
Required journals not available	18	19.2
Subscription is very costly	38	40.4
Total	94	100.0

A survey of reasons (Table 1.64) (Diagram 10) for not subscribing to journals in electronic formats reveals a mixed response. According to 40.4 per cent librarians (38) they do not subscribe to electronic journals because subscription is very costly, whereas according to 20.2 per cent (19) librarians readers resist the use of electronic formats. 19.2 per cent (18) staff in libraries have cited the problem of not finding journals of their interest in electronic formats. This is particularly true in case of most of the Indian journals which are excluded from all presently available databases. There is a need for proper user orientation and also requisite training for library staff to handle the electronic formats.

Analysis of Question No. 48 and 49 (Related to Problems, Solutions and Suggestions)

The response of the librarians to the above question are mixed. Most of the librarians have stated the problem of late fulfilling of orders particularly in case of foreign publications. Library material not only arrive quite late but often it never arrives which leads to embarrassing situation. They have also mentioned about the rising cost of materials. Several librarians have stated that Indian publications are of very low quality and are also being priced very high.

In case of non-print materials, there is lack of proper bibliographical control due to which it is difficult to locate relevant and required material. In case of periodical publications, most of the librarians have mentioned about the problem non-supply of journals. Librarians have to constantly monitor the arrival of journals despite making payments well in advance. In cases of electronic publications, most of the librarians have stated that there are not much of acquisition problems except that they are quite costly because it involves substantial initial expenditure. Librarians have infact advocated the need for more digital resources. In matters related to other library material like patents, standards, reports and microforms, most of the librarians have stated that there is lack of suppliers due to which they find it to difficult to obtain these special formats. Such material is not properly listed in publishers' catalogues and also not obtainable for inspection.

Librarians have suggested the need for adequate bibliographical tools. They have also suggested that Indian publishing trade should rigorously evaluate the manuscripts before deciding them to publish so as to maintain high standards in publishing. Publishers should commission good studies by leading academicians and pay adequate compensation to authors so that they are sufficiently encouraged to write good publishing material. Librarians have also suggested to have some regulation for pricing the publications. Several suggestions have been given for regular interaction between librarians and publishing trade. Librarians have also suggested that GOC rates of discount should be accepted by all librarians but the mark up value should not be fixed arbitrarily. These findings have also been established during personal interaction with the librarians on the matter of electronic formats. A majority of librarians expressed the opinion that electronic formats are going to play a very important role in near future but they ruled out the possibility of print material being fully eliminated. According to majority of them print formats are going to stay in the libraries and can never be fully substituted by online databases or electronic journals on CD-ROMs.

Reasons for Not Subscribing Journals in E-Format

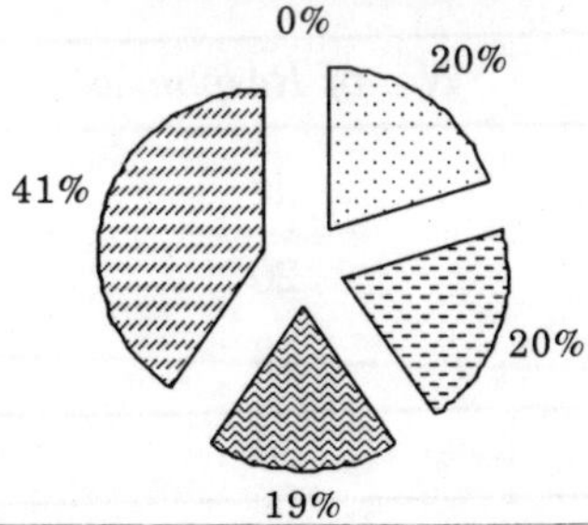

- Initial expenditure on infrastructure Is high
- Staff unwilling to handle
- Readers resist the use
- Required journals not available
- Subscription is very costly

Diagram 10

PART 2

Analysis of Responses Received from Publishers

Publishers play a very important role in developing the need-based, all round and up-to-date collection in libraries, comprising of traditional and non traditional documents. Libraries are their potential customers. Publishers keep their customers well informed by acting as an important linkage between libraries and users. To elicit important information about the role of publishers, a separate questionnaire (Appendix 2) was prepared. This questionnaire was distributed among 150 publishers out of which 70 (46.6%) have responded. Publishers for administering questionnaire were selected from the directory of publishers and also on the basis of consultation with senior persons in the library profession. The data received from these questionnaires has been analysed in Tables 2.1-2.36.

Profile of the Publishing Houses

In this section data has been collected about the profile of the publishing houses.

Table 2.1

Nature of Firms

Nature	*No. of Responses*	*Per cent*
Proprietorship	37	52.9
Partnership	20	28.6
Private Company	13	18.6
Total	70	100.0

According to data in Table 2.1 9 (Diagram 11), majority of the publishers i.e. 52.9 per cent (37) are the proprietors, followed by 28.6 per cent (20) of those who are having their publishing business in partnership and 18.6 per cent (13) publishers are private limited companies.

Table 2.2

Period of Establishment

Period	*No. of Responses*	*Per cent*
pre-independence	3	4.3
1947-60	2	2.9
1961-70	18	25.7
1971-80	23	32.9
1981-90	17	24.3
1991-2000	7	10.0
Total	70	100.0

Regarding the period of establishment, Table 2.2 (Diagram 11) reveals that 32.9 per cent (23) publishing houses were established during the period 1970-1980, followed by 25.7 per cent (18) and 24.3 per cent (17), established during 1961-70 and 1981-90 respectively. There were only 4.3 per cent (3) publishing houses established before Indian independence, which were owned by Britishers. Data does not reveal a steady growth of publishing companies during 1961-90.

Table 2.3

Strength of Staff

Strength	*No. of Responses*	*Per cent*
Upto 5	7	10.0
Upto 7	17	24.3
Upto 10	21	30.0
Upto 15	13	18.6
Upto 20	7	10.0
Upto 25	5	7.1
Total	70	100.0

To assess the size of publishing houses, a question about the strength of the staff was asked. The responses have been grouped on the basis of data provided by the publishers which reveals that in maximum publishing houses i.e. 30 per cent (21) staff strength is upto 10 persons, followed by 24.3 per cent (17) and 18.5 per cent (13) publishing houses having staff strength upto 7 and 15 respectively. Only 7.1 per cent publishing houses (7) have 25 employees. The finding reveals that 64 per cent publishers employ upto 10 employees only and are small publishing houses.

Period of Establishment

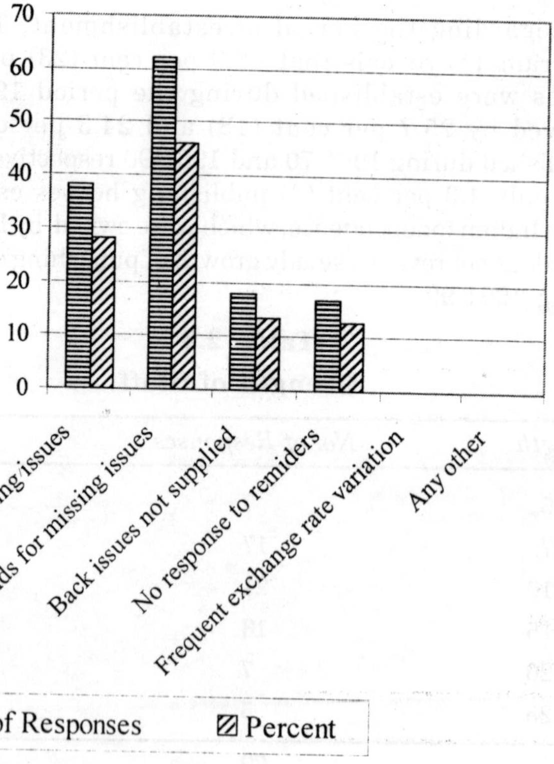

Diagram 11

Table 2.4
Annual Turnover

Annual Turnover (Rs.)	*No. of Responses*	*Per cent*
500000-1000000	1	1.4
1000001-1500000	1	1.4
1500001-2000000	6	8.6
2000001-2500000	10	14.3
2500001-3500000	12	17.1
3500001-5000000	18	25.7
5000001-7500000	10	14.3
7500001-10000000	9	12.9
>50000000	3	4.3
Total	70	100.0

The data relating to annual turnover of publishing houses presents wide variation in Table 2.4 (Diagram 12) Highest i.e. 25.7 per cent (18) publishing houses have an annual turnover of Rs. 35 lakh to 50 lakh, followed by 17.1 per cent (12) having a turnover ranging between Rs. 25 to Rs. 35 lakh. There are only 4.3 per cent(3) publishers having total turnover of more than Rs. 5 crore . Thus, findings reveal (Table 2.4) that majority (71.4 %) of the publishers (50) are having an annual turnover ranging between Rs. 20 to 75 lakh.

Type of Publishing

An attempt has been made to collect data regarding the type of books being published. This is for the purpose of understanding trends in publishing industry. The responses are analysed in this section.

Table 2.5

Area of Specialization

Specialization	*Yes*	*No*	*Total*	*% (Yes)*	*Rank*
The Humanities & Social sciences	62	8	70	88.6	1
Management	58	12	70	82.9	2
Computer & Engineering	43	27	70	38.6	3
Art & Culture	20	50	70	28.6	4
Natural Science	13	57	70	18.6	5
Medical Science	12	58	70	17.1	6

Annual Turnover

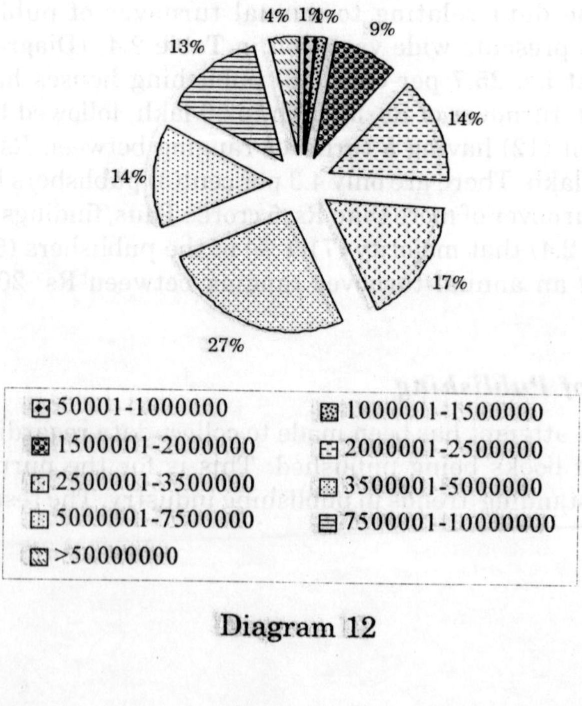

Diagram 12

Many of the publishers specialise according to disciplines. So to find what are the areas of popular choice among publishers, a question was asked. Response on this aspect has been analysed and presented in Table 2.5 which reveals that maximum i.e. 88.6 per cent (62) publishers are in the field of Humanities and Social Sciences, followed by 82.9 per cent (58) who publish Management books. The 3rd rank is occupied by Computer and Engineering books accounting for 38.6 per cent (43) publishers. Areas like Art and Culture, Natural and Medical Science occupy 4th, 5th and 6th ranks respectively. Thus, the data shows that the Humanities and Social Sciences, Management and Computer and Engineering are the areas of popular choice as they are more in demand in market.

Table 2.6

Kinds and Forms of Documents Published

Specialization	*Yes*	*No*	*Total*	*%(Yes)*	*Rank*
Text books	50	20	70	71.0	1
General books	40	30	70	56.8	2
Reference books	12	58	70	17.2	3
Novels/Fictions	3	67	70	4.3	7
Journals	5	65	70	7.1	5
Reports	4	66	70	5.7	6
CD ROMs	6	64	70	8.6	4
Audio Cassettes	2	68	70	2.9	8
Video Cassettes	3	67	70	4.3	7
Maps/Atlases	0	70	70	0.0	0

In response to question about the forms and kinds of (Table 2.6) documents being published, the responses received reveal that highest number of publishers i.e. 50 (71%) are publishing text books. It is followed by general academic books (56.8%) and reference books (17.2%).Only 7.1 per cent (5) publishers undertake publishing of journals, whereas there are 8.6 per cent (6) CD-ROM publishers. 7.2 per cent (5) publishers dealing in audio-visual material. Research reports are brought out by 5.7 per cent (4) publishing houses. Thus, data reveals that there is lack of publishing houses dealing in non-print materials.

Table 2.7
Total Number of Titles Published

No.	*No. of Responses*	*Per cent*
1-25	13	18.6
26-50	7	10.0
76-100	1	1.4
101-150	6	8.6
151-200	8	11.4
201-300	10	14.3
301-400	14	20.0
401-500	11	15.7
Total	70	100.0

Data in Table 2.7 (Diagram 13) reveals that 18.6 per cent (13) publishers have published titles ranging between 1-25 followed by 10 per cent (7)publishers who have published 26 to 50 titles so far. The highest number of publishers,20 per cent (14), have published titles between 301-400 whereas there are 15.7 per cent (11) publishing houses who have published titles between 401-500. The smallest percentage is of 1.4 per cent (1) publisher publishing 76 to 100 titles in all. Thus, a majority have published less than 300 titles.

In question nos. 4 and 5, publishers were asked if they bring out reprints of their publications. All the 70 publishers have reported that they have a policy for reprinting titles in case there is further demand for a particular title.

Most of the text book publishers like Prentice-Hall of India, Tata McGraw-Hill and Vikas Publishing House regularly bring out reprints to meet the demand for a publication. The data reveals that a sizeable number of publishers, 25 (35.7%) have published reprints of text book in the range of 81-100. The data shows that there exists sufficient demand for text books and other popular readings warranting reprints. Similarly bringing out revised editions is a regular process. Almost all publishers regularly revise the titles which are prescribed as text books.

Total Number of Titles Published

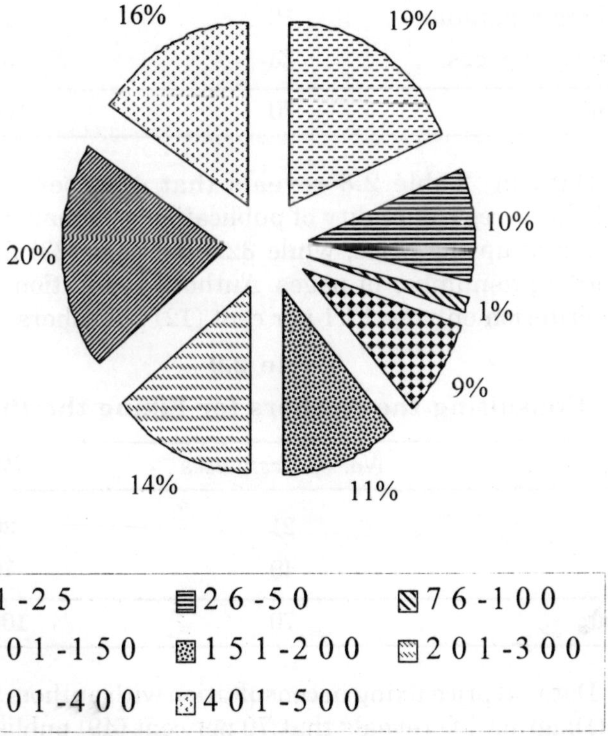

Diagram 13

Pricing of Publications

This section deals with the questions related with the pricing of their publications by the publishers. Pricing is an important area as it has direct bearing on the collection development process in libraries. The rising cost of publications is badly affecting the capacity of libraries to buy requisite material.

Table 2.8

Criteria Used for Fixing Prices of Publications

Criteria	*No. of Responses*	*Per cent*
Quality of publication	29	41.4
Demand for publication	6	8.6
Authors' reputation	12	17.1
Number of pages	23	32.9
Total	70	100.0

Data in Table 2.8 reveals that 41.4 per cent (29) publishers regard quality of publication as a main criterion for fixing up the price, while 32.9 per cent (23) fix prices according to number of pages. Author's reputation is taken as a criterion only by 17.1 per cent (12) publishers.

Table 2.9

Consulting the Authors for Fixing the Price

Response	*No. of Responses*	*Per cent*
Yes	21	30.0
No	49	70.0
Total	70	100.0

Data on price fixing in consultation with authors in Table 2.9 (Diagram 14) reveals that 70 per cent (49) publishers do not consult authors while fixing the prices of their publications. On interaction with the publishers it was found that even if they consult, they do not go by authors' opinion on the price of publication. Publishers take decision on their own while determining the price. It seems that they are guided more by their business interests rather than by the academic value of a publication.

Prices of Documents : Consulting the Authors

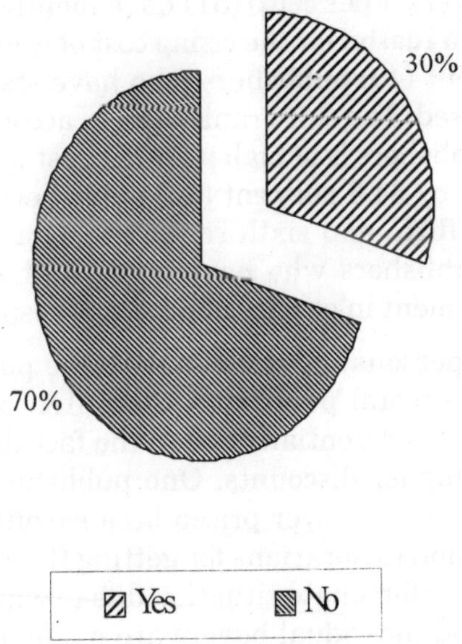

Diagram 14

Table 2.10

Reasons for Rising Prices of Publications

Reasons	*Yes*	*No.*	*Total*	*%(Yes)*	*Rank*
Decreased sales	49	21	70	70.0	2
Rising paper cost	45	25	70	64.3	4
Decreased print run	51	29	70	71.4	1
Costly printing	48	22	70	68.4	3
Royalty has gone up	21	49	70	30.0	6
Quality has improved	29	41	70	41.4	5

The data in Table 2.10 shows that highest percentage of respondents (71.4 per cent) (51) have mentioned decreasing print run as a reason for the rising cost of books. It is followed by 70 per cent (49) publishers who have stated that sales have decreased. The third rank reason, according to 68.4 per cent (48) publishers is of high printing cost while fourth rank reason cited by 64.3 per cent (45) publishers is rising paper cost. In the fifth and sixth ranks are 41.4 (29) and 30 per cent (21) publishers who have given higher royalty rates and improvement in quality of products respectively.

During personal interaction with the publishers, it was revealed by several publishers that often publications are over priced. It is essentially due to the fact that libraries are demanding higher discounts. One publisher informed that publications are also over-priced because often they have to pay commission to librarians for getting their books selected. This is most unfortunate situation due to which both honest librarians and individual buyers are made to suffer.

Selection of Manuscripts for Publications

Quality of books is an important matter for libraries. A library is known not only by the size of its collection but also by rich contents of the acquired material. An effort has been made to understand the parameters which publishers use to select publishing material. If they do not follow a rigorous quality control, the quality of books available in the market will also not be good. The data related to this problem is presented in Tables 2.12-2.16.

The analysis of data received for question 9 has revealed that in majority of cases authors themselves contact the publishers for getting their manuscripts published. But publishing houses themselves contact the authors in case the person is well known expert in a particular area. The practice of literary agents acting as facilitators like in western countries is not prevalent in the country.

Table 2.11

No. of Manuscripts Received (Annually)

Number	*No. of Responses*	*Per cent*
Upto 10	0	0.0
Upto 20	0	0.0
Upto 30	0	0.0
Upto 40	23	32.9
Upto 50	31	44.3
More than 50	16	22.9
Total	70	100.0

32.9 per cent (23) publishers receive up to 40 manuscripts (Table 2.11) annually. According to 44.3 per cent (31) publishers, upto 50 manuscripts are submitted annually for publication while according to 22.9 per cent (16) publishers, more than 50 manuscripts are received for the purpose of publication. Given the fact there are approximately 10,000 publishers in the country, the number of manuscripts submitted is a clear indication of a high publishing activity in the country.

Table 2.12

Percentage of Selected Manuscripts

Percentage	*No. of Responses*	*Per cent*
Upto 10%	0	0.0
Upto 20%	7	10.0
Upto 30%	11	15.7
Upto 40%	11	15.7
Upto 50%	29	41.4
> 50%	12	17.1
Total	70	100.0

The highest response i.e. in 41.4 per cent (29) cases (Table 2.12) the rate of acceptance of manuscripts for actual publication is upto 50 per cent whereas according to 17.1 per cent (12) publishers it is more than 50 per cent.The lowest acceptance rate is upto 20 per cent as per 10 per cent (7) publishers. Publishers like Oxford University Press, Sage Publication, Cambridge University Press and Rupa and Company etc., have a very rigorous editing module and accordingly the rate of acceptance is around 30 per cent or less.

Table 2.13

System of Evaluation of Manuscripts

System	*No. of Responses*	*Per cent*
Refer to panel of experts	21	30.0
Editorial Board	22	31.4
Evaluate on own	26	37.1
Any other	1	1.4
Total	70	100.0

Majority of publishers i.e. 37.1 per cent (26) (Table 2.13) (Diagram 15) have indicated that they evaluate manuscripts themselves, followed by 31.4 per cent (22) who get the manuscripts evaluated through their editorial board and another 30 per cent (21) have indicated that they refer the manuscripts to panel of experts.

The data thus reveals that ironically a large percentage of publishers do not have any editorial board nor they refer the manuscripts to subject experts or have a regular editorial panel for the evaluation of manuscripts. This is a serious drawback of Indian publishing industry and is largely responsible for lack of quality publishing.

The above finding was also established during personal interaction with the publishers. Publishers agreed that a good number of publishers are neither professionally qualified nor have any training required for the publishing job. This has an added adverse impact on the quality of publications.

Table 2.14

Criteria for Selection of Manuscripts

Criteria	*Yes*	*No.*	*Total*	*%*	*Rank*
Subject of Mss	70	0	70	100	1
Quality of Mss	65	5	70	92.9	2
Reputation of author	57	23	70	81.4	3
Demand of subject	0	0	0	0	0
Any other reasons	0	0	0	0	0

Mss =Manuscript

Subject of manuscript (ranked 1) is the prime factor as indicated by all the publishers for accepting a manuscript for publishing as it is always taken into consideration while taking a decision for publishing. For 92.9 per cent (65) publishers quality of manuscript is another important factor (ranked 2) taken into consideration while accepting a manuscript for publication. Reputation of author is the third ranking criteria taken into consideration for selecting a manuscript for publication.

Table 2.15
Reasons for Rejection

Reasons	*No. of Responses*	*Per cent*
Low demand of subject	11	15.7
Rejected by editors	14	20.0
Not of general interest	9	12.9
Rejected by panel of experts	21	30.0
Author is not well known	0	0.0
Author's first work	0	0.0
Subject is too specialised	15	21.4
Any other reason		
Total	70	100.0

According to 15.7 per cent (11) manuscripts (Table 2.15) are rejected for the low demand of subject whereas 20 per cent (14)manuscripts are rejected by editors. In 30 per cent (21)cases there is rejection by panel of experts. According to 21.4 per cent (15) publishers one more reason for rejection is that subject is too specialised whereas in 12.9 per cent cases(9) it is not of general interest and hence can not be published. Thus the major reason is the rejection by panel of experts.

Evaluation of Manuscripts

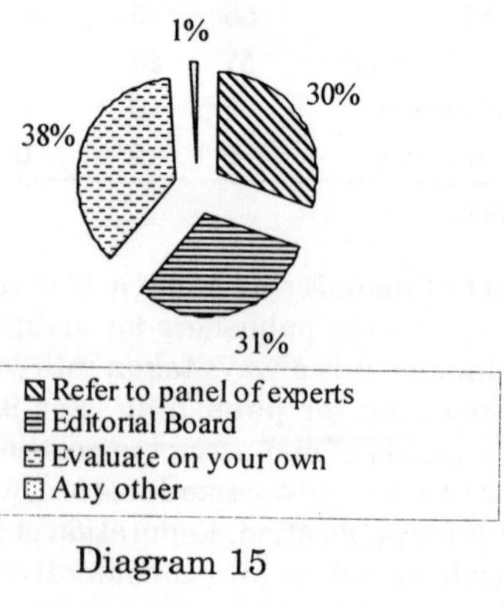

Diagram 15

Financial Difficulties

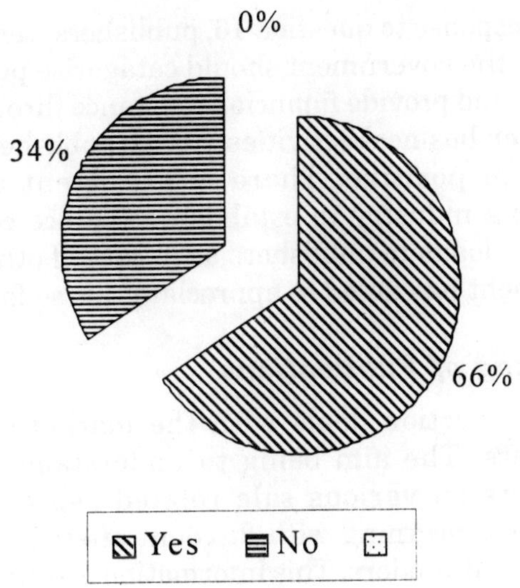

Diagram 16

Table 2.16
Financial Difficulties Faced in Publishing Assignment

Response	*No. of Responses*	*Per cent*
Yes	46	65.7
No	24	34.3
Total	70	100.0

According to 65.7 per cent (46) (Diagram 16) publishers, they face financial difficulties (Table 2.16) while undertaking publishing assignments. For the existence of healthy publishing activitiés, need for regular inflow of funds is essential. This is specially important because incoming proceeds from sale are relatively slow and money gets blocked proceeds from sale are relatively slow and money gets blocked for a very long time.

In response to question 16, publishers were asked if they feel that the government should catagorise publishing as an industry and provide financial assistance through bank loans as in other business activities. All the publishers (100%) have replied in positive. There is persistent demand from publishing industry to establish a finance corporation for providing loans to publishers as in case of other trades. But government has failed to appreciate this so far.

Marketing of Publications

This section deals with the marketing strategy of publishers. The aim being to understand viewpoint of publishers on various sale related aspects. It includes questions concerning with discount offered to distributors, libraries and vendors. This information is primarily intended to understand the internal dynamics of publishing industry.

Table 2.17

Priority of Business Customers

(Total Responses 70)

Priority	*Yes*	*No.*	*% (Yes)*	*Rank*
Wholesalers/ Distributors	70	0	100.0	1
Vendors	24	46	34.28	2
Libraries	14	56	20.0	3

For all publishers, wholesalers/distributors are their primary business customers (rank 1), followed by vendors and libraries. 20 per cent (14) publishers (Table 2.17) consider libraries as their business customers (rank 3) whereas 34.28 per cent publishers (24) consider vendors as important business customers (rank 2).

Table 2.18
Discount Offered to Wholesalers/Distributors

Discount	*No. of Responses*	*Per cent*
25%	2	2.8
25+5%	8	11.6
30%	10	14.3
33%	7	10.0
40%	42	60.0
	1.4	Missing
Total	70	100.0

In 60 per cent cases (42) publishers' discount to distributors (Table 2.18) is 40 per cent whereas in rest of the cases it varies between 25 to 33 per cent. The amount of discount, however also depends upon number of copies being purchased. Some publishers like McGraw-Hill, New York and Sage (International), London, are very conservative in their discount rates. Some Indian publishes have started over pricing their books to pay more discount to distributors. As regards discount to individual and institutional (other than libraries) sales, there are not much customers and discount varies on situation to situation basis.

Table 2.19
Discount Offered to Vendors

Discount	*No. of Responses*	*Per cent*
25%	10	14.3
25+5%	12	17.1
30%	19	27.1
33%	24	34.3
40%	5	7.1
Total	70	100.0

The data in table 2.19 reveals that 33 per cent discount is being given to vendors by 34.3 per cent (24) publishers while 7.1 per cent (5) publishers pay 40 per cent discount to vendors. The lowest discount is 25 per cent as per 14.3 per cent (10) publishers. Thus, the discount offered by publishers to vendors varies between 25% and 33% and is largely same as offered to distributors.

Table 2.20
Reaching Publications the Major Cities

Response	*No. of Responses*	*Per cent*
Yes	42	60
No	28	40
Total	70	100

As regards distribution of books (Table 2.20) (Diagram17), 40 per cent publishers (28) have indicated that books do not reach all parts of the country. This is probably the biggest challenge before Indian publishing industry. There does not exist any national level distribution channel for supplying books at all India basis.This has a serious implication on the publishing business as well as for collection development activities of libraries situated in remote areas or small towns.

Reaching Publications the Major Cities of the Country

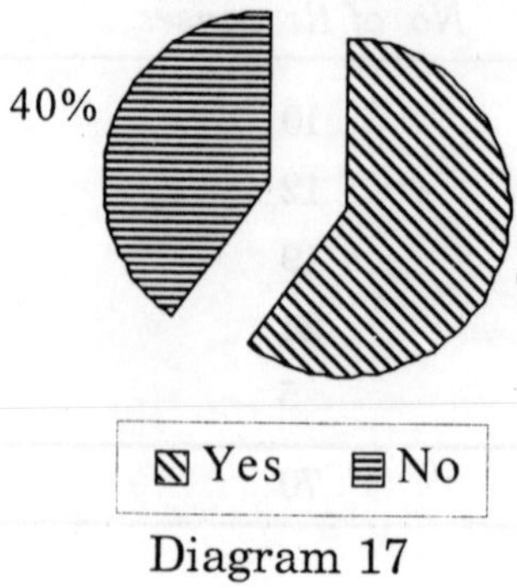

Diagram 17

Table 2.21

Reasons for Not Reaching the Major Cities

Response	*No. of Responses*	*Per cent*
National level distribution network does not exist	21	75.0
Outstation booksellers do not make payaments in time	0	0.0
There is a risk of not getting the payments from outside distributors	7	25.0
Sending material directly involves high freight/postage cost	0	0.0
Total	28	100.0

According to 75 per cent (21) (Table 2.22) publishers, there is no viablc national level distribution network which can supply books to all major towns and cities of the country, whereas 25 per cent (7) publishers have stated that there is a problem in getting payments from out station distributors which affects the supply of books.

Table 2.22

Supply of Books to Libraries Directly

Response	*No. of Responses*	*Per cent*
Yes	30	42.0
No	40	58.0
Total	70	100.0

About supply of books directly to the libraries, 42 per cent (30) publishers (Table 2.20) have stated that they supply books directly to libraries. These are mostly those publishers who deal in distributorship also. However, 58 per cent (40) publishers do not directly deal with the libraries.

Table 2.23

Discount Offered to Libraries

Discount	*No. of Responses*	*Per cent*
10%	6	20.0
15%	7	23.3
20%	8	26.7
25%	9	30.0
Total	30	100.0

According to data in Table 2.21, the discount rates vary between GOC rate of 10 per cent to 25 per cent. 20 per cent publishers (6) give 10 per cent discount while 23 per cent (7) publishers give 15 per cent. 26 per cent (8) and 30 per cent(9) give 20 and 30 per cent discount to libraries respectively.

In their response to question that under what conditions books are supplied directly to libraries, 73 per cent publishers (22) have stated they supply books directly to libraries only on confirmed order basis. Rest 27 per cent (8) publishers supply books on approval basis also. It shows that an overwhelming majority of publishers are not interested in supplying books to libraries on their own.

Table 2.24

Facing Problems in Getting Payments From Libraries

Response	*No. of Responses*	*Per cent*
Yes	14	46.7
No	16	53.3
Total	30	100.0

The data in Table 2.22 reveals that 46.7 per cent (14) publishers face problems in getting payment of their bills from libraries. Bills are not cleared for long time which adversely affect their schedule of payment as well as business. This is serious matter and librarian must see to it that payments are made in time. However, 53.3 (16) publishers do not have any problem with payment of their bills.

Table 2.25

Time Taken by Libraries to Clear Bills

Time	*No. of Responses*	*Per cent*
Upto One Week	0	0.0
Upto two Weeks	0	0.0
Upto three weeks	4	13.0
Upto one month	6	20.0
Upto two months	8	26.0
Upto three months	9	30.0
More than three months	3	10.0
Total	30	100.0

Out of 30 publishers who supply books directly to libraries, 13 per cent (4) have indicated that they get payment in upto 3 weeks time whereas 20 per cent publishers (6) have stated upto 1 month's time. 40 per cent (12) publishers get payment of bills after more than two months. The time taken to clear bills must be reduced so that publishers are in a position to improve their service.

Table 2.26

Decrease in Demand for Books in Special Libraries

Response	*No. of Responses*	*Per cent*
Yes	41	58.5
No	29	41.5
Total	70	100.0

According to data in Table 2.26, 58.5 per cent (41) publishers have stated that there is a decrease in demand of books in special libraries in the last five years, whereas according to 41.5 per cent (29) publishers, there is no decrease in demand. It can be said that the response is fairly mixed and a generalisation is not possible to infer. Probably some special libraries have reduced their library budgets leading to the above response.

The analysis of responses received for question no. 25 reveals that demand for printed journals has not gone down in last five years in special libraries. All the five publishers who supply journals to libraries have stated that demand for printed journals has not gone down.

Table 2.27

Reasons for Decreasing Demand

Reasons	*No. of Responses*	*Per cent*
Acquiring more non-print material	4	9.8
Fast acceptability of electronic formats	13	31.7
Increased resource sharing	10	24.4
Any other reason (budgets reduced)	14	34.4
Total	41	100.0

According to a high percentage of publishers i.e. 34.4 per cent(14) (Table 2.27) (Diagram 18) the demand for books has decreased because of reduced library budgets, whereas 31.7 per cent(13) publishers have stated that libraries are spending more money on electronic formats. Increasing resource sharing is also leading to lesser purchases as stated by 24.4 per cent (10) publishers. Network like DELNET provide document delivery service which often eliminates the need for purchasing certain costly titles.

In regard to a question as to whether demand for printed journals has gone down in special libraries during the last five years, all the 5 publishers undertaking publishing of journals. All of them have stated that demand for journals has not gone down in special libraries. This is basically due to the fact that researchers and user harbour protective feelings towards journals and resist in most cases any deletion. They constantly put pressure for higher allocations in this area.

Reasons for Decreasing Demand

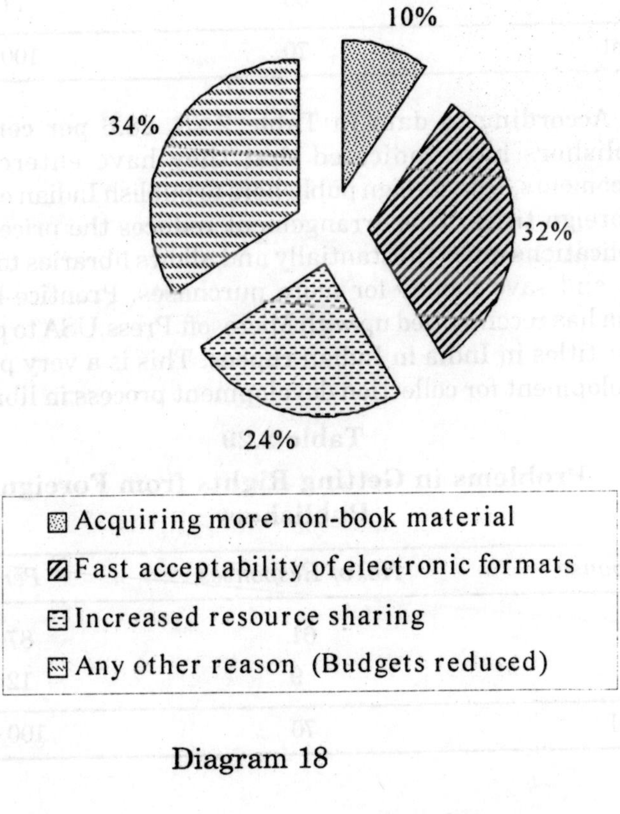

Diagram 18

Foreign Publications

Tables 2.29-2.34 deal with questions related to foreign publishers. As collection of foreign materials is a very important part of special libraries, questions were asked to get information related to process of acquiring such material by the publishers.

Table 2.28

Tie up With Foreign Publishers

Response	*No. of Responses*	*Per cent*
Yes	20	28.6
No	50	71.4
Total	70	100.0

According to data in Table 2.28, 28.6 per cent (20) publishers have indicated that they have entered into agreements, with foreign publishers to publish Indian editions of foreign titles. This arrangement reduces the price of the publications quite substantially and allows libraries to spend less and save money for more purchases. Prentice-Hall of India has recently tied up with Microsoft Press,USA to publish their titles in India in Indian rupees. This is a very positive development for collection development process in libraries.

Table 2.29

Problems in Getting Rights from Foreign Publishers

Response	*No. of Responses*	*Per cent*
Yes	61	87.1
No	9	12.9
Total	70	100.0

But getting rights for bringing out Indian editions is not an easy exercise. According to 87.1 per cent publishers (61), they face problems in getting into agreements with foreign publishers.

Table 2.30
Nature of Problems

Problem	*No. of Responses*	*Per cent*
Demand for heavy advance	36	59.0
Rights granted for text books	6	10.0
Rights not for latest editions	19	31.0
Total	61	100.0

The biggest problem as revealed by 59 per cent (36), (Table 2.30) publishers is of heavy advance payments which foreign publishers demand for granting rights. The amount ranges between Rs. 5 to 10 lakh which most of the publishers find difficult to meet. The other problem as revealed by 31 per cent (19) publishers is that rights arc granted for selected text books only and not for research level publications. Even in text books, according to 10 per cent (6) publishers permission is not given for the latest editions.

Table 2.31
Export of Books

Response	*No. of Responses*	*Per cent*
Yes	19	27.1
No	51	72.9
Total	70	100.0

According to 27.1 publishers (19), they export books (Table 2.31) whereas 72.9 per cent (51) do not export their publications to foreign countries. In case of those who export, over 50 per cent of export are to USA and Britain and rest goes to countries with large Indian immigrant population. But slowly new markets are also coming up in countries like Singapore, Malaysia, Sri Lanka, Bangladesh, Nepal, Middle-East and Africa. This is a good opportunity to develop global business for Indian publishing industry.

Table 2.32

Annual Export Turnover

Turnover	*No. of Responses*	*Per cent*
<500000	5	26.0
500000-1000000	8	42.0
100001-1500000	6	32.0
Total	19	100.0

According to 26 per cent publishers (5) their annual turn over (Table 2.32) is upto 5 lakh whereas 42 per cent publishers (8) have reported a turnover of Rs. 5 to 10 lakhs. 32 per cent (6) publishers have annual turnover ranging between Rs. 10 to 15 lakhs . Thus, majority of publishers have an annual turnover of less than Rs.10 lakh.

Table 2.33

Subsidy for Export

Response	*No. of Responses*	*Per cent*
Yes	22	100.0
No	0	0.0
Total	22	100.0

All the 22 publishers(100%) have reported that government provides subsidies for all those publishing houses who export books and earn foreign exchange. Subsidy is provided by way of rebates in income tax and also bank loans for the purpose of exports. This is in keeping with the government policy of providing incentives to those organisations including publishers who are earning foreign exchange for the country.

Relationship between Publishers and Librarians

No library can develop its collection without continuous supply of good reading material. Publishers, booksellers and libraries depend upon and are affected by the products, requirements or services of one another. For the smooth functioning of the system it is necessary that good relations exist between librarians and publishers. In the following section data has been presented regarding the level of relationship that prevails between librarians and publishers.

Table 2.34

Kind of Relationship Between Librarians and Publishers

Response	*No. of Responses*	*Per cent*	*WI**	*Rank*
Very good	12	17.1	0.84	3
Good	26	37.2	1.48	1
Neither good nor poor	28	40.0	1.2	2
Poor	4	5.7	0.11	4
Very poor	0	0.0	0	5
Total	70	100.0		

Note: *Weighted Index is calculated on a Five Point scale with weights assigned as : Very Good = 5; Good= 4; Neither good nor poor= 3; Poor= 2; Very Poor= 1.

The existence of cordial relationship between publishers and librarians is an important factor in building a good library collection. In fact librarians need to establish a good rapport with Personal equation always help librarians in securing prompt service. The data in Table 2.34 (Diagram 19) reveals that 17.1 per cent (12) and 37.2 per cent (26) publishers have 'Very good' and 'Good' relations respectively whereas 40 per cent (28) publishers regard their relations with librarians 'Neither good nor poor'. 5.7 per cent (4) publishers have categorised the relationship as 'Poor'. Thus, majority of publishers have indicated that relationship with librarians is 'Neither good nor poor'.

Kind of Relationship Between Librarians and Publishers

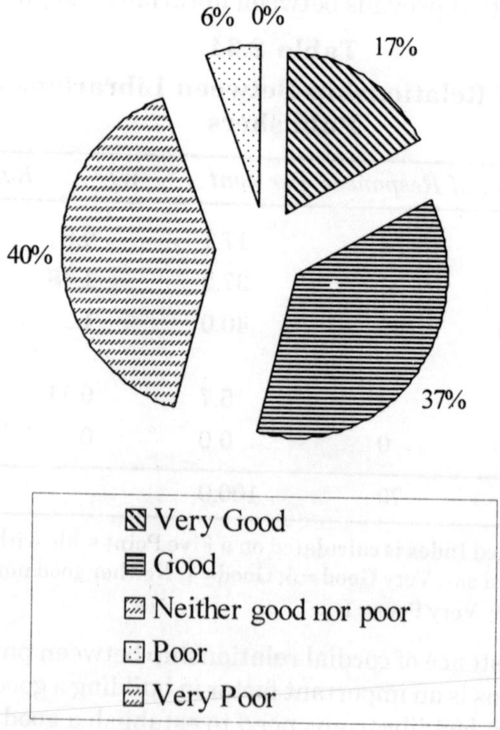

Diagram 19

Some of the above information has also been supplemented and confirmed during the personal interaction with the publishers. Though in most of the cases relations between librarians and publishers are of professional nature but in some cases librarians are also biased in their dealings. Several publishers stated that often librarians look for favours while placing their orders or getting their books approved in their libraries.

Table 2.35

Usefulness of GOC's Role between Publishers and Libraries

Response	*No. of Responses*	*Per cent*
Yes	45	64.3
No	25	35.7
Total	70	100.0

Good Offices Committee (GOC) established to regulate book supply activities and conversion rates is considered to be playing a useful role between libraries and publishers as indicated by 64.3 per cent (45) publishers while 35.7% (25) do not think so. The main reason for this negative impression is because of GOC's failure in enforcing discount rates. Even the conversion rates recommended by GOC are not being followed due to some dispute between Indian Library Association (ILA) and GOC. These findings have also been established during personal interaction. While some publishers expressed their satisfaction with the functioning of GOC, several other were totally dissatisfied particularly in the matters related to enforcing discount rates. They stated that GOC should be given more teeth by government and action should be taken against both the suppliers and librarians who violate GOC norms.The situation relating to the functioning of GOC has further worsened with Indian Library Association withdrawing itself from the original body and fixing its own conversion rates in the name of ILA-Good Offices Committee.

Analysis of Question Nos. 32-37

In response to question about role of GOC, a majority of the publishers have criticised GOC for its failure in enforcing uniform discount rates. They have recommended that GOC be made a statutory body so that rates fixed by it may be implemented all over the country.

Regarding the status of publishing in India, the publishers have mentioned that government does not have any policy about the promotion of publishing trade as publishers do not find any place either in educational or cultural policies of the Indian government. They have also mentioned the threat from piracy and violation of copy rights by photo copying activities. Publishers have suggested that copy right laws should be strictly implemented. These suggestions were also received while having personal interaction with the publishers.

About the future of publishing trade, most of the publishers have described the situation in negative terms. They are concerned by the wide acceptance of electronic formats in special libraries. However a sizeable number of publishers have stated that they are optimistic about the future of publishing trade as educational activities are expanding in the country.

Regarding suggestions for promoting development of collection in special libraries, most of the publishers have suggested increase in library budgets in proportion to the rising cost of publications.

These findings have also been established during personal interaction with the publishers. Publishers informed that they are not often able to sell all the copies published due to which they suffer heavy losses in their business. The publishers agreed that this is happening largely due to indiscriminate publishing without any regard to maintaining quality of publications. There is lot of duplication in terms of contents of material being published.

PART 3

Analysis of Responses Received From Distributors

Distributors are an important part of the library acquisition process. It is through distributors that books reach all the parts of the country. Without a strong distribution network, it will be impossible for individual publishers to sell their books. A separate questionnaire (Appendix 3) was designed to understand the functioning of distributors which has a direct bearing on library collection development programmes. 75 questionnaires were distributed among reputed distributors out of which 32 (46.6%) questionnaire were received back duly filled in.The responses received have been analysed in following sections.

Profile of Firms

Table 3.1

Nature of Firms

Nature	*No. of Responses*	*Per cent*
Proprietorship	21	65.6
Partnership	3	9.4
Private Company	8	25.0
Total	32	100.0

65.6 per cent (21) distributors (Table 3.1) have proprietorship firms, whereas 25 per cent(8) are private companies. Only 3 distributors are having partnership firms. Indian distribution houses are small time entrepreneurs with limited capital. Most of them operate locally. Majority are proprietorship firms.

Table 3.2
Academic Qualifications

Qualification	*No. of Responses*	*Per cent*
Graduate	24	75.0
Post Graduate	6	18.8
Matriculate	2	6.3
Total	32	100.0

Data (Table 3.2) reveals that 75 per cent (24) distributors are graduates while 18.8 per cent(6) hold Master degrees. 6.3 per cent (2) distributors are just matriculates, which indeed is surprising.

Table 3.3
Period of Establishment

Period	*No. of Responses*	*Per cent*
1961-70	6	18.8
1971-80	10	31.2
1981-90	8	25.0
1991-2000	8	25.0
Total	32	100.0

The data relating to year of establishment (Table 3.4) shows that maximum i.e. 31.2 per cent (10) distribution houses came into existence between 1971-1980. 18.6 per cent (6) firms were established during 1961-70 and during 1980-90 and 1991-2000 8 firms each came into existence. Thus, there were very few firms in 1960s, majority of them came into being during the last 30 years.

The distributors were asked about the total strength of staff members working in their firms.

Table 3.4
Strength of Staff

Staff	*No. of Responses*	*Per cent*
Upto 5	17	53.1
Upto 7	4	12.5
Upto 10	10	31.3
Upto 15	1	3.1
Total	32	100.0

Data in Table 3.4 shows that most of Indian distribution firms are small in size having 5 to 15 staff members. However, majority of them i.e. 53.1 per cent (17) have just 5 or less employees. There is just 1 (3.1 %) distribution house having upto 15 employees.

Table 3.5
Annual Turnover

Turnover (Rs.)	***No. of Responses***	***Per cent***
1500000-2000000	1	3.1
2000001-2500000	3	9.4
2500001-3500000	3	9.4
3500001-5000000	9	28.1
5000001-7500000	8	25.0
7500001-10000000	5	15.6
<10000000	3	9.4
Total	32	100.0

The data reveals (Table 3.5) that 9.4 per cent (3) firms have an annual turnover of more than Rs.1 crore whereas turnover of Rs. 35 to 50 lakh is shared by 28.1 per cent (9) firms, followed by 25 per cent firms (8) who have annual turnover of Rs. 50 Lakh to Rs. 75 Lakh.

Procurement of Books

Questionnaire asked about the procurement of books, number of publishers dealt with and importing of books. These are important questions to know the working of distribution houses having a vital bearing on libraries.

Table 3.6

Subjects and Kinds of Documents Supplied

Kinds	*No. of Responses*	*Per cent*
Social Sciences	9	28.2
Humanities		25.1
Scientific/ Technical	8	25.0
Journals	3	9.4
CD-ROMs	0	0.0
Reports and Government Publications	4	12.3
Audio-Visual Material	0	0.0
Total	32	100.0

The data indicates (Table 3.6) that 28.2 per cent (9) distributors deal in social sciences subjects while second highest category of distributors, (25 per cent) (8) distribute subjects related to humanities. An equal number of distributors deal in scientific/technical books. 12.5 per cent (4) distribute governmernt publications while 9.4 per cent (3) deal with journals.

Table 3.7

No. of Indian Publishers Whose Books You Distribute

Number	*No. of Responses*	*Per cent*
25-50	1	3.1
50-75	5	15.6
75-100	8	25.0
100-150	6	18.8
150-200	4	12.5
200-300	3	9.4
>1000	5	15.6
Total	32	100.0

The number of Indian publishers whose books are distributed by distributors (Table 3.7) range between 25 and 1000. There are 15.6 per cent (5) distributors distributing books of more than 1000 Indian publishers. The maximum i.e. 25 per cent distributors (8) deal with 75 to 100 publishers. Given tho fact that there are more than 10,000 publishers in the country, the data shows lack of really a large distribution company. Thus, a large number of publishers do not distribute through well established distributors become their own distributors.

Table 3.8

No. of Foreign Publishers Whose Books You Distribute

Number	*No.of Responses*	*Per cent*
1-20	3	9.4
21-40	5	15.6
41-60	11	34.4
61-80	11	34.4
81-100	2	6.3
Total	32	100.0

The figure related to number of foreign publishers distributed is relatively moderate (Table 3.8). The total publishers being distributed by individual distribution houses are between 1 to 100 only. There are 2 groups of distributors consisting of 34.4 per cent (11) distributors each who distribute the books of 41 to 60 and 61 to 80 foreign publishers respectively. Only 6.3 per cent distributors (2) deal with upto 100 publishers. It is obvious that a large number of foreign publishers do not have their distributors in India as a result it becomes more difficult to get books published by such publishers.

Table 3.9

Main Source of Getting Books

Sources	*No. of Responses*	*Per cent*
Import directly	20	62.5
From local publisher	12	37.5
From Indian publishers outside Delhi	0	0.0
Total	32	100.0

The data reveals that 62.5 per cent (20) distributors (Table 3.9) import directly from abroad while rest of 37.6 per cent (12) take books from local publishers. Importing books from abroad ofcourse requires very heavy investments and lot of spadework to handle the work very professionally. A majority of distributing concerns are small enterprises not well equipped with requisite professionalism.

Table 3.10

Time Taken to Procure Foreign Books

Time	*No. of Responses*	*Per cent*
4 weeks	8	40.0
6 weeks	7	35.0
8 weeks	5	25.0
Total	20	100.0

Procurement of foreign titles is a problem area and the biggest challenge to collection development process. The data (Table 3.10) reveals that on an average suppliers take 4 to 8 weeks' time to procure foreign titles. According to 40 per cent(8) distributors, they take 4 weeks time to procure books from abroad whereas 35 per cent (7) distributors take 6 weeks. Highest time of 8 weeks is taken by 25 per cent (5) respondents. A general complaint by libraries is that suppliers do not stick to given schedules and accumulate orders to reduce their own expenses.

Table 3.11

Approval Period for Books Received from Foreign Publishers

Period	*No. of Responses*	*Per cent*
90 days	6	18.8
Six months	13	40.6
Nil	13	40.6
Total	32	100.0

The approval time granted by foreign publishers to Indian distributors varies from 90 days to 6 months (Table 3.11). But approval period is not granted by all publishers and in all cases. According to 40.6 per cent (13) distributors, approval period granted is upto 6 months whereas another 40.6 per cent (13) have indicated grant of no approval time. Once books are procured, they can not be returned whether sold or not. In certain cases distributors have to suffer heavy losses.

Table 3.12

Average Discount Received

Discount	*No. of Responses*	*Per cent*
33%	8	25.0
40%	10	31.3
upto 45%	14	43.8
Total	32	100.0

The highest discount (Table 3.12) that distributors get from publishers, according to 43.8 per cent (14) vendors is upto 45 per cent whereas in 25 per cent cases (8), it is 33 per cent. 40 per cent discount is received by 31.3 per cent (10) distributors. The average discount received varies from 33 per cent to 45 per cent.

Table 3.13
Percentage of Discount Depends Upon

Factors	*No. of Responses*	*Per cent*
Type of publisher	19	59.4
No of copies ordered	13	40.6
Total	32	100.0

According to 59.4 per cent (19) distributors (Table 3.13), discount varies from publisher to publisher. Some publishers are very conservative while some are relatively liberal and offer higher discount. For 40.6 per cent distributors (13) discount also depends upon number of copies ordered. Distributors who place orders for large number of copies get little higher discount as a result of which they reduce the price of publication in the local market.

Table 3.14
Average Discount Offered to Vendors

Discount	*No. of Responses*	*Per cent*
25+5%	7	21.9
27.5%	10	33.6
30%	8	25.0
35%	7	19.5
Total	32	100.0

Discount on books has been a vexed issue, particularly for libraries. The discount on foreign books varies between 25% to 30% and in case of Indian publications it goes up to 35% (Table 3.14). 33.6 per cent (10) distributors have stated that the discount given by them to vendors is 27.5 per cent whereas according to 25 per cent (8), the discount rate is 30 per cent. If a vendor makes cash payment, he is likely to get 3 to 5 per cent extra discount.

Table 3.15

Problems Faced in Importing Books

Problems	*No. of Responses*	*Per cent*
Demand heavy investment	10	31.3
Respond very late	3	9.4
Accumulate orders for long	4	12.5
Publishers change frequently	6	18.8
Shipment charges are high	7	21.9
Custom clearance takes time	2	6.3
Total	32	100.0

Importing books from foreign publishers is full of hassles. According to 31.3 per cent (10) (Table 3.15) it requires lot of investments on the part of distributors and often they are handicapped by the lack of requisite finance. Situation is aggravated by the fact that there are no funding institutions for the book trade. 21.9 per cent (7) have stated that shipment charges have gone up due to which they are not able to import freely. According to 18.8 per cent (6) there is a problem of frequently changing publishers on account of mergers and acquisitions of companies, which often creates problem in placing orders.

Sale of Books

This Section (Tables 3.16-3.23) present analysis of questions related to sales of books by distributors, discount given to vendors and approval period granted.Since the usual system is that vendors take books from distributors for supplying to various libraries, an open-ended question was asked to find the number of vendors usually associated with distributing agencies.

Table 3.16

Number of Vendors Taking Books

Number	*No. of Responses*	*Per cent*
Between 1-10	1	3.1
Between 10-20	2	6.3
Between 20-30	3	9.4
Between 30-40	6	18.8
Between 40-50	2	6.3
Between 50-60	5	15.6
Between 60-70	6	18.8
Between 70-100	2	6.3
More than 100	5	15.6
Total	32	100.0

The data relating to number of vendors (Table 3.16) taking books from distributors for supplying to libraries varies between 1 to more than 100. 3.1 per cent (1) distributors have 1-10 vendors, 6.3 per cent(2) 20-30 vendors.There are 18.8 per cent distributors (6) having each 30-40 and 60-70 group of vendors. There are 15.6 per cent (5) distributors who have more than 100 vendors on their list of vendors.

Table 3.17

Period of Approval Granted to Vendors

Category	*No. of Responses*	*Per cent*
Upto 2 weeks	0	0.0
Upto 4 weeks	24	75.0
Upto 6 weeks	8	25.0
Upto 8 weeks	0	0.0
Upto 3 months	0	0.0
Upto 6 months	0	0.0
Total	32	100.0

According to data given in Table 3.17, in 75 per cent cases (24), the maximum period of approval granted to vendors by the distributors is upto four weeks while 25 per cent distributors (8) give six weeks time.

Table 3.18

Variations in Approval Period

Response	*No. of Responses*	*Per cent*
Yes	15	46.9
No	17	53.1
Total	32	100.0

According to 46.9 per cent distributors (15) (Table 3.18) approval period varies in some cases whereas in majority of cases i.e. 53.1 per cent (17), there is no variation. The reason for variation in approval period is of course the amount of business given by a vendor to the distributor.

Table 3.19

Selling Strategy

Strategy	*No. of Responses*	*Per cent*
Sell what is available	2	6.3
Procure and sell recent and most needed books	7	21.9
Offer more discount to vendors	4	12.5
Increase the publicity		
Through advertisements	11	34.4
Establishing good rapport with		
Libraries through effective service	8	25.0
Total	32	100.0

34.4 per cent (11) distributors have emphasised the need for increasing publicity as their main selling strategy (Table 3.19) whereas 25 per cent (8) distributors consider establishing good rapport with publishers and vendors as their main selling strategy which basically means increasing the number both of publishers and vendors. 21.9 distributors (7) have emphasised on getting recent books as their main selling strategy. Only 12.5 per cent (4) distributors consider higher discount as a main selling strategy.

Table 3.20

Selling Books Available Locally Only

Response	*No. of Responses*	*Per cent*
Yes	14	43.8
No	18	56.3
Total	32	100.0

A sizeable 43.8 (14) vendors (Table 3.20) prefer to sell books available locally only, whereas 56.3 per cent (18) distributors acquire books from all over the country and abroad for distribution.

Table 3.21

Reasons for Selling Locally Available Books

Reasons	*No. of Responses*	*Per cent*
Difficult to obtain non-local books	3	21.0
Books available against payment	7	50.0
Approval period is short	4	29.0
Total	14	100.0

According to 21 per cent distributors (3) (Table 3.21) it is difficult to obtain non-local books. There does not exist any effective national level distribution network. 50 per cent distributors (7) have stated that books are available against advance payment only which is again a serious handicap. In 29 per cent (4) cases, the approval period granted by the publisher is very short on account of which the distributors fail to obtain books and sell them in this short period.

Table 3.22

Facing Conflict with the Publishers

Issues	*No. of Responses*	*Per cent*
On discount aspect	21	65.6
For not complying with the agreement	7	21.9
On sudden cessation of publication	4	12.5
On lack of effective feedback and communication	0	0.0
Total	32	100.0

In response to question 13, all the 32 distributors (100%) have stated that the face conflict with the publishers. According to data in Table 3.22 a majority of distributors i.e.

65.6 per cent (21) have reported that they confront the publishers on discount issue, followed by 21.9 per cent (7) having some conflict on the issue of non-compliance of orders. Sudden cessation of a publication is also a problem area for some distributors as reported by 12.5 per cent (4)respondents.

Table 3.23

Supplying Books to Libraries Directly

Response	*No. of Responses*	*Per cent*
Yes	8	25.0
No	24	75.0
Total	32	100.0

Normally distributing firms do not supply books directly to libraries (Table 3.23). It has been mentioned by 75 per cent(24) distributors that they do not supply books directly to libraries. Being wholesalers, distributors avoid getting into retailing.

Linkages Between Libraries and Book Trade

For a healthy publishing industry a harmonious relationship between publishers, distributors and vendors is essential. If any of these do not co-operate with others, the entire process will be derailed. In this section questions related to all these issues have been analysed.

Table 3.24

Lack of Co-operation Between Publishers, Distributors and Vendors

Response	*Publisher / Distributor*	*Distributor / Vendor*	*Libraian / Vendor*
Yes	8 (25)	9 (28.1)	19(59.3)
No	24 (75)	23 (71.9)	13(40.7)

Data in Table 3.24 reveals that according to 75 per cent (24) distributors there is no lack of cooperation between publishers and distributors whereas 25 per cent (8) distributors have reported that there is lack of co-operation between the two. But according to 59.3 per cent (19) distributors, there is lack of cooperation between vendors and librarians. This is based on their interaction with vendors. On the same aspect, 28.1 per cent (9) distributors have reported lack of co-operation between distributors and vendors. This is indeed a serious matter, which needs to be looked into.

Table 3.25

Reasons for Lack of Cooperation

Reasons	*No. of Responses*	*Per cent*
Librarians busy in their professional activities	0	0.0
Distributors are not interested	8	22.2
Publishers are not interested to cooperate	13	36.2
Vendors do not cooperate	15	41.6
Total	36	100.0

22.2 per cent (8) publishers have held distributors responsible for lack of co-operation (Table 3.25) whereas 36.2 per cent (13) distributors think that publishers do not co-operate with them. 41.6 per cent distributors (15) have stated that vendors do not co-operate.

In response to question 16, all the distributors i.e. 100 per cent (32) have emphasised the need for regular interaction to further improve relationship among the distributors, vendors and librarians.

Table 3.26

Important Methods for Improving Relations

Methods	*No. of Responses*	*Per cent*
By offering higher discounts	5	29.4
By organising meetings/ seminars	6	35.2
By extending effective services	4	23.5
By providing latest information	2	11.7
Total	17	100.0

On the aspect of ways for improving the relationship, 29.4 per cent distributors (5) (Table 3.26) have stated that relations between publishers, distributors, and vendors can improve if publishers offer more discounts while according to 35.2 (6) per cent publishers, they think that there should be regular interaction by way of meetings and seminars so that the issues can be discussed and resolved. 23.5 per cent (4)distributors have stated the need for effective services while according to 11.7 per cent (2) distributors relations can be improved by providing latest information about publications.

Table 3.27

Membership of Booksellers' Associations

Response	*No. of Responses*	*Per cent*
Yes	25	78.1
No	7	21.9
Total	32	100.0

78.1 per cent (25) distributors have indicated (Table 3.27) that they are members of booksellers association, while 21.9 per cent (7) distributors are not members of any of such association.

Table 3.28

Provision of Assistance by Association/Federation

Response	*No. of Responses*	*Per cent*
Yes	20	80.0
No	5	20.0
Total	25	100.0

A majority of 80 per cent distributors (20) (Table 3.28) have stated that their association provides help by way of taking advocacy role on behalf of booksellers at various platforms. The association regularly holds conferences, seminars and meetings to discuss various issues confronting the book trade. 5 respondents (20%) have reported that association does not help them in promoting their business interests.

Table 3.29

Impact of Information Technology

Impact	*`No. of Responses*	*Per cent*	*WI**	*Rank*
To a very great extent	5	15.6	0.78	2
To a great extent	3	9.4	0.37	3
To some extent	16	50.0	1.5	1
To a little extent	5	15.6	0.31	4
Not affected	3	9.4	0.09	5
Total	32	100.0		

Note: *Weighted Index is calculated on a Five Point scale with weights assigned as: To very great extent = 5; To great extent= 4; To some extent= 3; To a little extent= 2; Not affected= 1.

The arrival of Internet and full text online databases has posed a challenge to publishing industry. Maximum i.e. 50 per cent (16) distributors (rank 1) (Table 3.29) have reported that their business has been affected 'To some extent' by electronic information whereas 15.6 per cent(5) each have stated that their business has been affected 'To a very great extent' and 'To a little extent'. According to 9.4 per cent (3) each, distributors think that their business has been affected 'To a great extent' and there is no impact of IT on their business.

Analysis of question nos. 19-20, regarding financial constraints the distributors face in conducting their business, 75 per cent (24) distributors have replied in affirmative. Only 8 (25%) per cent distributors have stated that they do not face any financial difficulty. Regarding the extent of financial difficulty, all the 24 distributors (100%) have stated that they 'mostly' face the financial constraints.

In response to question 20 regarding procurement of books, most of the distributors have suggested that orders should be placed well in advance with the vendors so to give distributors sufficient time for procuring library material. They have also stated the need for providing complete bibliographical information while placing the orders. Distributors have also suggested that books received on approval by libraries from their suppliers should be cleared within reasonable time so that vendors may clear their account with their distributors. They have also suggested that libraries should clear the bills of suppliers within a certain definite time frame. All the distributors have emphasised the need for adhering to the GOC rates of discount and conversion rates of foreign currency.

Distributors have suggested that there should be constant and regular interaction between librarians, publishers, distributors and vendors so that matter of mutual concern may be discussed and clarified.

PART 4

Analysis of Responses Received from Vendors

The complex process of handling library materials from the point when they leave the publisher to the point when they are acquired by a library can not be performed without vendors. Much of the order fulfillment by publishers depends upon the vendor. Libraries have to make selection of vendors very carefully. A separate questionnaire (Appendix 4) was developed for vendors to understand how they function. 100 questionnaires were distributed among library vendors out of which 55 were received back. The data obtained from these responses is analysed in following tables.

Profile of the Firms

In this section questions related to the profile of the vendors' firms have been analysed.

Table 4.1

Nature of Firms

Nature	*No. of Responses*	*Per cent*
Proprietorship	50	90.9
Partnership	5	9.1
Private Company	0	0.0
Total	55	100.0

90.9 per cent (50) (Table 4.1) vendors are proprietors of the firms whereas remaining 9.1 per cent (5) are doing their business on partnership basis.

Table 4.2

Academic Qualifications

Qualification	*No. of Responses*	*Per cent*
10+2	17	30.9
Graduate	38	69.1
Post Graduate	0	0
Total	55	100.0

Data pertaining to academic qualifications reveals (Table 4.2) that 69.1 per cent (38) vendors are graduates while 30.9 per cent (17) are holding 10+2 qualification only. It can be said that the requirement of the business is to meet educated people or group of people who has proper understanding of library requirements. If a supplier holds good academic qualification, he is likely to understand the needs of the customers in a much better manner.

Table 4.3

Period of Establishment

Period	*No. of Responses*	*Per cent*
1947-60	1	1.8
1961-1970	14	25.5
1971-1980	22	40.0
1981-1990	7	12.7
1991-2000	11	20.0
Total	55	100.0

40 per cent(22) vendors (Table 4.3) started their work related to supply of books during 1971-80 while 25.5 per cent (14) came into existence during 1961-70. 20 per cent (11) firms have been established during 1991-2000. None existed

before 1947. It can be said that establishment of firms has been fairly keeping pace with the establishment of libraries and publishing houses.

Table 4.4
Strength of Staff

Strength	*No. of Responses*	*Per cent*
Upto 5	28	50.9
Upto 7	10	18.2
Upto 10	17	31.0
Total	55	100.0

The data reveals that 50.9 per cent (28) vendors (Table 4.4) have upto 5 staff members while 18.2 per cent (10) have upto 7 employees. Highest number of staff is upto 10 in 31 per cent (17) cases. Thus majority of them have 7 or less staff members.

Table 4.5
Annual Turnover

Turnover (in Rs.)	*No. of Responses*	*Per cent*
100000- 500000	11	20.0
500001- 1000000	3	5.4
1000001-1500000	5	9.1
1500001-2000000	9	16.4
2000001-2500000	12	21.8
2500001-3500000	5	9.1
3500001-5000000	4	7.3
5000001-7500000	6	10.9
Total	55	100.0

The data relating to annual turnover of vendors (Table 4.5) shows a wide variance ranging from 1 lakh to 75 lakh. 20 per cent (11) vendors have an annual turnover Rs. 1 lakh to 5 lakh whereas 10.9 per cent (6) vendors are in the highest group of Rs. 50 to 75 lakh. The highest percentage of vendors i.e. 21.1 per cent (12) who have an annual turnover of Rs. 20 to 25 lakh. Majority of vendors have an annual turnover ranging between 1 lakh and 20 lakh.

Procurement and Supply of Books

Vendors play a very important role in meeting day to day requirements of the libraries. In this section questions related to their method of procuring books for onward supply to libraries, issues related to time taken to fulfill orders and discount have been analysed.

Table 4.6

Subjects and Kinds of Document Supplied

Subject and Kinds	*No. of Responses*	*Per cent*
Social Sciences and Humanities	20	36.4
Management	11	20.0
Scientific/ Technical	17	30.9
Government Publications and Reports	6	10.9
Audio-Visual Material	1	1.8
Total	55	100.0

A fairly large majority (36.4%) (20) of vendors (Table 4.6) supply social science and humanities documents followed by 30.9 per cent (17) vendors supplying scientific and technical books and 20 per cent (11) vendors dealing in management books. 10.9 per cent (6) deal in government documents and research reports.There is 1 vendor (1.8%) who supplies audio-visual material. Though most of the vendors have their respective specialization, but there is lot of overlapping when it comes to actually supplying material to libraries.

Table 4.7

Main Sources of Getting Books

Source	*No. of Responses*	*Per cent*
Distributors-Indian	24	43.6
Distributors-Foreign	14	25.
Local Publishers	17	30.9
Total	55	100.0

The data reveals that 43.6 per cent (24) vendors (Table 4.7) take Indian books from distributors while 25.5 per cent (14) take foreign books from distributors. About one third of vendors forming 30.9 per cent (17) get books from direct from publishers and supply directly to libraries.

In response to question no. 3, regarding preference to sell books available locally only, 100 per cent (55) vendors have stated in negative.

Table 4.8

Average Time Taken to Procure Books

Time	*No. of Responses*	*Per cent*
2-3 days	2	3.6
Upto 1 week	10	18.2
4 weeks	17	31.0
6 weeks	8	14.0
8 weeks	18	32.3
Total	55	100.0

The data indicates that 3.6 per cent (2) vendors (Table 4.8) take 2-3 days' time for supplying books. This is in case of local Indian books or foreign books which are readily available in local market. In case of foreign books the procurement time varies between 4 weeks to 8 weeks. Maximum of number of vendors i.e. 32.3 per cent (18) have mentioned 8 weeks time while 31 per cent (17)have stated that they take 4 weeks time. The procurement time also varies from publisher to publisher. Some publishers have the tendency to accumulate the orders to save handling charges which leads to delay.

Table 4.9

Average Discount Received

Discount	*No. of Responses*	*Per cent*
20 per cent	1	1.8
20+5 per cent	6	10.9
25 per cent	9	16.4
30 per cent	14	25.5
33 per cent	13	23.6
40 per cent	12	21.8
Total	55	100.0

The data related to discount received by vendors reveals that 25.5 per cent (14) (Table 4.9) vendors receive 30 per cent discount whereas 23.6 per cent (13) get 33 per cent discount followed by 21.8 per cent (12) vendors who get 40 per cent discount. This is in case of Indian publications. There are 10.9 per cent (6) vendors in the category of 20+5 per cent and 16.4 per cent (9) vendors who are getting 25 per cent. This is in case publishers like McGraw-Hill International and Sage publication who are very conservative in their discount rates. Thus discount varies between 20% and 40% depending upon various factors.

Table 4.10

Approval Period Granted

Approval	*No. of Responses*	*Per cent*
4 weeks	32	58.2
6 weeks	10	18.2
8 weeks	13	23.6
Total	55	100.0

According to 58.2 per cent (32) vendors (Table 4.10) they get 4 weeks as approval time from distributors while 18.2 per cent (10) get 6 weeks time as approval period. Maximum period of approval is 8 weeks as stated by 23.6 per cent (13) vendors. Thus, there is substantial variation between approval period granted to different vendors. Interaction with vendors has also revealed that variation is largely in case of Indian publications.

Table 4.11

Kinds of Problems with Publishers and Distributors

Problems	*No. of Responses*	*Per cent*
Varying discounts	5	9.1
Demand advance payments	22	40.0
Approval period varies	8	14.5
Supply against cash	10	18.2
Offer low discount	10	18.2
Do not take back the unsold books	0	0.0
Charge higher prices	0	0.0
Any other	0	0.0
Total	55	100.0

In response to the question regarding problems faced by vendors (Table 4.11), maximum percentage of (40 per cent) (22) vendors have stated the problem of demand of advance payments. Small vendors are not in position to afford heavy advance payments due to which they are not able to fulfill the orders. According to 18.2 per cent (10) vendors each, they have to make cash purchases and discounts rates are also comparatively low whereas according to 14.5 per cent (8) there is problem of variation in approval period which they have to face. All these problems have adverse impact on the collection building activities of libraries.

Table 4.12

Number of Libraries Where Books Supplied

Number	*No. of Responses*	*Per cent*
Between 1-5	9	16.4
Between 6-10	12	21.8
Between 11-15	15	27.3
Between 16-20	14	25.5
Between 21-25	5	9.1
Total	55	100.0

It is an open-ended question and responses have been grouped accordingly (Table 4.12). The number of libraries which are supplied books by a vendor vary between 1 to 25. Maximum i.e. 27.3 per cent (15)vendors supply books to libraries ranging from 11 to 15, followed by 25.5 per cent (14) vendors supply books to 16-20 libraries. The maximum number of libraries covered are between 21 to 25. The number of vendors who have stated this category are 9.1 per cent (5). Majority of vendors supply books to libraries ranging between 5-20 libraries.

Table 4.13

Average Discount Given to Libraries

Discount	*Indian Books*		*Foreign Books*	
	No. of Responses	*Per cent*	*No.of Responses*	*Per cent*
10 per cent	15	27.3	26	47.2
15 per cent	28	52.5	21	38.1
20 per cent	12	20.2	8	14.5
Total	55	100.0		

In respect of Indian books, 27.3 per cent (15) vendors (Table 4.13) are giving GOC rate of discount (i.e. 10 per cent) whereas 52.5 per cent (28) vendors give 15 per cent discount. 20.2 per cent (12)vendors are offering 20 per cent discount. The discount given to libraries on Indian books vary but majority of vendors give 15% discount. For foreign books, maximum number of vendors i.e. 26 (47.2%) give 10 per cent discount while 21 vendors (38.1 %) give 15 per cent discount. The highest discount is 20 per cent mentioned by 8 respondents (14.5 %) vendors.

Table 4.14

Time Taken by Libraries to Finalise Orders

Time	*No. of Responses*	*Per cent*
Upto one week	0	0.0
Upto two weeks	0	0.0
Upto three weeks	0	0.0
Upto four weeks	13	23.6
Upto six weeks	7	12.7
Eight weeks	24	43.6
More than eight week	11	20.0
Total	55	100.0

In response to question 8, regarding discount, 100 per cent (55) vendors have stated that the percentage of discount depends upon type of publisher and number of copies ordered. Some publishers are liberal in their discounts while others are very conservative.

The time taken by libraries to finalize orders varies from four weeks to more than eight weeks time (Table 4.14). This is in case of books brought on approval basis by the vendors to the libraries. Highest number of vendors i.e. 43.6 per cent (24) are in the 8 weeks category while 23.6 per cent (13)have stated four weeks time. According to 20 per cent vendors (11) libraries are taking more than 8 weeks time to finalize orders which is definitely very long. The delay largely takes place due to highly bureaucratic system which some libraries adopt in purchase related matters. This is a serious impediment in the way of collection development activities.

Table 4.15

Impact of Delay in Finalising Orders on Business

Impact	*No. of Responses*	*Per cent*
Yes	45	81.8
No	10	18.2
Total	55	100.0

According to 81.8 per cent (45)vendors (Table 4.15) the delay in finalizing orders affects their business. Only 18.2 per cent (10)vendors have stated that it does not affect their business. These are large firms which have the capacity to bear delay in orders.

According to 24.5 per cent (11)vendors (Table 4.16) their business is affected 'To a very great extent' while 31.2 (14) per cent vendors have indicated that business is affected 'To a great extent'. According to 28.8 per cent (13) vendors their business is affected 'To some extent' whereas 13.3 per cent

(6)vendors have stated their business is affected 'To a very little extent' by delay in finalizing orders by libraries. Thus, business is affected to a great extent due to delay in finalising orders.

Table 4.16

Extent to Which Business is Affected

Extent	*No. of Responses*	*Per cent*	*WI**	*Rank*
To a very great extent	11	24.5	1.22	2
To a great extent	14	31.2	1.24	1
To some extent	13	28.8	0.86	3
To little extent	6	13.3	0.26	4
To very little extent	1	2.2	0.02	5
Total	45	100.0		

Note: *Weighted Index is calculated on a Five Point scale with weights assigned as : To very great extent = 5; To great extent= 4; To some extent= 3; To little extent= 2; To very little extent= 1.

Table 4.17

Frequency of Books supplied by Your Firm Rejected, Others' Selected?

Response	*No. of Responses*	*Per cent*	*WI*	*Rank*
Always	0	0.0	0.0	5
Mostly	5	9.1	0.36	3
Sometimes	21	38.1	1.45	1
Rarely	19	21.8	0.69	2
Never	10	18.2	0.18	4
Total	55	100.0		

Note: *Weighted Index is calculated on a Five Point scale with weights assigned as : Always = 5; Mostly= 4; Sometimes= 3; Rerely= 2; Never= 1.

According to 9.1 per cent (5) (Table 4.17) vendors such cases take place with them 'mostly' that their books are rejected while same books supplied by other vendors are approved whereas according to 38.1 per cent (21) vendors such cases take place only 'sometimes'. According to 21.8 (19) per cent of total vendors such problem comes only 'rarely'. There are only 18.2 per cent (10) vendors who have never faced such situation. It can be said the problem is of peripheral nature and does not take place as a routine matter. Sometimes librarians are biased in their selection. A vendor who provides relatively better service does need some support.

In response to question 12 regarding reaction of vendors in such cases, all 45 vendors (100%) have stated that they registered protest with the librarians.

Table 4.18

Tendency of Selling Only High Profit Titles

Response	*No. of Responses*	*Per cent*
Strongly agree	15	27.3
Agree	11	20.0
Neither agree nor disagree	7	12.7
Do not agree	13	23.6
Strongly disagree	9	16.4
Total	55	100.0

There is a strong tendency in some bookseller (Table 4.18) to sell only high profit titles. They do not bring to libraries low priced books due to which libraries are sometimes deprived of good material. When this question was posed to library suppliers, highest i.e. 27.3 per cent (15) of them 'Strongly agree' whereas 20 per cent (11) 'Agree'. 12.7 per cent (7) vendors 'Neither agree nor disagree' while 23.6 per cent (13) vendors 'Do not agree' with the statement. 16.4 per cent vendors 'Strongly disagree'. It can be said that there is a fairly mixed response on the part of vendors to the question but a large percentage (47.3%) of vendors agree that the problem exists.

Table 4.19

Preference to Take Direct Faculty Recommendations

Prefer	*No. of Responses*	*Per cent*
Yes	37	67.3
No	18	32.7
Total	55	100.0

67.3 per cent vendors (37) prefer (Table 4. 19) to get their books directly approved from concerned faculty members whereas 32. 7 per cent (18) vendors have stated that they do not favour getting their books directly approved by faculty members.

Table 4.20

Reasons for Direct Faculty Recommendations

Reasons	*No. of Responses*	*Per cent*
Requirements known on the spot	16	43.2
Evaluation of stock	7	19.0
Getting suggestions	6	16.2
They recommend us to other customers	0	0.0
Direct recommendation saves time	8	21.6
Any other reason	0	0.0
Total	37	100.0

According to 43.2 per cent (43) vendors (Table 4.20) they prefer to take direct recommendation as requirements are known whereas 19 per cent (7) vendors have indicated that their stock gets evaluated on the spot. It is followed by 16.2 per cent (6) vendors according to whom it helps them to get suggestions for new books and improves their business prospects. 21. 6 per cent (8) vendors have indicated that it saves their time as books get recommended on the spot.

Table 4.21

Ability to Supply All the Ordered Books

Response	*No. of Responses*	*Per cent*
Yes	37	67.3
No	18	32.7
Total	55	100.0

67.3 per cent (37) vendors (Table 4.21) have stated that they are able to supply all the books for which they receive the orders whereas 32.7 per cent (8) have expressed their inability in supply all the requisite books.

Table 4.22

Reasons for Not Supplying All Books

Reasons	*No. of Responses*	*Per cent*
Publishers respond late	4	22.2
Lack of complete details	4	22.2
books are out of print	3	16.6
Custom clearance takes time	2	11.7
Any other reason	5	27.7
Total	18	100.0

According to 22.2 per cent (4) vendors, foreign publishers (Table 4.22) respond very late for fulfilling the orders while an equally 22.2 per cent (4) vendors have stated that there is lack of complete bibliographical details. 16.6 per cent (3) vendors have indicated that books are out of print while according to 11.7 per cent (2) vendors, custom clearance takes long time due to which sometimes they fail to fulfill the orders in time. 27.7 per cent vendors (5) have cited different reasons like cease of publication, merger and acquisition of publishing house.

In response to question 16, regarding type of titles being supplied by vendors to libraries, 40 per cent (22) vendors have stated that they supply only Indian books while 54.5 per cent (30) vendors supply only foreign books. Remaining 5.5 (3) vendors supply only selected titles in their specialised area.

Table 4.23

Declining Capacity of Special Libraries to Buy Books

Response	*No. of Responses*	*Per cent*
Yes	23	41.8
No	32	58.2
Total	55	100.0

A majority of 58.2 per cent (32) vendors (Table 4.23) have stated that buying capacity of special libraries is not going down whi le 41.8 per cent (23) vendors have agreed that the buying capacity of special libraries has gone down.

Table 4.24

Reasons for Decreasing Paying Capacity

Reasons	*No. of Responses*	*Per cent*
Rising cost of publications	3	13.0
Budgetary cuts in libraries	5	21.8
IT leading to more resource sharing	4	17.3
Increase in foreign exchange rates	11	47.9
Total	23	100.0

As vendors interact with librarians on day to day basis, a question was asked to from them about reasons for decreasing paying capacity (Table 4.24). According to 13 per cent (3) vendors the reason for decreasing buying capacity is rising cost of publications whereas 21.8 per cent (5) vendors have indicated that there are budgetary cuts in libraries. According to 17.3 per cent (4) vendors demand for publication is decreasing due to increased resources sharing among librarians due to application of IT. However, highest percentage of vendors i.e. 47.9 per cent (11) have stated that buying capacity of libraries is declining due to rising conversion value of foreign currencies.

Table 4.25

Dealing in Electronic Formats

Response	*No. of Responses*	*Per cent*
Yes	7	13.1
No	34	86.9
Total	55	100.0

Data in Table 4.25 reveals that 86.9 per cent (34) vendors do not deal in electronic formats. Only 13.1 per cent (7) vendors have given answer in affirmative. These are basically data base vendors who deal in information related products. Thus, it can be said that there is shortage of vendors dealing in electronic formats.

Table 4.26

Effect of Electronic Formats on Business

Effect	*No. of Responses*	*Per cent*
Yes	11	20.0
No	44	80.0
Total	55	100.0

Increased use of electronic formats in the form of CD-ROM databases, online databases and information available through Internet has a direct bearing on the sale of hard copy version. Even books are now being printed electronically. According to 20 per cent vendors (11) (Table 4.26) this has affected the supply of books whereas 80 per cent (44)vendors have responded in negative. The impact of IT is more visible in libraries situated in big cities due to availability of supporting infrastructure. There too it is partial and on supplementary basis. There is a long way to go before IT based products are able to substantially replace printed books and journals in libraries.

Table 4.27

Extent to Which Business Affected

Extent	*No. of Responses*	*Per cent*	*WI**	*Rank*
To a very great extent	0	0.0	0.0	3
To great extent	7	63.6	0.50	1
To some extent	4	36.4	0.21	2
To Little extent	0	0.0	0	3
To very little extent	0	0.0	0	3
Total		55		100.0

Note: *Weighted Index is calculated on a Five Point scale with weights assigned as: To very great extent = 5; To great extent= 4; To some extent= 3; To little extent= 2; To very little extent= 1.

The analysis of data relating to impact of electronic formats reveals that 63.6 per cent (7) (Table 4.27) vendors have stated that their business has been affected 'To a great extent' while remaining 36.4 per cent (4) vendors think that their business has been affected 'To a little extent' by the electronic formats. Thus it can be concluded that electronic formats have still not been able to influence substantially the business of library suppliers.

Payments and Discounts

For maintaining efficiency in supplying books to libraries and fulfilling library requirements in time, it is also necessary that vendors get the payment of their bills in time. In this section responses to the questions related to payments have been analysed.

The situation about payments to book suppliers is not very satisfactory in most of the libraries. 38.2 per cent (21) vendors (Table 4.28) have indicated that it takes about 3 months to get payments. While according to 18.2 per cent (10) vendors it takes more than 6 months' time to get payments of their bills. According to 30.9 per cent (17) vendors, it takes 4 to 6 weeks time to get payments. The shortest time for getting payments has been mentioned by 10.9 per cent vendors (6) which is 2 to 4 weeks. 1 vendor (1.8%) has even mentioned 1 year's time. In majority of cases, it takes about 3 months on average. Libraries must look into the payment problems so that book suppliers are not made to wait for long which has an adverse impact on book supply process.

Table 4.28

Time Taken to Get the Payments

Time	*No. of Responses*	*Per cent*
2 to 4 weeks	6	10.9
4 to 8 weeks	17	30.9
About 3 months	21	38.2
About six months	10	18.2
About 1 year	1	1.8
Total	55	100.0

Table 4.29

Reasons for Not Getting Timely Payment

Reasons	*No. of Responses*	*Per cent*
Lack of sufficient funds	14	25.5
Bills held up for lot of clarifications	17	32.0
Finance branch puts objections	12	21.8
For claiming extra postal and handling charges	7	12.7
For not producing publishers price proofs	5	9.0
Total	55	100.0

According to 25.5 per cent (14) vendors (Table 4.29) there is lack of sufficient funds in libraries to release payment in time. Whereas 32 per cent (17) vendors think that in library itself bills are held up for a very long time for lot of clarifications which delays the payments. It is followed by 21.8 per cent (12) vendors who have indicated that finance branch put unnecessary objections in passing the bills. According to 12.7 per cent (7) vendors, the delay takes place for claiming extra postal and handling charges while according to 9 per cent (5) vendors payment is delayed for not producing publishers price proofs. First three reasons as given in the table are the main reasons for not getting timely payments. Librarians should expedite payment by getting in touch with vendors to get objections removed and clarifications given.

Linkages between Libraries and Book Suppliers

There exists regular interaction between libraries and book suppliers. It is important that cordial professional relations are maintained between the two as they have to depend on each other for their requirements. Questions related to mutual relationship were asked in the questionnaire and the responses have been analysed in Tables 4.30-4.36.

Table 4.30
Criteria on Which Special Libraries Select You As Library Supplier

Criteria	*No. of Responses*	*Per cent*
Good service	11	20.0
Quality of books	12	21.8
High discount	10	18.2
Providing quick feedback	2	3.6
Maintaining punctuality	20	36.4
Establishing cordial rapport	0	0.0
Any other reason	0	0.0
Total	55	100.0

According to 20 per cent (11)vendors (Table 4.30), they have been chosen on the basis of good service which they provide to libraries. Another 21.8 per cent (12) have stated that quality of their books is the reason of their being chosen while 18.2 per cent vendors regard discount factor responsible for their selection. Highest percentage of vendors i.e. 36.4 per cent (20) have indicated that they maintain punctuality in fulfilling orders and library requirements due to which they have been chosen as suppliers. In the order of ranking the criteria appear to be maintaining punctuality, quality of books and good service in descending order.

According to 34.5 per cent (19) vendors (Table 4.31) their relationship with librarians is 'very good' while 38.2 per cent(21) vendors have described it as 'good'. The remaining 27.3 per cent (15) have indicated that their relationship with librarians is average. Right kind of relationship between librarians and the suppliers is very much desirable for timely supply of books and other library material. Personal rapport between suppliers and librarians always helps in getting timely procurement.

Table 4.31

Nature of Your Relationship With:

Relation	*Librarians*		*Publishers*		*Distributors*	
	No. of Responses	*%*	*No. of Responses*	*%*	*No. of Responses*	*%*
Very good	19	34.5	37	67.3	29	52.7
Good	21	38.2	15	27.3	12	21.8
Average	15	27.3	3	5.5	13	23.6
Not Good	0	0	0	0	1	1.8
Bad	0	0	0	0	0	
Total	55	100.0				

With regard to their relationship with publishers 67.3 per cent (37) vendors have indicated that their relationship with publishers is 'very good' while as per 27.3 per cent (15) vendors, it is in "good" category. According to remaining 5.5 per cent (3) vendors their relationship with publishers is just average. This relationship is essentially in respect of Indian publishers. Right kind of relationship between vendors and the publishers is very much desirable for timely supply of books and other library material.

In response to a question regarding the relationship between vendors and distributors 52.7 per cent (29) vendors have indicated that their relationship with distributors is very good while 21.8 per cent (12) vendors have indicated it to be 'good' whereas 23.6 per cent (13) vendors have described the relationship as average. 1 vendor (1.8 per cent) has described the relationship as 'not good'. It can be concluded that majority of vendors have very good relations with publishers and distributors. On the other hand a high percentage (38.2) of vendors have good relation with librarians.

Table 4.32

Discrimination in Placing Orders

Response	*No. of Responses*	*Per cent*	*WI*	*Rank*
Always	8	14.5	0.72	2
Mostly	9	16.4	0.65	3
Sometimes	24	43.6	1.30	1
Rarely	12	21.8	0.43	4
Never	2	3.6	0.03	5
Total	55	100.0		

Note: *Weighted Index is calculated on a Five Point scale with weights assigned as : Always = 5; Mostly= 4; Sometimes= 3; Rarely= 2; Never= 1.

Librarians are often accused of discriminating between various vendors while giving confirmed orders. The analysis of data related to this question reveals that according to 14.5 per cent (8) vendors (Table 4.32) librarians 'always' discriminate between various suppliers whereas 16.4 per cent (9) have stated that discrimination is 'mostly' there. Highest percentage of vendors i.e. 43.6 (24) has indicated that librarians discriminate 'sometimes'. According to 21.8 per cent vendors the cases of discrimination are 'rare'. Only 3.6 per cent(2) vendors have stated that there is no discrimination at all by librarians.

This issue of discrimination is quite difficult to understand and a generalisation can not be made on the basis of few cases. At times there are very professional reason for not giving orders to a particular supplier in the larger interest of library services. However, it can be concluded that 30.9% vendors feel that there is always/mostly discrimination by librarians in placing orders. There is need to have a dialogue so that better understanding can be created.

Table 4.33

Discussion with Librarians on Following Issues

Issues	*No. of Responses*	*Per cent*
Problem of late payments	21	38.2
Fund position of library	10	18.2
Promotion of sales	19	34.5
Other professional matters	3	5.5
On forthcoming publications	2	3.6
Total	55	100.0

There is regular interaction between vendors and librarians on various matters. 38.2 per cent(21)vendors discuss problem (Table 4.33) related to payment of bills while 34.5 per cent (19) discuss matters related to promotion of sales. According to 18.2 per cent vendors (10) they also discuss funds position of libraries. 5.5 per cent (3)and 3.6 per cent (2) vendors have discussion on other professional matters and forthcoming publications respectively. It is a healthy sign that discussion takes place between librarians and vendors to resolve issues.

Table 4.34

Issues on which there has been Argument with Librarian

Issues	*No. of Responses*	*Per cent*
More discount than approved by GOC	10	18.2
Deducting of postage charges	3	5.5
For making delay in payments	15	27.3
For variation in conversion rate	9	16.4
For not fulfilling order	11	20.0
For not getting confirmed orders	7	12.7
Total	55	100.0

An attempt was has been made to find out potential areas of conflict between vendors and librarians through a question asked in the questionnaire. According to 32.7 per cent (18) vendors (Table 4.34) argument takes place between them and librarians for not fulfilling library orders whereas 27.3 per cent (15) vendors have indicated that rift takes place on matters related to late payments. According to 18.2 per cent (10) vendors discount is another area of conflict. Variation in conversion rates is one more area of conflict as indicated by 16.4 per cent (9) vendors. 12.7 per cent (7) vendors have stated that not getting confirmed orders is also an issue of conflict. The organization of vendors and librarians should sit together to resolve these conflicts. Hence, mutual discussion, GOC, Indian Library Association and publishers can play an important role.

Data in Table 4.35 reveals that according to 81.8 per cent (45) vendors there is no lack of co-operation between publishers and distributors whereas 17.2 per cent (10) distributors have reported that there is lack of co-operation between the two. 72.7 per cent vendors (40) have reported lack of co-operation between vendors and librarians.

Table 4.35

Lack of Co-operation Between Publishers, Distributors and Vendors

Response	*Publisher / Distributor*	*Distributor / Vendor*	*Librarian / Vendor*
Yes	45 (81.8)	30(54.5)	40(72.7)
No	10 (17.2)	25(44.5)	15(27.3)

In response to question 28 regarding the need for regular interaction between vendors, librarians publishers and distributors, all 55 (100 per cent) vendors have responded positively.

Table 4.36

Membership of Booksellers'Association

Response	*No. of Responses*	*Per cent*
Yes	32	58.2
No	23	41.8
Total	55	100.0

Maximum 58.2 per cent (32) (Table 4.35) vendors are members of booksellers association. Some libraries insist on taking books from only those suppliers who are members of Booksellers and Publishers Association. But this condition sometimes creates hurdle in getting service from a variety of sources.

Table 4.37

Professional Assistance provided by Association/ Federation in your Work

Response	*No. of Responses*	*Per cent*
Yes	19	59.3
No	13	40.7
Total	32	100.0

The analysis of data in table 4.36 reveals that 59.3 per cent (19) vendors have stated that the association does provide help in their business while 40.7 per cent (13) vendors have said that they do not get any assistance from the federation. According to views expressed during personal interaction with vendors, it has been found that booksellers' association has been quite active and vocal in matters related to conversion rates and discount. However, it has singularly failed to enforce uniform discount rates all over the country and booksellers are themselves violating the discount rates as fixed by GOC for their small gains. Booksellers' association needs to take up these issues seriously as it gives bad name to the profession itself.

In response to question 30, regarding impact of recent development in information technology and its impact on book suppliers 63.6 per cent (35) vendors have stated that these development have affected their business to 'some extent' while 26.4 per cent (20) vendors have stated that it has not affected their business.

Analysis of Question No 31

In response to above question related to suggestions by the vendors about procurement of library material, a majority of vendors have stated that librarians should be fair in their dealing while placing orders with the vendors. They have stated that librarians should take into account the services being rendered often without any income to vendors. The vendors have suggested that librarians should maintain due proportion among various suppliers while selecting the books brought on approval. Vendors have also stated that often librarians hold up books for months without any reason which badly affects their business.

Regarding supply of books, vendors have suggested that librarians should give them sufficient procurement time. Even in case of local books, they should be given 2-3 so as the vendors can meet their own schedule. The librarians should plan acquisition of library material well in advance.

Some vendors have also suggested that librarians should allow them to meet concerned faculty member/ researcher so that library material can be selected on the spot.

Regarding payments and discount, vendors have stated that books are not processed in library in time due to which bills are not cleared in time. They have suggested that vendors should get payment of their bills within 30 days time of submission of bills. In the matters of discount, some vendors have suggested that some librarians do not follow uniform rate of discount. They have suggested that all the vendors should be asked to supply books only on GOC terms.

Regarding improvement of relations between vendors

and librarians, vendors have suggested the need for fair play on the part of librarians. They have also stated that vendors should be treated with dignity.

With regard to their relations with distributors/ wholesalers, the vendors have stated that distributors too should follow uniform discount policy. They have also suggested the need for increasing approval period. The vendors have also made useful suggestion that distributors should be liberal if due to some reason their payment are delayed.

The analysis of above four questionnaires has revealed a lot of important information about the working of Indian special libraries and also of Indian book trade. It has enabled to draw several important findings on the basis of which recommendations have been made. In most of the cases information and opinion furnished by respondents has been very clear. It has enabled to put the issues related to acquisition of documents in special libraries in India in a proper perspective and draw important conclusion. The data furnished by librarians, publishers, distributors and vendors has also enabled to establish linkages between acquisition of documents and publishing trade.

10

Findings, Recommendations and Areas for Further Research

Introduction

The history of special libraries in India is linked with the establishment and growth of research institutions in the aftermath of Indian Independence. Since Independence in 1947, there has been steady expansion of research activities. The majority of special libraries came into being only during the last five decades or so. They are largely concentrated in major towns like Delhi, Mumbai, Kolkata, Chennai and Bangalore etc. The number of special libraries has been increasing steadily in the fields of social sciences and the humanities during the last two decades. However, this growth is at much faster pace in science and technology due to the growth of technical education.

Findings

The main findings of the research study, based on analysis and interpretation of data received, have been given below in four different parts based on respective questionnaires.

Findings Related to Libraries

Special libraries are fast catching up with the application of new information technologies in their operation and services. There is sizeable collection of new storage media like CD-ROMs and floppies (Table 1.7). They are also increasingly subscribing to electronic databases to meet users' information needs. Some of the libraries have separate budgetary allocation. Similarly audio-visual material is also finding its importance as an alternate learning and teaching aid. There is no separate allocation for maps and atlases (Table 1.12).

As far as budget for library material is concerned, there is wide variation and it is not possible to make any generalisation in this regard (Tables 1.9-1.11).

It has been observed that budget allocation in terms of amount of money is sizeable, it is the rising cost of library material which leads to its insufficiency. When sufficient budget is not available, special libraries are increasingly depending upon inter-library loans to meet users' requirements. (Table 1.13).

A substantial majority of special libraries have written collection development policies to guide them in their quest for developing need-based library material (Table 1.14). All responding 135 libraries do follow some policy informally in their collection building programme (Table 1.15). These collection development policies are revised from time to time to incorporate required changes (Table 1.16). It has been found that most of the special libraries have well defined and clear cut aims and objectives pertaining to development of collection (Table 1.19).

The findings reveal that well known authors have top most priority in terms of ranking, followed by faculty recommendations. Well known publishers are third in ranking while scholarly publications have got 4th rank. (Table 1.20). Data in Table 1.21 reveals that despite the fact that electronic formats are gaining fast acceptability in the market and library, paper format still constitutes the preferred choice as indicated by 96.3 per cent (130) libraries. There are only 3.7 per cent (5) librarians who have opted for electronic format as their first choice. No preference has been given for microforms. It clearly establishes the precedence of hard copy over soft copy version or electronic format. Although, there is a high acceptance for electronic source but paper form is still most popular (Table 1.21).

Libraries use several sources to identify new material and a large number of them have access to online electronic sources. There is heavy involvement of faculty members in this exercise. Special libraries are also increasingly purchasing various library material from online vendors though not to a large extent (Tables 1.22-1.23). This is largely due to the fact that online vendors do not provide services similar to those being provided by traditional library suppliers. The ranking order of the sources used for book identification and selection of library material reveals that faculty members' recommendations have highest ranking followed by books received on approval basis. Booksellers' list and online databases have 3rd and 4th rankings respectively. Standard bibliographies, publishers' catalogues and book reviews have lower ranks in order. The selection of documents is largely done by concerned faculty members, library committee and head of the organisations. As far as librarians' role in approval of library material is concerned, it is not confined to merely to preparing approval lists but there are substantial number of cases where they have recommendatory powers (57.8%), largely because of their first hand knowledge of users' requirements. (Tables 1.26 to 1.28).

In most of the libraries documents are procured on approval basis though there are a large number of libraries which acquire material on confirmed order basis only. This shows the well defined nature of their requirements (Table 1.30). It happens largely in libraries attached to scientific and industrial institutions having R&D programmes.

Non-print material is an important part of library collections. There are reliable and well established booksellers available for the supply of books and periodicals, but there are very few suppliers of non-print materials. The lack of comprehensive and up-to-date selection tools for non-print material further adds to the problem of libraries. A majority of non-print materials still comes from abroad. Majority of libraries have got them listed with vendors to keep themselves up-to-date and informed about the availability of non-print material like audio-video cassettes and databases on CD-ROMs.

As a channel for acquiring library materials, vendors have occupied first rank (1.32).

As far as criteria for selection of book supplier for the supply of library material is concerned, service provided by vendors has been found to be the most important criteria followed by timely procurement (Table 1.33).

One important finding of the study is that in majority of libraries, there exists substantial vendor-wise variation in spending their budget amount. It depends upon the performance and service provided (Table 1.37). Libraries place order with suppliers whom they consider best possible supplier for that particular order.

The study has revealed that there is lot of failure and delay in fulfilling the library orders by the suppliers (Table 1.41). This is largely true in cases where library requirements are small and profit margin is not very high.

In majority of the cases librarians themselves are sending booksellers directly to faculty members/researchers for getting books recommended as it saves the time of library staff (Table 1.45-1.46).

There exist a strong tendency among booksellers to push high margin books (Tables 1.50-1.51). This tendency has an adverse impact on library collection development process. The library is deprived of cheap but valuable material which booksellers do not bring to the notice of librarians.

Majority of the libraries subscribe journals through subscription agencies. Placement of single order and easy renewal are two factors revealed for this (Tables 1.56-1.57), despite librarians having problems with them. Librarians regularly face the problem of missing issues and also not getting refunds for missing issues. But librarians do not usually change their subscription agency as the problem is almost universal (Table 1.58-1.59).

Electronic journals are not still very popular. Most of the libraries subscribe journals in traditional paper format only. There are several reasons for this tendency but primarily the prohibitively subscription costs act as major handicap (Tables1.61-1.63).

Findings Related to Publishers

Most of the publishing houses are privately owned firms. The process of corporatisation in Indian publishing is very slow and there are only few companies. Most of the publishing houses are employing on an average 5 to 10 persons (Tables 2.1, 2.3).

There are only few publishers dealing in non-print materials (Table 2.6).

Quality of publication is the most important criteria for fixing the prices of publications (Table 2.8). In majority of cases, authors are not consulted (Table 2.9). In majority of cases publishers evaluate the manuscripts on their own (Table 2.13) as most of them do not have any editorial assistance available to them. This obviously has an adverse impact on the quality of publications.

All publishers face difficulties in accepting assignment for publication as they face financial difficulties. They need assistance by government in the form of loans (Table 2.16).

The discount offered by publishers to wholesalers and vendors is almost same. Maximum discount on Indian publications is 40 per cent (Table 2.18-2.19). However the discount offered to libraries is not at par with vendors and wholesalers (Table 2.23).

Majority of publishers do not supply books directly to libraries (Table 2.22).

There does not exist any effective national level distribution network and a sizeable number of publishers (40%) are not able to sell their books in all major cities (Table -2.20-2.21).

The demand for books in special libraries is decreasing. This is due to increased resource sharing and also emphasis on electronic formats in these libraries (Table 2.26-2.27).

To meet the rising cost of foreign publications, several Indian publishers are entering into agreement with these publishers to bring out low priced Indian reprints. There is lot of problem in getting these rights primarily because foreign publishers are demanding heavy advances. Moreover, they do not grant rights for latest editions (Table 2.29).

Several Indian publishers are increasingly exploring foreign markets for their publications particularly in African countries and in Indian sub continent (Table 2.31).

Majority of the publishers have an annual export turnover of less than Rs. 10 lakh (Table 2.32).

Some of the above information has also been supplemented and confirmed during the personal interaction with the publishers. Though in most of the cases relations between librarians and publishers are of professional nature but in some cases librarians are also biased in their dealings. Several publishers stated that often librarians look for favours while placing their orders or getting their books approved in their libraries (Table 2.34).

Findings Related to Distributors

Most of the distributors (53.1%) are employing upto 5 persons (Table 3.4). About annual turnover, there are only 3 (9.4%) distribution firms whose annual turnover exceeds

Rs. 1 crore (Table 3.5). There are 5 (15.6%) distributors who stock books of more than 1000 Indian publishers (Table 3.7). In case of foreign books, there are 2 distributors(6.3%) who stock books of 81 to 100 publishers (Table 3.8-9).

The average procurement time for foreign books is upto 6 weeks (Table 3.10). The highest discount received by distributors is 45 per cent (Table 3.12) and amount of discount depends upon type of publisher and number of copies ordered (Table 3.13).

One of the major problems in importing books from foreign as reported by distributors is that it needs heavy investment and high shipment charges (Table 3.15).

There are 5 distributors (15.6%) who supply books to more than 100 vendors (Table 3.16).

In 75% cases the approval period granted to vendors is 30 days (Table 3.17).

One main finding of this study is that distributors face conflict with the publishers on the matters related to discounts (Table 3.22).

75 per cent distributors do not supply books to libraries directly (Table 3.23).

Another finding is that most of the distributors are members of bookseller's association which provides professional assistance to them (Tables 3.27-28).

Findings Related to Vendors

Most of the book suppliers are having proprietorship. Regading academic qualifications, no one is holding post-graduate degree. More than 50 per cent vendors have upto 5 employees (Tables 4.1 to 4.2,4.4). The annual turnover ranges between Rs. 1 lakh to 7.5 lakh. The highest percentage of vendors (36.4%) supply social science and humanities books. Regarding formats, the lowest percentage (1.8%) supply audio-visual material (Table 4.5 to 4.6). The highest percentage of vendors (43.6%) take books from Indian distributors (Table 4.7). The highest percentage of discount received by 21.8 per cent Vendors is 40 per cent (Tables 4.9).

Maximum approval time granted by publishers and distributors to vendors is 4 weeks (Table 4.10). This is the time by which vendors have to settle their accounts. The biggest problem which vendors (40%) face is that distributors and publishers demand advance payment while registering the orders (Table 4.11).

The number of libraries to which books are supplied by vendors ranges from 5 to 25 (Table 4.12).

The majority of vendors do not follow GOC guidelines in the matter of discount given on books supplied to libraries. The highest rate of discount is 20% and is being given by 20.2 per cent vendors only (Tables 4.13).

According to 20 per cent vendors, libraries take more than eight weeks to finalize orders for books received by them on approval basis. According to 81.8 per cent vendors, the delay in finalizing orders affects their business and in 24.5 per cent cases it affects to a very great extent (Tables 4.14-16).

The unfair practice of getting books from one vendor on approval and actually buying from different vendor, according to maximum (38.1 per cent) vendors, happens only 'sometimes'. Thus we can say that librarians are mostly fair in their dealing with vendors in this matter (Table 4.17).

One interesting finding of this study is that 27.3 per cent vendors have strongly agreed to the statement that there is tendency among vendors to supply only high profit titles (Table 4.18).

There is also strong tendency among vendors to get the books directly approved from faculty members. As high as 67.3 per cent vendors prefer this practice and the reason for this tendency as given by a high percentage of vendors (43.2%) is that requirement is known on the spot (Table 4.19-4.20).

The main reasons for not fulfilling complete order of books are 'publishers respond late' and 'lack of complete details' (Table 4.22).

According to a majority of vendors, (58.2%) the capacity of special libraries to buy books has not declined (Table 4.23).

The electronic formats have yet not been able to make much dent. Only 13.1 per cent of them are dealing in this kind of format. According to an overwhelming majority of vendors (80%), electronic formats have not affected their business (Tables 4.25-4.26).

The payment situation is not satisfactory in libraries. As high as 38.2 per cent vendors have reported that it takes upto 3 months in getting payments of bills. The highest period as quoted by only 1 vendor is 1 year. Libraries need to improve the situation to get good service from vendors. The main reason for late payment, according to 32 per cent vendors is that bills are held up for lot of clarifications (Table 4.28-4.29).

The main reason for their selection for supplying books by librarians, according to vendors is maintaining punctuality in their library services (Table 4.30). The relationship between librarians and vendors, according to them is 'very good' (Table 4.31).

Findings Related to Hypotheses

Hypothesis 1: "The acquisition of documents in majority of special libraries is being fully guided by a written and comprehensive collection development policy".

Tables 1.14-1.19 are related to collection development policy. It reveals that majority of special libraries (71.9 per cent) have a written collection development policy as a tool to guide them while developing their library collection. Data analysis regarding consistency in following the prescribed collection development policy reveals that 62 per cent libraries (60) 'mostly' stick to it whereas 36 per cent libraries (35) 'always' follow their prescribed policy. Thus, the findings support the hypothesis.

Hypothesis 2: "Librarians are influenced by many variables while purchasing library material ranging from favourable reviews, to inclusion on a vendor's approval plan, to publishers advertising, to faculty request. They also order materials through many different channels; direct from publishers; through a varied number of booksellers, both wholesalers and retailers and from subscription agents".

The data in Table 1.22 reveals that Publishers' catalogues, as source for identifying, acquiring and building library collection, are used by more than 50 per cent (68) libraries. Booksellers send the select list of books to libraries to promote their sale. 73.3 per cent (99) libraries use these lists for identifying books. Standard bibliographies are used by 57 per cent libraries. Although book reviews are considered highly valuable sources for identifying the quality books but only 26.7 per cent (36) libraries refer to book reviews for selecting library books. Usually the time-lag between releasing of a title and publication of its review has a very wide gap, therefore the response for this category seems low. Almost all libraries receive books on approval basis which provides an opportunity to see and scan the books physically. Therefore It is regarded as most popular way of selecting books by 85.9 per cent (116) libraries.

Faculty members in special libraries tend to send their recommendations for library material, regularly providing a help to develop need- based collection. Therefore, their recommendations for selecting library material are regarded to be the most valuable in this regard. All the 135 responding libraries use this medium for identification and selection of material in the libraries.

Various Internet sites related to books such amazon.com, firstandsecond.com are being increasingly used as a book selection tool. However, only 58.5 per cent (79) libraries access this medium.

Majority of libraries i.e. 55.5 per cent (80) (Table 1.30) prefer receiving books on approval basis. This method gives them liberty to examine books physically and to select according to their respective requirements. 31.9 per cent (38) librarians have indicated that they acquire material against confirmed orders whereas in 12.6 per cent (17) libraries there is no fixed pattern for acquiring the library material (Table 1.30).

As per data in Table 1.32, booksellers (vendors) are the prime source of actual acquisition of books for libraries. Publishers and distributors are 2nd and 3rd choice for acquiring library books. Out of 55 per cent (74) libraries (Table 1.39) which have stated that they place orders directly with publishers for foreign books, it happens only when local sources decline to take orders. As far as acquisition of journals is concerned all libraries subscribe through agencies (Table 1.57). Thus the findings support the hypothesis.

Hypothesis 3: "Electronic formats and online databases, slowly but surely are becoming an important part of collection of special libraries".

Data in Table 1.7 indicates that more than 86 per cent (117) libraries have CD-ROMs and 7.4 per cent (10) libraries have more than 500 CD-ROMs. Given the fact that it is relatively a newer storage medium, CD-ROMs format is gaining fast acceptability in special libraries.

The collection of computer floppies ranges between 10 to 100 in 77.8 per cent (105) libraries. In 12.6 per cent (17) per cent libraries the number of floppies ranges between 200 to 400.

Separate budget is now being allocated for electronic formats (Table 1.12). Special libraries are also acquiring material from online vendors though in a limited way. Table 1.23 reveals that 29.6 per cent (40) libraries purchase library material from online vendors like amozon.com, fabmart.com or firstandsecond.com. Similarly data related to e-journals in Table 1.62 reveals that 30.4 per cent (41) libraries subscribe to journals in electronic format. Given the fact that electronic format is relatively a new medium, the percentage of libraries having access to e-journals is sizeable. Thus the findings support the hypothesis.

Hypothesis 4: "Special libraries are maintaining their traditional services and collections even as they use technology in new ways to deliver services and provide access to information on networks or through document delivery services".

Special libraries despite the availability of information in online and electronic formats are acquiring all traditional formats to a large extent (Table 1.21). Similarly special libraries are subscribing to large number of journals in paper format (Table 1.62).

It clearly establishes the precedence of hard copy over soft copy version or electronic format. Thus, the findings support the hypothesis.

Hypothesis 5: "Acquisition of documents in special library is dependent upon a strong book trade. Indian book trade has not been successful in fulfilling the requirements of special libraries for a need- based and up-to-date collection of library material".

According to data in Table 1.41, 53.5 per cent (72) librarians have stated that orders for Indian documents are fulfilled in upto 1 week's time. Maximum time taken for Indian documents is four weeks by 12.5 per cent (17) librarians. The time taken in fulfilling the orders in respect of foreign documents, has been mentioned as 1 week by 11.8 per cent (16) librarians. The maximum period has been mentioned as 12 weeks by 7.4 per cent (10) librarians. In case of non-supply of documents, 58.51 per cent (79) librarians have mentioned that upto 10 per cent orders are not fulfilled whereas 31.11 per cent librarians (42) have stated that upto 15 per cent orders remain unfulfilled. The highest percentage of unfulfilled orders is 20% as mentioned by 10.38 per cent (14) librarians.

According to data in Table 1.50, 51-9 per cent (70) librarians have stated that there is a tendency among booksellers to sell only high profit books. This tendency quite often deprives library of books which are cheap but of good reading. A majority of libraries, 57.8 per cent (78) have reported (Table 1.42) that vendors do not keep them informed if the fulfillment of orders is delayed.

Similarly, librarians face problems in acquisition of journals. According to 28.1 per cent (38) librarians, there is problem of missing issues, whereas 45.9 per cent (62) librarians have said that payments are not adjusted for missing issues. According to 12.6 per cent (17) librarians, there is no response to reminders (Table 1.58). This is a serious situation and affects the library services greatly. The data related to distribution of books (Table 2.20) reveals that that in 40 per cent cases (28) books do not reach all parts of the country. This is probably the biggest challenge before Indian book trade. There does not exist any national level distribution channel for supplying books at All India basis. This has serious implication on the publishing business as well as for collection development activities of libraries situated in remote areas or small towns. This problem is faced by distributors also. According to 21 per cent distributors (3), it is difficult to obtain non-local books. 50 per cent distributors(7) have stated that books are available against advance payment only which is again a serious handicap. In 29 per cent (4) cases, the approval period granted by publisher is very short on account of which distributors fail to obtain books and sell them in this short period (Table 3.21). Thus the findings support the hypothesis.

Hypothesis 6: "Publishing trade in India is a loosely organised, enterprise lacking both trained manpower and sufficient capital to run its operations."

A majority of the publishers 52.9 per cent (37) are the proprietors of their firms (Table 2.1). The data shows that most of the publishers are medium size enterprises not requiring incorporation. Similarly data provided by the publishers pertaining to the strength of staff reveals that in majority of the publishing houses i.e. 51 (72.9 per cent), it varies between 7-15 only. 7.1 per cent publishing houses (7) employ 25 people (Table 2.3). The data relating to annual turnover of publishing houses presents wide variation. For majority of the publishers i.e 71.4 per cent (50), it ranges between Rs. 20 Lakh to 75 Lakh (Table 2.4). There are only 4.3 per cent (3) publishers having total turnover of more than Rs. 5 crore . According to 65.7 per cent (46) publishers, they face financial difficulties while undertaking new publishing assignments (Table 2.16). For the existence of healthy publishing activities, need for regular inflow of funds is essential. This is especially important because incoming proceeds from sale, are relatively slow and money gets blocked for a very long time.

Most of the publishers do not have any editorial staff for evaluating the manuscripts. Majority of publishers i.e. 37.1 per cent (26) have indicated that they evaluate manuscripts themselves. The data, thus reveals, that ironically a majority of publishers neither have any editorial board nor they refer the manuscripts to subject experts for the evaluation of manuscripts. Thus, there is lack of trained manpower. This is a serious drawback of Indian publishing industry and is largely responsible for lack of quality publishing (Table 2.13).

Similarly, distributors face lot of problems in importing books from foreign publishers. According to 31.3 per cent (10), it requires lot of investments on the part of distributors and 21.9 per cent (Table 3.15) (7) have stated that shipment charges have gone up due to which they find it difficult to import books. As a result often they are handicapped by the lack of requisite finance. Situation is aggravated by the fact that there are no funding institutions for book trade. Thus, the findings support the hypothesis.

Recommendations

Building a need-based and up-to-date collection in special libraries involves relating the practice of librarianship with publishers and other book suppliers. Thus, without appropriate recognition of publishers and library suppliers to the library community on the part of librarians, this important link in the distribution network may be in serious trouble and could jeopardize the orderly and efficient flow of information from scholars to practitioners.

Based on the findings, the following recommendations are made:

Recommendations for Librarians

(i) Librarians expect library suppliers to be familiar with the programmes, policies and fiscal procedures and budget constraints in each of the libraries. They also expect that vendors should be aware of the vagaries of the publishing world and to serve as library's link to that market. In return vendors believe that librarians should reciprocate by managing their operation efficiently and objectively, and by being sensitive to vendors' needs for a return on their investment. For this purpose there is need for an increase in communication and dialogue among the publishers/vendors/librarians which can lead to creative solutions and better service.

(ii) Working at a time when fiscal resources are falling short, libraries need to enhance the quality of their services, using information technology in new ways to deliver services and provide access to information on networks or through document delivery services.

(iii) Managing budgets well and educating the users to perceive libraries and their services as essential to the institution are key survival skills for librarians. Effective public relations, communication and information on library services is part of this educational outreach. Libraries today also need to develop credibility in delivering services efficiently and to be pro-active in providing new services that other institutions or departments cannot or do not provide. Librarians need to anticipate customer needs for example, archiving of electronic materials.

(iv) Funding remains a key issue. The problems of continuing lack of resources in the face of increased volumes and costs of printed publications, and particularly the mounting pressure on book funds from serials, are now compounded by the extra demand to acquire new media. Collection Development should be geared to properly identified needs and must be responsive to the needs of the users. It should consider all information formats for inclusion.

(v) The acquisition of library material should be guided by a comprehensive written policy, developed with the advice and involvement of all library users so as to make process smooth and problem free by clarifying dimensions and limits of material being acquired.

(vi) Libraries increasingly need a collection development policy for electronic materials, paying particular attention to potential use.

(vii) Library institutions which have historically been responsible for providing access to printed information must adapt to new requirements and provide access to electronic media or they will be replaced by others as a primary source of information. New and expanded functions should include: access to electronic databases, online access to library resources, electronic referrals and access to resources in other libraries via networking.

(viii) Many vendors and librarians tend to develop personal relationships with one another for several reasons. Extra care should be taken to insure that those friendships do not lead to biased judgements.

(ix) Special libraries should co-ordinate their current collection development and acquisition activities and provide clearing houses for collection development information at national and international level.

(x) Programmes initiated by libraries to support bibliographic control should enlist the cooperation of publishers and also work together with paper manufacturers, the microfilming industry, the information technology industry and others to develop standards and implement them, and define software requirements that may serve to benefit libraries and publishers alike.

Recommendations for Book Trade

(i) Development of publishers' web sites can be a useful source for locating special material. Major subscription agents are slowly beginning to provide electronic journal information to libraries. Once relevant titles have been identified, selection criteria should follow the principles established for printed subscriptions, such as quality/peer-review, and relevance to research, teaching and learning. Freely available electronic journals have a zero subscription cost but they do have an upkeep cost once added to an electronic journal service.

(ii) The need exists for formation of an apex council of librarians, publishers, distributors and vendors at the national level to coordinate and discuss various common issues and problems related to supply of books, discount rates and timely payment of bills, encourage its members to establish and maintain bibliographic leadership by supplying bibliographic records for library and information service communities; promote the development and application of international bibliographic standards, (e.g., for machine-readable formats), encouraging international cooperation in this field through the establishment of international networks of bibliographic agencies;

(iii) Strengthening distribution network so as to extend the range and variety of information resources available throughout the country.

(iv) Government should recognise publishing trade as an industry and extend all facilities and privileges available to the industrial sector like loan from financial institutions.A separate financial corporation may be established for this purpose.

(v) Support should be provided to help establish a non profit international clearing house for publishers to register their business needs and ideas so as to allow publishers to introduce themselves to one another to explore the undertaking of collaborative business ventures.

(vi) Government should take strong steps to check piracy of publications and violation of copyrights.

(vii) Urgent improvement needs to be made in the infrastructure of the book trade to encourage independent indigenous publishers; development of an effective distribution system and use relevant technologies for the production of books.

(viii) GOC should be made a statutory body with due representation from all sections of libraries and book trade and its decisions pertaining to discount and conversion rates should be made legally binding both on book trade and libraries

Areas of Further Research

The findings of the study offer several new areas which could be the themes of further research. It will help to strengthen and validate the findings of the present study.

Following are some of the important areas in which further research is recommended:

(i) Given their disparate nature, acquiring special formats (non-print and electronic publications) is true test of a librarian in special library. It is an area which needs to be researched further in minute details.

(ii) Impact of electronic revolution on publishing trade has far reaching implications. This area needs to be looked into quite exhaustively.

(iii) The problems of acquisition of documents from foreign countries needs to be researched fully and comprehensively.

(iv) Development of a distribution mechanism to a point which makes procurement of foreign material easy.

(v) Library literature does not deal extensively with out-of-print market. Because print runs are comparatively short and publishers do not hold stocks for many years, problem is faced in finding recently out-of-print titles. A future researcher may look into this problem in depth.

(vi) Vendor performance study should be carried out to establish a methodology to measure the performance of vendors. Such study may develop measures for the performance of a vendor by type of material, location of vendor in terms of speed of order fulfillment.

(vii) Designing of an electronic national database and bibliography of all types of library material with complete details of their availability.

(viii) Social and interpersonal processes affecting the acquisition of documents.

(ix) Principles of identifying, selecting, acquiring, managing, and evaluating information resources.

Bibliography

Aguilar (W). Application of relative use and interlibrary demand in collection development. *Collect Manag*. 8; 1986; 15-24.

Alison (Scammell), *Ed. Handbook of library management*. Ed 8. 2001. ASLIB, London.

Arlen (Shelley) et al. Web tools for collection managers. *Collect Build*. 17; 1998; 65-70.

Ashcroft (Linda) and Colin (Langdon). Electronic journals and university library collections. *Collect Build*. 19; 1999; 105-113.

Batt (F). Folly of book reviews. *In* Kathman (M D) and Massman (V F), *Ed. Options for the 80s*. 1981. Jai Press, Greenwich.

Bernstein(J. R.). Corporate annual reports: The commercial vendors. *Coll Res Libr*. 47; March 1986; 178-80.

Block (D) and Kalyoncu (A). Selection of word processing software for library use. *Inf Technol Libr*. 2; September 1983; 252-60.

Bonk (S C). Towards a methodology of evaluating serials vendors. *Libr Acquis Prac Th*. 9, 2; 1985; 51-60.

Bonk (S). Rethinking the acquisitions budget: Anticipating and managing change. *Libr Acquis Prac Th*. 10, 2; 1986; 97-106.

Calmes (A). New confidence in microfilm. *Libr J*. 111; 15 September 1986; 38-42.

Chaberlain (C E). Automating acquisitions. *Libr Hi Tech*. 3, 3; 1985; 27-29.

Chan (Liza). Electronic journals and academic libraries. *Libr Hi Tech*.17; 1999; 10-16.

Chapman (Liz). Managing acquisitions in libraries and information services. 2001. Library Association Publishing, London.

Curley (A).Building library collections. 1985. Scare Crow Press, N. J.

Day (M) and Revill (M). Towards the active collection: The use of circulation analyses in collection evaluation. *J Libr Inf Sc*. 27; 1995; 149-157.

Dessauer (J P). Book publishing : What it is, What it does. 1983. R R Bowker, New York.

Drury (F). Book selection. 1930. American Library Association, Greenwich.

Eaglen (A). Trouble in kiddy land : The hidden costs of O P and O S. *Collect Build*. 6; Summer 1984; 26-28.

Electronic collections development. www.library.yale.edu/~okerson/ecd.html.

Ellison (J W). Non-print selection: A combination of methods. *Cathol Libr World*. 54; October 1982; 119-21.

Evans (G. Edward). Developing library and information center collections. Ed. 3. 1995. Libraries Unlimited, Littleton, Colorado.

Evans (R W). Collection development policy statements. *Collect Manag*. 7; Spring 1985; 63-73.

Furnham (A). Book reviews as a selection tool for librarians : Comments from a psychologist. *Collect Manag*. Spring 8; 1986; 33-43.

Futas (E). Issues in collection building: Why collection development policies. *Collect Build*. 3, 1; 1981; 58-60.

Gilbert (D L). Complete guide to starting a used book store.1986. Review Press, Chicago.

Grant (J). Librarian and the purchasing function. *Libr Acquis Prac Th*. 9, 4; 1985; 305-6.

Hamlin (J B). The selection process. *In* Stuert (R D) and Miller (G B), *Ed*. Collection development in libraries. 1980. Jai Press, Greenwich.

Hannigan (J A). Evaluation of software. *Libr Trends*, 23; Winter 1985; 327-48.

Hoffmann (E). Defining information. *Inf Process Manag*. 18, 3; 1982; 115-23.

Holmes (L S.). Systems acquisitions and vendor expectations. *Libr Hi Tech*. 2, 2; 1984. 110-12.

Hurt (C D). Important literature identification in science. *In Advances in librarianship*. 13; 239-58. New York. Academic Press, 1984.

Intner (Shoila S). and Elizabeth (Futas). Evaluating public library collections: Why do it, and how to use the results. *Am Libs*. 1994; 410-411.

Katz (B). Who is the reviewer. *Collect Build*. Spring 7; 1985; 33-35.

Katz (W A). *Collection development: The selection of materials for libraries*. 1980. Rinehart and Winston, New York.

Lancaster (F W). *Libraries and librarians in an age of electronics*. 1982. Information Resources Press, Arlington, Va.

Lane (A H). Gifts and exchange manual. 1980. Greenwood Press, Westport, Conn.

Leiserson (Anna Belle). Acquisition web: Book buying in the age of the Internet. *Libr Hi Tech*. 15; 1997; 438-44.

Line (M B). UAP and audiovisual materials. *IFLA J*. 12; 1982; 91-103.

Lucas (Thomas). Verifying the conspectus: Problems and progress. *Coll Res Libr News.* 51; March 1990; 199-201.

Magril (R M) and Hickey (D J). *Acquisition management and collection development in libraries*. 1984. American Library Association, Chicago.

Magrill (Rose Mary) and Corbin (John). *Acquisition managing and collection development in libraries.* Ed.2. 1989. ALA, Chicago.

Mann (Peter). Library acquisitions : The economic constraints. *The Bookseller*; 14 June 1986; 2338-44.

Maple (Amanda) and MORROW (Jean). Guide to writing collection development policies for music. *Music Libr Assoc Tech Rep Series*. 26, 2001.Scarecrow Press, NJ.

Martin (S). Ordering after selection. *The Bookseller*. 4218; 24 October 1986; 1674-78.

McCleary (H). Practical guide to establishing a business intelligence clearing house. *Database*. 9; June 1986; 40-46.

McGrath (W E). Collection evaluation theory and the search for structure. *Libr Trends*. 12; Winter 1985; 241-66.

McLaure (C R). and Reifsnyder (B). Performance measures for corporate information centes. *Spl Libs*. 75; July 1984; 193-204.

Melin (N). The book on library uses : CD-Rom. *CD-Rom Rev.* 1; October 1986; 36-38.

Moddy (M). State documents : Basic selection sources. *Collect Build*. 7; Spring 1985; 41-44.

Mosher (P H). Quality and library collections: New directions in research and practice in collection evaluation. *Adv in Librship.* 13; 1984; 65-76.

Moskowitz (M) and Alcorn (C W). Collection managers *Technicalities.* 5; March 1985; 11-14.

Mulliner (B K). Library of Congress acquisitions policies. *Libr Acquis Prac Th.* 6, 2; 1982; 103-6.

Nisonger (T E). Electronic journal collection management issues. *Collect Build.* 16, 1997; 58-65.

Norton (R) and GAUTSCHI (D). User survey of an international library : Expectations and evaluation. *Aslib Proc.* 37; April 195-206.

Nugent (W R). Optical disc: An emerging technology for libraries. *IFLA J.* 12; August 1986; 175-81.

Oakeshott (P). *Impact of new technology on publication chain.* 1987. Pontish Library, London.

Oulton (A J). Measuring book supply efficiency. *The Bookseller.* 4206; 2 August 1986; 493-95.

Parker (R H.). Bibliometric models for management of an information store. *Inf science.* 33; March 1982; 124-38.

Presley (Roger L). Firing an old friend, painful decisions: The ethics between librarians and vendors. *Libr Acquis Prac Th.* 17,1993; 53-59.

Rossi (P H) and Freeman (H E). *Evaluation: A systematic approach.*1985. Sage Publications, California.

Rouse (W B). Optimal selection of acquisitions sources. *J Am Soc Inf Sc.* 25; July 1974; 227-31.

Rowley (Gordon) and BLACK (Wiliam K). Consequences of change: The evolution of collection development. *Collect Build.* 15; 1996; 22-30.

Ryland (J). Collection development and selection : Who should do it? *Libr Acquis Prac Th.* 6, 1; 1982; 13-17.

Samore (T). Acquisition of foreign materials for U.S. libraries.1982. Scarecrow Press, Metuchen, NJ.

Sauter (H E) and REA (R H). Place of research/classified reports in a special library. 1980. Scarecrow Press, Metuchen. NJ.

Schauer (B). Economics of managing library services.1986. American Library Association, Chicago.

Scheschy (Virginia M). Publishers on the web: From Addison to Ziff. *Libr Coll Acq Tech Serv*. 23; 1999; 73-78.

Schmidt (F) and Welsch (H W). Acquisition guide : Technical reports and other non-GPO publications. *Government Publications Rev* . 8, 4; 1981; 175-79.

Schottlanender (Brian E C). The development of national principles to guide librarians in licensing electronic resources. *Libr Acquis Prac Th*. 22, Spring 1998; 49-54.

Schuman (Patricia Glass). Librarians and publishers: An uneasy dance. *Wilson Libr Bull*. 69; December 1994; 40-43.

Segel (J A). Journal deselection : A literature review and an application. *Sci Technol Libr*. 6; Spring; 1986; 25-42.

Shalini (R). Journal acquisition and cost effectiveness in special libraries. *Int Libr Rev*. 13, April; 1981; 181-94.

Sive (M R). Media selection handbook.1983. Libraries Unlimited; Littleton.

Spiller (D). Book selection : An introduction to principles and practice. Ed 4.1986. Clive Bingley, London.

Stiffler (S A). Core analysis in collection management. *Collect Manag*. Fall/Winter, 5; 1983; 135-49.

Stueart (R D), *Ed*. Collection development. 1980, Jai Press, Greenwich.

Tephens (A). British national bibliography: Aims and uses. *The Bookseller*. 4219; 31 October 1986; 1780-85.

Tyckoson (D A). On the convention circuit. *Technicalities*. 4; September 1984; 14-15.

Veatch (J R). Automating government documents orders with a microcomputer. *Government Publications Rev.* 12 March, 1985; 137-41.

Wagers (R). Online sources of competitive intelligence. *Database.* 9; June 1986; 28-38.

Weihs (J), Lewis (S) and MacDonald (J). Non-book materials: The organisation of integrated collections. Ed.2. 1980. American Library Association, Chicago.

Welsch (E). A social scientific view of collection development. *Collect Manag.* 4; Fall 1982; 71-84.

Williams (S F). Reporting book prices. *Book Research Q.* 1. No. 4 1986; 85-88.

Wood (L B) and Perry-Holmes (Claudia). Libraries practice prior censorship to avoid the flak. *Libr J* . 107; 1982; 1711-1715.

Index

□□□